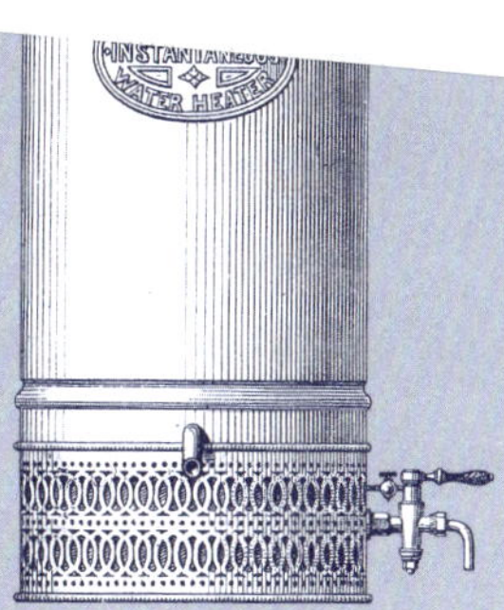
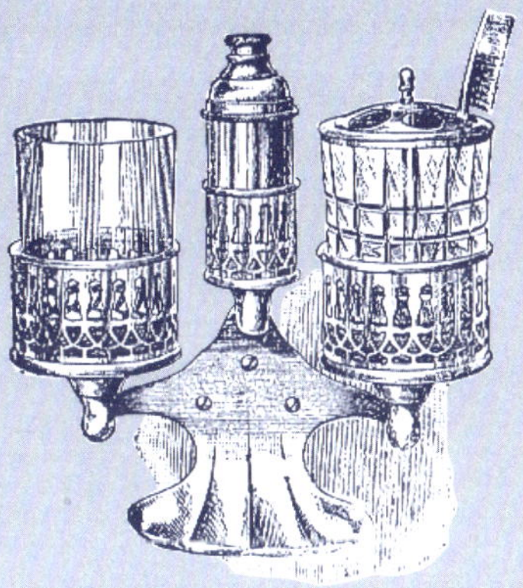
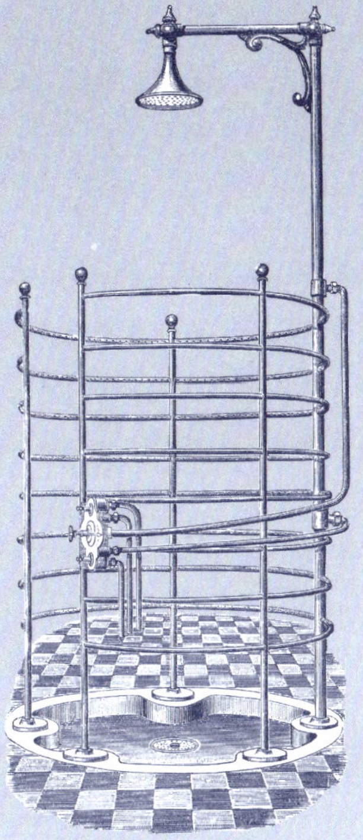

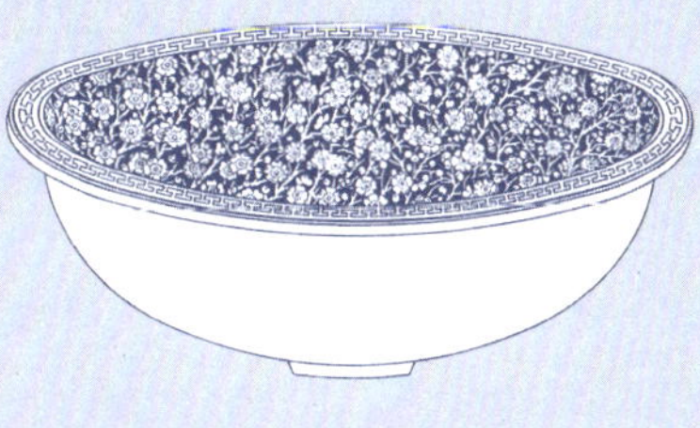
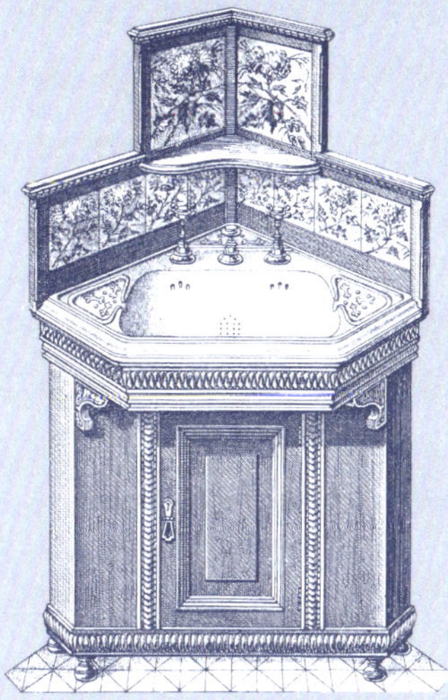

The VICTORIAN BATHROOM Catalogue

A Treasury of
over 1,000 Baths, Showers,
Fixtures and Fittings

INTRODUCTION BY
KIT WEDD

STUDIO
EDITIONS

First published in 1996 by Studio Editions,
an imprint of Random House UK Ltd,
20 Vauxhall Bridge Road, London SW1V 2SA

ISBN 1 85891 583 X

Printed and bound in Great Britain by BPC Hazell Books Ltd
A member of The British Printing Company Ltd

The publishers extend their grateful thanks to Mr Carol Hogben for supplying the original material from which this volume has been compiled, and also to Dorothy Bosomworth for her valued contribution.

CONTENTS

Illustrated Catalogue
of
Sanitary Appliances
MANUFACTURED BY
SHANKS & Co.
TUBAL WORKS
BARRHEAD NEAR GLASGOW.
BATHS & BATH FITTINGS
LAVATORIES AND
LAVATORY FITTINGS
WATER CLOSETS & URINALS
SINKS. SANITARY EARTHENWARE
PORCELAIN ENAMELLED WARE
BATH-ROOM CABINET WORK.
BRASS WATER FITTINGS &c.
LONDON OFFICE & SHOWROOMS, 46 Cannon St. E.C.
LONDON WAREHOUSE & STORES, 384 Old St. Shoreditch. E.
MANCHESTER, Grosvenor Buildings, Deansgate.
GLASGOW, 26 West Nile Street.
DUBLIN, 48 Lower Sackville Street.
ABERDEEN. SHOWROOM, 12 Meal Market Street.
Entered at Stationers' Hall.
William Gorman & Co., Lith. Glasgow.

INTRODUCTION

The illustrated pages reproduced in this book have been selected from six manufacturers' catalogues published in Britain, France and the United States between about 1885 and 1900. They represent the state of the sanitary ware industry in an era when the provision of efficient and elegant bathrooms was of unprecedented importance in the design and marketing of houses.

The need to dedicate at least one room of the house to bathing was widely accepted when the first of these catalogues was published, but only a couple of generations earlier the purpose-built bathroom had still been a novelty. A mere handful of bathing rooms survives from the eighteenth century. In the basement of No. 7 Great George Street (The Georgian House Museum) in Bristol, built for a prosperous sugar merchant in the 1790s, there is a deep plunge pool, lined with closely jointed masonry, which would have been filled with icy spring water in readiness for the bather to take an extremely bracing dip. A similar bath, supplied with hot as well as cold water, was installed by the architect John Soane at Wimpole Hall, Cambridgeshire. Baths of this kind were used for occasional health-giving stimulation and exercise, rather than to ensure day-to-day personal cleanliness.

Before the advent of the plumbed-in bathroom, the simplest rituals of personal hygiene were laborious. In middle-class houses, each bedroom was furnished with a chamber pot and a wash-stand. The chamber pot might be housed in a purpose-built cupboard or fitted into a chair with a hinged seat, known as a 'close stool'. Its contents were collected every morning and disposed of, either into closed cess pits beneath the houses or into open middens. In towns and cities, these collection points were emptied by specialists, night-soil men who carted away the sewage and sold it as fertiliser to market gardeners and farmers in outlying areas. Rural householders would simply strew the contents of their privies onto the land.

The wash-stand, or 'lavatory', was a narrow table on which stood a china or metal basin, with a shelf below for a ewer or water can. The table top would often be made of marble and it might have a circular hole cut out of it, into which the basin fitted and was held steady. The more expensive examples had tiled splash-backs, fitted soap trays, towel rails and built-in pot cupboards, but however elaborate the design, the chore of fetching the water to and from the basin was inescapable.

When a full bath was required, a tin or copper hip bath would be carried into the bedroom and placed in front of the hearth. Hot water had to be brought up in cans from the basement where the boilers were situated. It took several cans to fill a bath, and several return trips to carry the dirty water away once the bather had finished. The heavy cans of hot water and the slop pails were carried up and down stairs by housemaids and footmen, whose physical strength and fitness were their principal qualifications for the job.

In middle-class households where few servants were employed, the housemaid was expected to bring up the water for the morning wash but the hard labour of providing hot baths might be shared between the servants and the family in a way that was not possible in an aristocratic house where the servant-master relationship was strictly observed. Mrs. Caddy, the author of *Household Organisation* (1877), implicitly recognised the resentment that bath-time drudgery could cause: 'When a man likes to have his bath regularly, he should think of the labour that half a dozen or more baths entail, and in the evening prepare his can of water for tomorrow's use, place his own bath on his piece of oilcloth, enjoy his tub to his heart's content, pour away the water, put up his tub, and say nothing about it.'

Families in more modest circumstances would have a weekly (or less frequent) 'bath night', when a tin bath was taken down from its hook by the back door and placed in front of the kitchen range. Sheets were draped over clothes-horses to protect the bathers from draughts and to preserve their modesty, and the children – the cleanest going first and the grubbiest last – took it in turns to use the same water while a fresh supply of hot water for the adults' baths was being heated.

For the very poor, even a weekly bath was an undreamed of luxury. Few working class households had their own water supply or private closet. Most families had to share a pump and a communal latrine with several others. In the country, cottagers used water from wells that might be polluted by seepage from nearby privies, while in the densely populated tenements of the great industrial cities the problems of water supply and sewage disposal were sometimes overwhelming. Those districts of London which did have a primitive sewer system discharged their sewage untreated into the Thames. The river was, of course, also the main water supply for the city, but any stream or puddle might be viewed as a legitimate source of water by the destitute, as one observer noted in the 1850s: 'In Jacob's Island [a notorious slum in Bermondsey] may be seen at any time of the day women dipping water, with pails attached by ropes to the backs of the houses, from a foul and foetid ditch, its banks coated with a compound of mud and filth, and with offal and carrion – the water to be used for every purpose.'

A campaign for sanitary reform began to gain ground in the 1840s, but it was not until 1854, when Dr. John Snow traced the source of an outbreak of cholera in Soho to a single water pump shared by the victims' families, that the connection between public health and clean water was officially recognised. Reform became inevitable after the hot summer of June 1858, when Parliament was forced to suspend business because the stench from the Thames was unbearable. In the 1860s the Metropolitan Board of Works under Sir Joseph Bazalgette revolutionised London's sewage disposal system. The old cess pits and middens were replaced by a network of brick-built sewers that sloped towards the Thames. Before they reached the river, however, they were intercepted by a grand sewer, running parallel to the riverbank, which led to outfalls far outside the city. The dirty water was pumped out on the falling tide to be carried out to sea and the solid waste was dumped further down the estuary. Bazalgette's 1,400 miles of sewers, built using 318 million bricks, provided a model for other major cities throughout the world and continue to serve London to this day.

Even after the prerequisites for the development of the modern bathroom – a reliable supply of clean water and an adequate system of sewage disposal – were in place, the development and distribution of bathrooms continued in a very piecemeal fashion. It was many years before every house was provided with a plumbed-in bath and water closet as a matter of course. Some aristocratic families had begun to install recognisably modern plumbing in their country houses in the early nineteenth century. As Mark Girouard has pointed out, 'By the late 1830s and early 1840s the dukes of Buckingham were equipping Stowe with plumbing almost as lavishly as their predecessors had equipped it with temples. By 1844 it had at least nine water-closets, a shower-bath and four bathrooms.'

It was easier to incorporate a bathroom in the plan of a house from the beginning than to try to squeeze one into any redundant space in an existing house. The country house building boom of the 1850s and 60s gave fresh impetus to bathroom design and provision, as wealthy clients began to expect their architects to provide water closets and plumbed-in baths. They were following the example of the highest in the land, since at the royal family's country seat of Osborne on the Isle of Wight, built in 1848 according to the most up-to-date principles, both Queen Victoria and Prince Albert had a bath and shower in their respective dressing rooms.

The royal approval implicit in the provision of these personal bathrooms ensured that similar arrangements would be provided as a matter of course in subsequent country houses. In *The Gentleman's House*, the architect Robert Kerr declared that 'no house of any pretensions will be devoid of a general Bath-room'. He dealt with water closets under a separate heading, and dismissed the economical practice of installing a closet and bath in the same room as unfit for the 'superior' house.

The same point was emphasised thirty years later by Hermann Muthesius, whose systematic survey of new domestic architecture in England, *The English House*, included this remark on bathroom planning: 'The lavatory naturally adjoins the bathroom. But we must stress the fact that in England a lavatory is never actually in the bathroom. Fifty years ago it may still have been permissible to put both in one room, but today it would be considered barbarous and is, we repeat, totally inadmissible'. The illustrations of complete bathrooms in manufacturers' catalogues seem to contradict this by showing bath and closet in the same room, but this may reflect the manufacturers' desire to promote as many of their products as possible within a single image.

Muthesius was writing about the latest crop of country houses by leading architects, whose clients had the money to pay for large numbers of separate bathrooms and closets, and the space to accommodate them. In the urban terraced house or the suburban semi, however, lack of space and the persistence of old attitudes meant that it was many years before a water closet was provided inside the house as a matter of course, whether or not it was in the same room as the bath. The possession of an indoor closet was largely a matter of class and partly one of geographical location. As late as the 1890s, London building regulations still permitted the building of new 'working class' houses with closets in the back yard

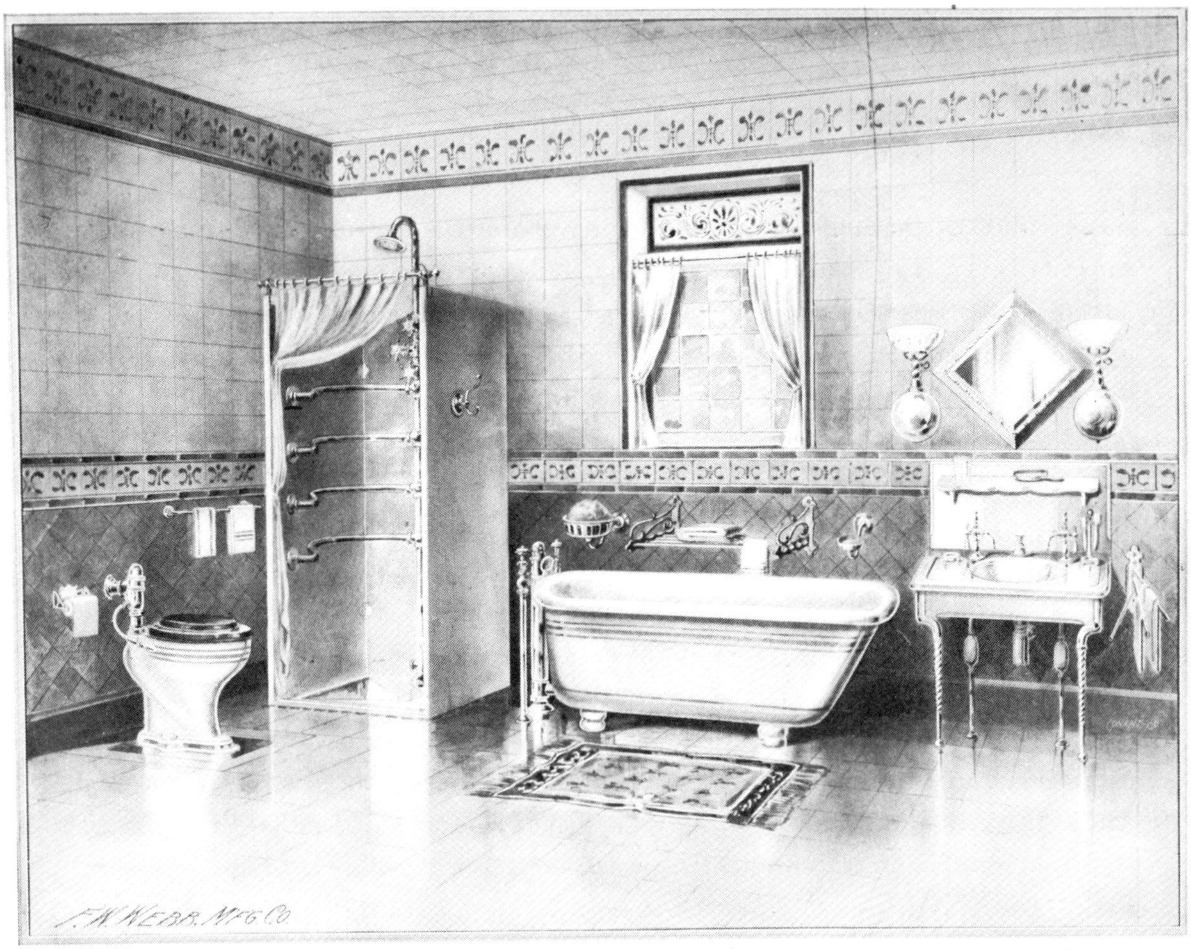
F.W. WEBB. MFG. CO.

rather than in the house itself, while in turn-of-the-century Leeds one outside closet for every two houses was considered adequate. In the north of England, an outside closet was acceptable in middle-class housing decades after it had become unthinkable in London. It was not until after the First World War that the provision of indoor closets became almost universal in new housing, and as late as the 1960s some local authorities were still providing grants for the installation of indoor closets in old houses which had been built without them.

Manufacturers were quick to respond to the demand for sanitary appliances to furnish all these new bathrooms. Although a plumbed-in bath with hot and cold running water did not become a standard feature of the Victorian home until the 1870s, there had been earlier attempts to make the hip bath more convenient by combining it with a shower. One manufacturer, George Jennings, published a catalogue illustrating 'the universal high-back taper bath. An ingenious model complete with shower and heating stove'. A sleigh-shaped bath with an integral shower, along the lines Jennings proposed, is preserved in a Regency bathroom at Plas Teg in Wales.

By the mid-nineteenth century Britain's iron and ceramics industries were well placed to supply everything that the modern bathroom required (for example, in 1820 Britain produced only 400,000 tons of iron, but by 1852 her annual output was 2,701,000 tons). Although some tin, zinc and copper baths were on sale, most of those illustrated in the catalogues are cast iron, as are many of the urinals, cisterns and shower enclosures. Cast-iron baths were first introduced around 1880. This comparatively late date is due to the technical difficulty of minimising thickness and weight while achieving a one-piece casting. The interior of the bath was stove-enamelled and the exterior (if it was not to be encased in panelling) was galvanised or painted. The ball-and-claw or scrolled feet were separately cast and bolted onto lugs cast into the underside of the bath.

Although some cast-iron models did exist, most lavatories and closets were made of porcelain, earthenware or fireclay. Clay also appeared in many other guises in the modern bathroom. Floors could be covered with a mosaic of geometric tiles in natural earth colours or in smart black-and-white chequer patterns, while walls were clad in tiles, glazed to make them hygienic and resistant to condensation. Even the handle on the end of the chain was made of glazed ceramic.

Ceramic bodies readily lent themselves to elaborate decoration, and the techniques used to embellish tableware and ornamental porcelain were adapted for the larger scale of sanitary ware. The clay bodies were impressed with relief decoration, fired with transfer-printed patterns or highlighted with gold – sometimes all three at once. The decoration sometimes had an aquatic theme: dolphins, scallop shells and waterlilies appear regularly in the manufacturers' catalogues. The classical vocabulary of ornament was also plundered, perhaps as a tribute to the ancient Greeks and Romans, whose baths were the stuff of legend: key patterns, acanthus leaves and Vitruvian scrolls suggestive of billowing waves are all present in the catalogue illustrations. However, plenty of the decorative designs were unrelated to water or to the history of bathing: birds of paradise outnumber kingfishers or swans, and chrysanthemums, daisies or peach blossoms appear more frequently than waterlilies.

Having come into possession of a bathroom fitted out with the very best that the manufacturers had to offer, the proud householder was free to decorate and personalise the room as he or she saw fit. Bathroom decoration reflected the prevailing fashions in interior decoration, and manufacturers provided sanitary ware that would fit into 'Renaissance' or neoclassical revival settings. In the 1880s and 90s, the Aesthetic Movement was a particularly powerful influence on bathroom decoration. The division of the wall into dado, filling and frieze that was a hallmark of the Aesthetic style could easily be achieved using bands of contrasting tiling or one of the new washable wallpapers. Muthesius remarked on the growing trend towards decorating the bathroom to the same standard as the other rooms in the house: 'The bathroom ... is a room that should be as agreeably appointed as possible, for bathing is pleasurable and not a necessary evil. Hand in hand with the increasing importance that is being attached to hygiene in our time, there has been a growing tendency to furnish the bathroom handsomely, as ... an inviting place in which to linger.'

The feeling that elaborate ornament was incompatible with hygiene led to a simplification of bathroom design and decoration in the early 1900s, with an emphasis on clean lines and cold, polished surfaces that mocked the idea of lingering any longer than necessary over one's ablutions. Only the Webb Manufacturing Co. catalogue, the latest in date and also (perhaps more significantly) the only American catalogue in the present selection, manages to combine modernity with cosiness by including large, heated towel rails and Oriental rugs in their suggested bathroom schemes.

Many British bathrooms remained chilly, austere and uninviting, especially those in aristocratic households, where the spartan discomfort of the public school determined the character of the family's bathing arrangements. Deborah Mitford, later the Duchess of Devonshire, recalled her first surprised encounter with transatlantic ideas of bathtime comfort when she visited the American hostess Nancy Lancaster at Ditchley Park: 'The bathrooms were little works of art, much more like sitting rooms than bathrooms ... A far cry from the cracked lino and icy draughts to which I was accustomed.'

Bathroom fixtures and fittings were provided by numerous manufacturers, a representative selection of whose work is shown in this book. The illustrations have been drawn from the catalogues of Shanks and Co. of Barrhead, near Glasgow (published in about 1885-90), Thomas W. Twyford of the Cliffe Vale Pottery, Hanley (1889); Morrison, Ingram and Co. of the Hygeia Works, Manchester (about 1893); Doulton and Co. of Lambeth (1895); Établissements Porcher of Paris (1899); and the F. W. Webb Manufacturing Co. of Boston, Massachusetts (1900). The size and magnificence of the catalogue volumes are a testament to the rapid growth of this relatively new industry in the nineteenth century, and to the intense competition between manufacturers eager to exploit the expanding market for sanitary appliances.

The catalogues are copiously illustrated in a variety of formats: line engravings are used to illustrate baths, showers and closets in plan, section, elevation and perspective, while chromolithography is used with extravagant generosity to show the full range of colour decoration available. The depth of moulding round a bath panel and the glossy sheen of the French polish on a lavatory cabinet are evoked by engraved shadows and highlights in the perspective views and in many of the plates the artistic effect has been enhanced by the inclusion of decorative accessories – usually an asymmetrical arrangement of 'Art' pottery or a Japanese print in the Aesthetic taste – in the scene.

Colour is used in all the catalogues. The expense of colour printing was offset by savings on the cost of the artwork, since the same basic drawing of one model of lavatory, bath or closet is reprinted several times on one page, each time overprinted with a different pattern or colour. Schematic as these pages are, their dazzling juxtapositions of colour and pattern grab the reader's attention just as the manufacturers intended. Text pages are headed in the 'Art' typography fashionable in the last quarter of the nineteenth century.

Each volume is handsomely bound, with a cover and title page that bespeak the dignity and extent of the manufacturer's enterprise. The branch offices are proudly listed: Shanks had branches in London, Manchester, Glasgow, Dublin and Aberdeen; Thomas Twyford had outlets in Berlin and New York; Doulton and Co. could be found in Paisley and Paris. The gold medals won at international exhibitions and trade fairs are prominently reproduced with metallic ink on the title page of Shanks's catalogue, while Doulton's states, '106 gold medals and first class awards. 102 silver medals and other awards'. The frontispieces to the catalogue of Morris, Ingram and Co. are full-page perspectives of notable public buildings in which their products have been used: Alfred Waterhouse's Refuge Assurance Buildings, Manchester ('with accommodation for 900 clerks') and the New General Hospital, Birmingham, by William Henman.

These manufacturers were right to be proud of their achievements. They established a brand-new category of consumer products, introduced technological innovation and decorative diversity into domestic and public bathrooms, and made possible a revolution in public health and private comfort. The confident prose and bold illustrations of their splendid catalogues stand as both a reproach to the bland timidity of current bathroom design and as an inspiration to architects, interior designers and householders in search of authentic Victorian bathroom style today.

A Note on Terminology

The terminology used to describe bathroom fittings has changed over the years, which can be confusing for anyone studying the history of the subject. Throughout the nineteenth century, the word 'lavatory' was used to refer to a wash basin. What we would now call a 'lavatory' or a 'toilet' was always termed a 'closet', and like the modern words, it could refer either to the item itself or to the room in which it was installed. To avoid confusion, and to be consistent with the text of the original catalogues, the nineteenth-century practice has been followed in this book.

CHAPTER ONE

BATHS & SHOWERS

Plumbed-in baths, in proper bathrooms with running hot water, first made their appearance in the 1850s. These baths were press-moulded in sheet metal, which was galvanised or painted with simple wood grain or marble finishes, or adorned with stencilled decoration. When the technology for casting baths was perfected in the 1880s, cast iron superseded all other materials; only a handful of the models in subsequently printed catalogues were available in other materials, such as zinc or copper. Not shown at all after 1885 are the portable, tin or zinc baths that were brought into temporary use in households that had no room specifically dedicated to bathing: by this date, sanitary appliance manufacturers assume that their clients will have at least one plumbed-in bath per household.

Baths could be supplied with straight top edges for enclosing in wood panelling, or with roll tops. The roll could be cast in the same metal as the body of the bath, or else a wooden, ceramic or marble moulding could be fitted around the edge. Tops in various materials and finishes, 'architect-designed' panelling, a wide range of stencilled decorations – in fact, everything to make the bath the stylish focus of the room – were available through the catalogues.

Not all baths were cast iron: George Vanderbilt's bathroom, installed in his New York house in 1855, had a porcelain bath. Such baths were durable and easy to clean, but heavy, fragile and cold to the skin until they had been thoroughly warmed by the water. Even more chilly and impressive were marble baths: the Marquess of Bute could easily afford the extravagance of his silver-inlaid, solid Roman marble bath at Cardiff Castle, but there was also a cheaper version made from sheets of white marble in the relatively modest, middle-class terraced house in Kensington occupied by Edward Linley Sambourne and his family in the 1870s.

Showers, which could be freestanding or attached to the tap end of the bath, were as complex as any modern Jacuzzi. One manufacturer, Ewart, in 1882 introduced an 'improved spray bath' with a hooded shower compartment at one end. Both bath and shower were encased in wood panelling, and ten control handles allowed the bather to experience a variety of water sensations. Shanks' 'Independent' plunge, spray and shower bath had a semi-cylindrical shower enclosure of sheet zinc, double-shelled and perforated inside to give a fine spray. This was 'metallic enamelled' white inside and japanned outside, and had an exterior painted with a decorative border design. The water sensations offered by such contraptions included hot and cold showers (from an overhead rose), spray (from small holes in the horizontal pipes surrounding the bather's body), a douche (which on some models could be swung into position from the side of the shower and returned home when no longer in use), wave (a flattened stream of water which would create ripples in the bath), sitz or plunge baths.

At first, there was little attempt to conceal plumbing; all the pipework was exposed, with fittings reduced to the essentials. In the 1880s, pipework was tidied away behind elaborate wooden panelling, tiled splashbacks and mahogany-framed mirrors. Shanks catered to both tastes by offering nine different styles of panelling for baths and showers alongside one example of a shower with completely exposed pipework. Around the turn of the century, the bathroom acquired a more functional aspect. Expensive, mahogany-encased hooded baths were replaced by all-metal counterparts and simpler showers with tubular metal cage frames became fashionable. These could be either freestanding, with their own drip tray and waste, or fixed over one end of a bath. Both types had ring frames carrying waterproof curtains. Co-ordinating lavatories were also set on tubular legs. Heated towel rails, nickel-plated and polished, along with white enamel, tiles and marble, completed the appearance of these smaller, more hygienic bathrooms, that became more numerous in the home. Bathrooms in hotels, first introduced in the USA in 1853, became more frequent, too. By 1906 the Ritz in Paris had private baths for all its bedrooms – a foretaste of today.

CAST-IRON BATHS FOR WOOD ENCLOSURE.

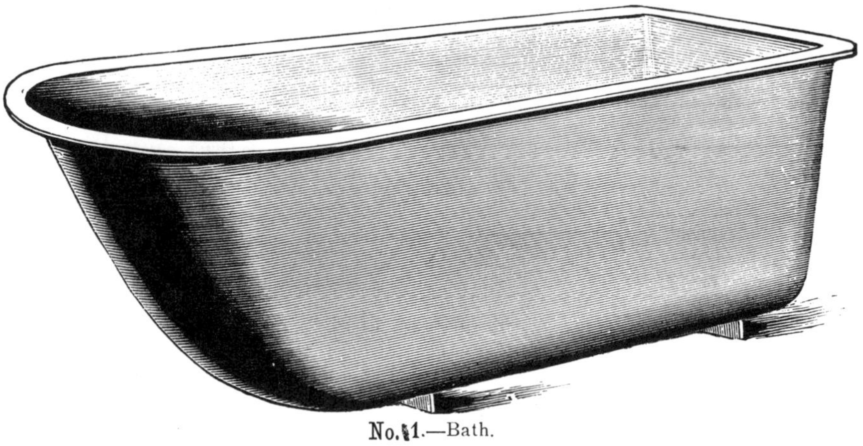

No. 1.—Bath.

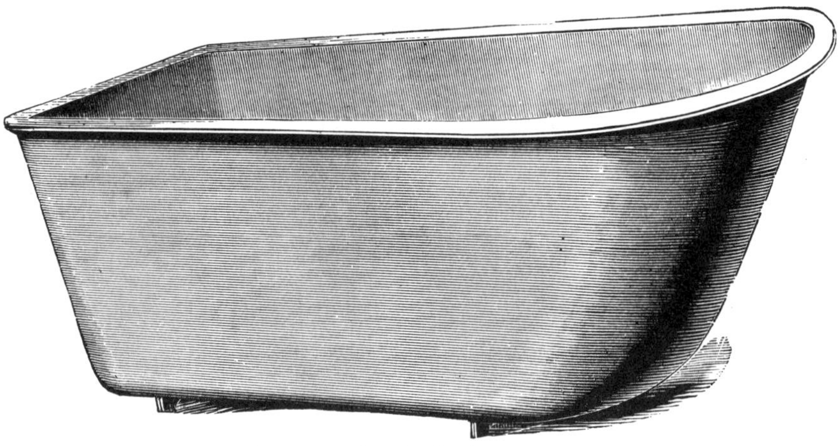

No. 2.—Bath.

Size... ...	Initial Letter indicates Quality only	No. 1.—Tapered Bath. 18½″ deep. 5′ 0″	5′ 6″	6′ 0″	No. 2.—Tapered Bath. 20½″ deep. 5′ 0″	5′ 6″	6′ 0″
Fine Cast	A	26/3	29/3	35/3	28/1	33/4	40/10
Plain Painted	B	27/-	30/4	36/9	28/10	34/6	42/4
3rd Class Japanned Sienna	C	32/3	35/3	44/3	34/6	39/9	48/9
2/2nd Class Japan Enamelled	D	43/10	45/9	55/6	45/9	53/3	61/6
2nd Class Japan Enamelled	E	46/6	50/3	60/-	49/6	56/3	69/-
1st Class Japan Enamelled	F	60/-	65/3	75/-	63/-	72/-	84/-

Baths Finished White, Cream, Pea Green, Sea Green, Shell Pink and Rose Antique, instead of Sienna, at same Prices.

Ordinary Overflow and Tap Holes cast in end of Bath free.

HOME-TRADE PACKING CHARGED AT **5/6** NETT EACH BATH.

Baths Packed for Shipment according to Port. Price on application. Best Shipping Packing, **10/9** Nett per Bath.

No. 1 Bath, 5 6″, packed for shipment, measures 5′ 8″ × 2′ 5″ × 1′ 9″; gross weight about 2cwt. 0qrs. 24lbs.

Interior of A, B, C and D Finished Baths may be utilised for packing light goods.

CAST-IRON BATHS, CURLED RIM.

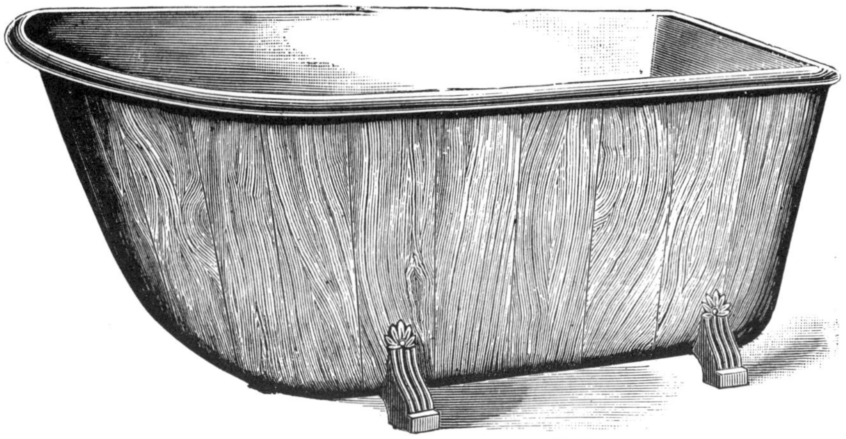

Decoration Design No. 134.

No. 3.—Curled Edge, or Roman Bath.

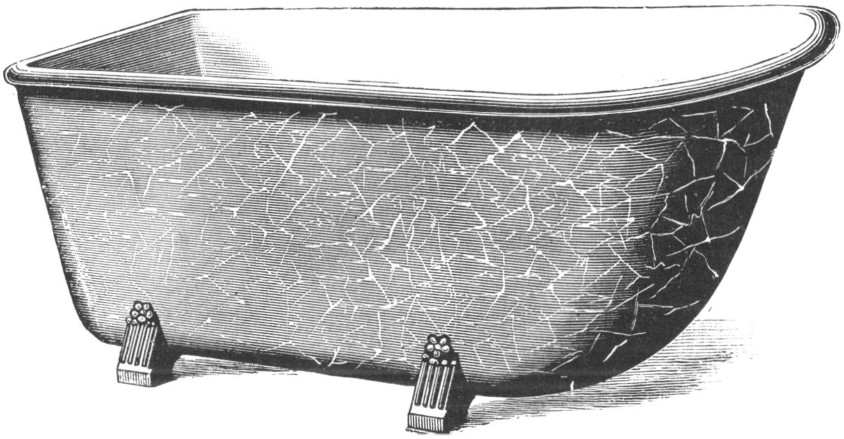

Decoration Design No. 135.

No. 4.—Curled Edge, or Roman Bath.

Size—	Initial Letter indicates Quality only	No. 3. Tapered Bath, 18½″ deep. 4′ 0″	5′ 0″	5′ 6″	No. 4. Tapered Bath 20½″ deep. 5′ 0″	5′ 6″	6′ 0″
Fine Cast	A	33/7	33/7	40/-	39/9	41/7	52/6
3rd Class Japanned Sienna Inside, and Plain Painted Outside ...	G	41/7	41/7	47/3	47/3	49/-	58/6
3rd Class Japanned Sienna Inside, and 3rd Class Outside ...	H	45/10	45/10	52/-	51/-	54/6	63/9
2/2nd Class Japan Enamelled Inside, and Plain Painted Outside	I	53/8	53/8	58/9	57/9	60/9	72/-
2/2nd Class Japan Enamelled Inside, and 3rd Class Outside ...	J	60/9	60/9	63/6	63/9	65/3	76/6
2nd Class Japan Enamelled Inside, and Plain Painted Outside...	K	60/9	60/9	63/6	63/9	65/3	76/6
2nd Class Japan Enamelled Inside, and 3rd Class Outside ...	L	65/3	65/3	69/1	68/3	71/3	84/-
2nd Class Japan Enamelled Inside, and 2/2nd Class Outside ...	M	80/7	80/7	84/-	84/9	87/9	99/-
1st Class Japan Enamelled Inside, and Plain Painted Outside...	N	70/10	70/10	76/6	75/9	78/9	90/-
1st Class Japan Enamelled Inside, and 3rd Class Outside ...	O	78/1	78/1	81/-	80/6	83/-	94/-
1st Class Japan Enamelled Inside, and 2nd Class Outside ...	P	106/-	106/-	108/-	108/9	112/3	126/6

Baths Finished White, Cream, Pea Green, Sea Green, Shell Pink, and Rose Antique, instead of Sienna, at same Prices.

Ordinary Overflow and Tap Holes cast in end of Bath free.

HOME-TRADE PACKING CHARGED AT **7/3** NETT EACH BATH.

Baths Packed for Shipment according to Port. Prices on application. Best Shipping Packing, **12/6** Nett per Bath.

No. 4 Bath, 5′ 6″, packed for Shipment, measures 6′ 3″ × 2′ 10″ × 2′ 4″; gross weight about 3cwt. 1qr. 0lbs.

Light Goods or Cotton Waste may be safely packed inside the A, G, H, I and J quality Baths, thus economising space and carriage.

SHANKS' PATENT "CITIZEN" COMBINED CAST-IRON BATH AND FITTINGS.

A BATH FOR THE MILLION—GOOD AND CHEAP.

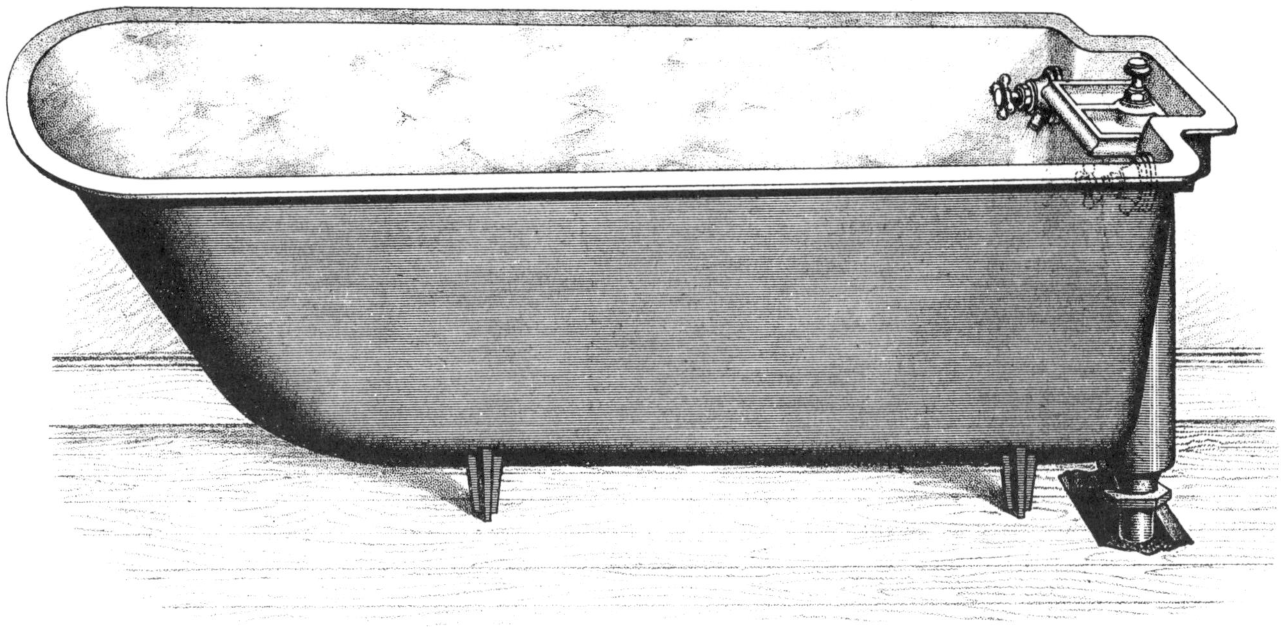

No. 97 Plain Flange Bath for fixing with Wood Enclosure.

Above Drawing shews the Bath as sent out of the Works, with Hot, Cold, and Waste Fittings, Soap Dish (Porcelain) draining into waste, Standing Waste Pipe cast on with Overflow, and Outlet connection complete.

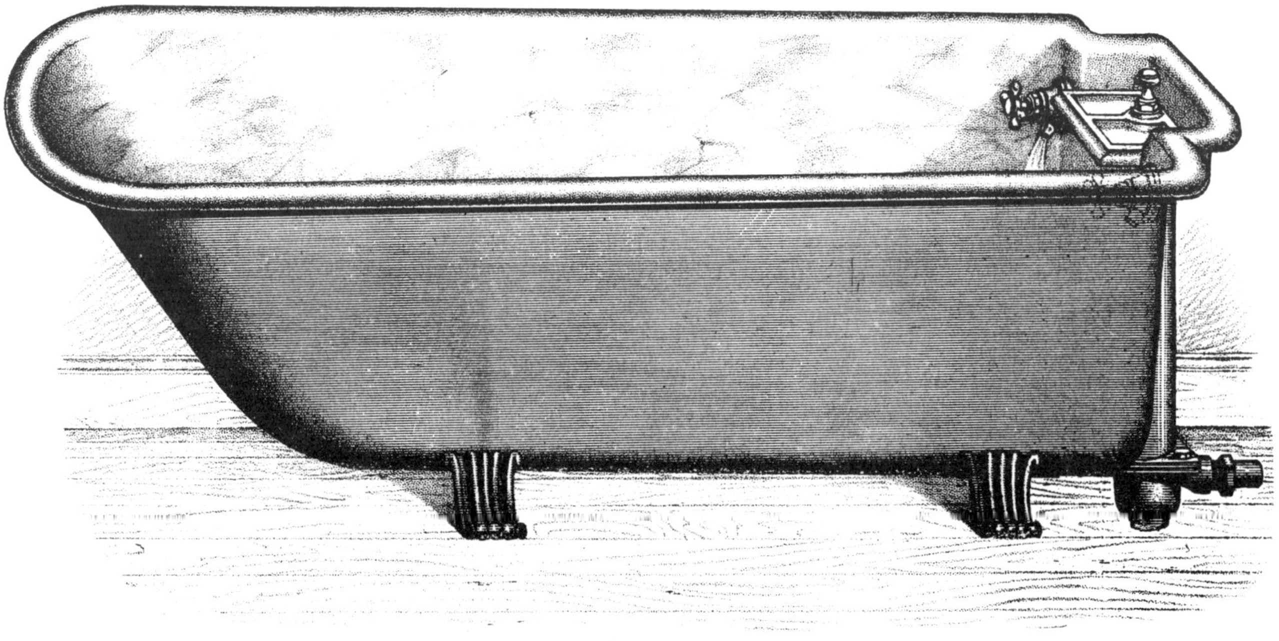

No. 99. Roll Edge Bath for fixing without Wood Enclosure.

Constructed with Ornamental Feet, and grained or painted outside.

The above drawing shews the "Citizen" Bath with Adjustable Trap above floor-line.

The Adjustable Outlet and Trap shewn on above Baths may be turned round in any position to suit the waste pipes, by slackening the nuts at bottom arranged for that purpose.

Made taper side and parallel, 5′ 0″, 5′ 6″, and 6′ 0″ long inside.

SHANKS' PATENT IMPERIAL COMBINED BATHS AND FITTINGS,

WITH SUPPLY OF WATER, HOT AND COLD, INTRODUCED NEAR THE BOTTOM OF BATH.

The object of this is to lessen the tendency of the hot water to evaporate and throw steam into the room. It also fulfils the requirements of those who prefer a bottom supply to a supply over edge.

No. 20, Cast-Iron Bath,
Made either with Rolled Edge or Plain Flange.

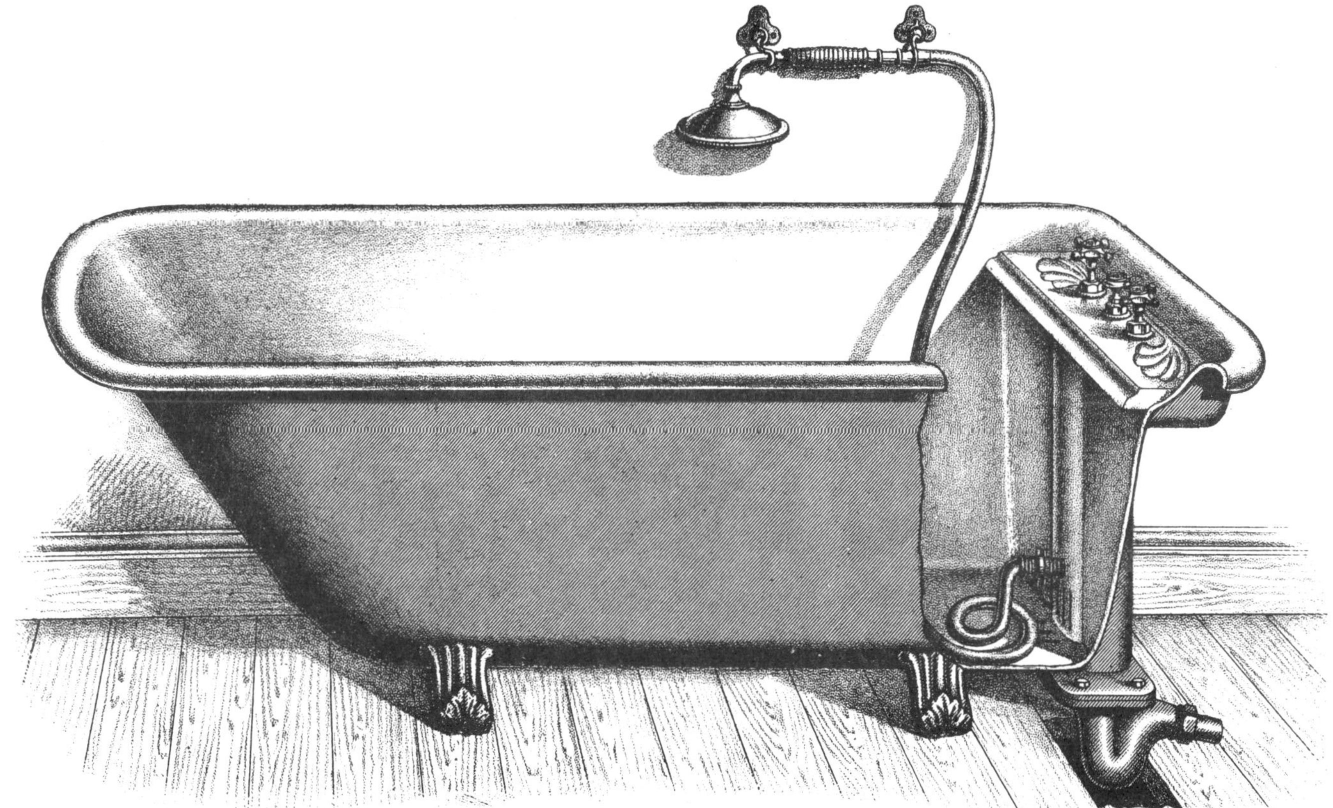

No. 20A. Cast-Iron Bath,
Same as above, but with Hand Spray.

The Taps are fixed exactly the same as on the other Imperial Baths, and covered with Porcelain, Soap and Brush Trays draining into waste; but instead of filling over edge, the water is conducted down a brass tube, fixed in the standing Waste Pipe, specially enlarged to hold it, and thrown into the Bath through Nozzlepiece, as shewn.

Price same as Nos. 1, 2, 5, and 6, according to Style, Shape, and Finish.

ROYAL PORCELAIN BATH.

Fitted for Hot, Cold and Waste, with marble cope, and resting on marble feet. To stand without wood enclosure.

No. 108.

The above Fittings are made specially for Baths which are fixed without enclosure of any kind. The Taps and Mountings, including stand-pipe, are of polished or nickel-plated brass, and the side standards of wrought iron.

A really superior article for first-class work.

ROYAL PORCELAIN BATHS.

Fitted for Hot, Cold, and Waste, with Mahogany or Walnut-wood Roll, and resting on Marble Feet or Rests. To stand without wood enclosure.

No. 109.

The above is shewn with No. 135 Fittings, comprising Hot and Cold Screw-down Valves, Copper Stand-pipe and Overflow.

No. 110.

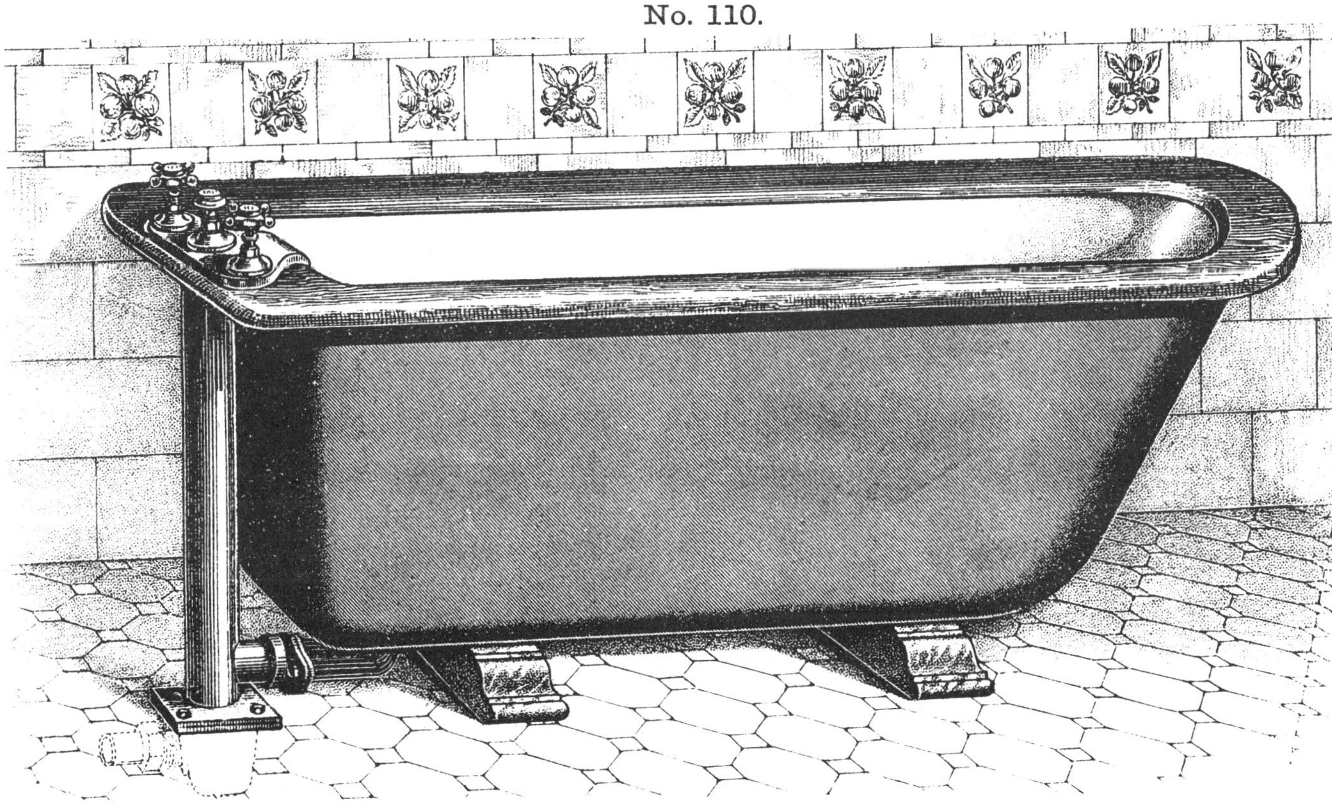

The above is shewn with No. 35A Bath Fittings for Hot, Cold, and Waste, with Cast-iron Stand-pipe and Trap

"EMPRESS" PORCELAIN-WARE BATH

Plate 1000-B.

"WINDHAM" EMPRESS PORCELAIN-WARE BATH TUB glazed inside and over roll-rim with "A" grade exterior finish and pond lily decorations; glazed feet 4½ inches high; Plate 1036-B nickel-plated "Princeton" combined waste and bell supply with china scalps on handles marked "Hot," "Cold" and "Waste;" Plate 1078-B nickel-plated shower complete with offset supplies.

Dimensions same as Plate 992-B.

Size of Tub	5 foot.	5½ foot.
Prices as described, Class "A"	$244.00	259.00
Prices as described, Class "B"	194.00	204.00

Add if with "Star" combined waste and bell supply with marked china scalps on handles	$9.50
Add if with thermometer and mixer on shower	9.00
Add if with wheel handle stops on supply pipes	3.00
If with gold lines instead of pond lily decorations, deduct	15.00

Can be furnished with glazed legs 5¼ inches high if desired at same price.

PATENT STEAMLESS & NOISELESS CLEOPATRA & EMPRESS BATHS

MADE IN CAST IRON, ENAMELLED.

Decoration Design No. 130.

No. 8.—Patent Cleopatra Bath.

Decoration Design No. 129.

No. 74.—Patent Empress Bath.

	Initial Letter indicates Quality only	No. 8.—Patent Taper* Cleopatra Bath, with $\frac{3}{4}''$ Hot and Cold Taps, Lift-up Waste, Earthenware Plate, Accessible Waste Valve, and $1\frac{1}{2}''$ Clear-way Trap and Union.			No. 74.—Patent Taper Empress Bath, with 1″ Hot and Cold Taps, Strong Lift-up Waste, Large Earthenware Plate, Accessible Waste Valve, and 2″ Clear-way Trap and Union.		
Size—		5′ 0″	5′ 6″	6′ 0″	5′ 0″	5′ 6″	6′ 0″
3rd Class Japanned Sienna Inside, and 3rd Class Outside	H	99/-	109/6	115/6	112/6	117/9	124/6
2nd Class Japan Enamelled Inside, and 3rd Class Outside	L	111/-	121/6	129/6	135/-	140/3	146/3
2nd Class Japan Enamelled Inside, and 2/2nd Class Outside	M	121/-	131/6	139/6	145/-	150/7	160/-
1st Class Japan Enamelled Inside, and 3rd Class Outside	O	133/6	144/-	157/6	146/3	152/-	162/-
1st Class Japan Enamelled Inside, and 2nd Class Outside	P	156/6	167/-	180/6	170/3	176/6	186/-
Porcelain Enamelled Inside, and 2nd Class Outside	S	—	—	—	237/-	248/6	265/6
Nickel-plating or Hygeia White Metal		No. 8 Bath, 3/5 extra.			No. 74 Bath, 5/8 extra.		

No. 8 Bath is also made with Secret Overflow, and No. 74 Bath is also made with Tell-tale Overflow, at same Prices.

*** No. 8 BATH, IF MADE PARALLEL, $7\frac{1}{2}$ PER CENT. EXTRA.**

NOTE.—No. 74 Bath is made with large outgo for quick discharge, and affords an excellent flush to house drain.

No. 8 Bath, 5′ 6″, when packed for shipment, measures 6′ 8″ × 2′ 10″ × 2′ 4″, and weighs about 4cwt. 0qr. 20lbs. gross. Best Packing charged 12/6 nett.

SHANKS' PATENT "EUREKA" BATH.

No. 2.

THE ACME OF LUXURIOUS BATHING.

The spray and shower canopies in use hitherto have been defective, because necessarily contracted in size and shape to fit the size and shape of ordinary Plunge Baths.

The hitherto accepted forms and methods of Bath fittings have been complicated, expensive, laborious to fit up, and ready to get out of order.

All these defects are obviated in the "EUREKA" BATH. The Plunge Bath of cast-iron enamelled, is made with a large circular end, as will be best seen in plan on page 26; the canopy is made to suit this, so that the spray jets all converge to the centre, and ample room is provided for the bather.

The system of fittings is more fully explained in the following pages; it mixes the hot and cold water, supplies all the various arrangements with a third of the number of pipes; it saves two-thirds of the labour of fitting; and beyond all, it is simpler and more certain of action than any system of bath fittings ever invented. The waste pull is on a new and improved style; and the waste pipe of Bath on Shanks' Patent Principle.

For description of Fittings, see page 27.

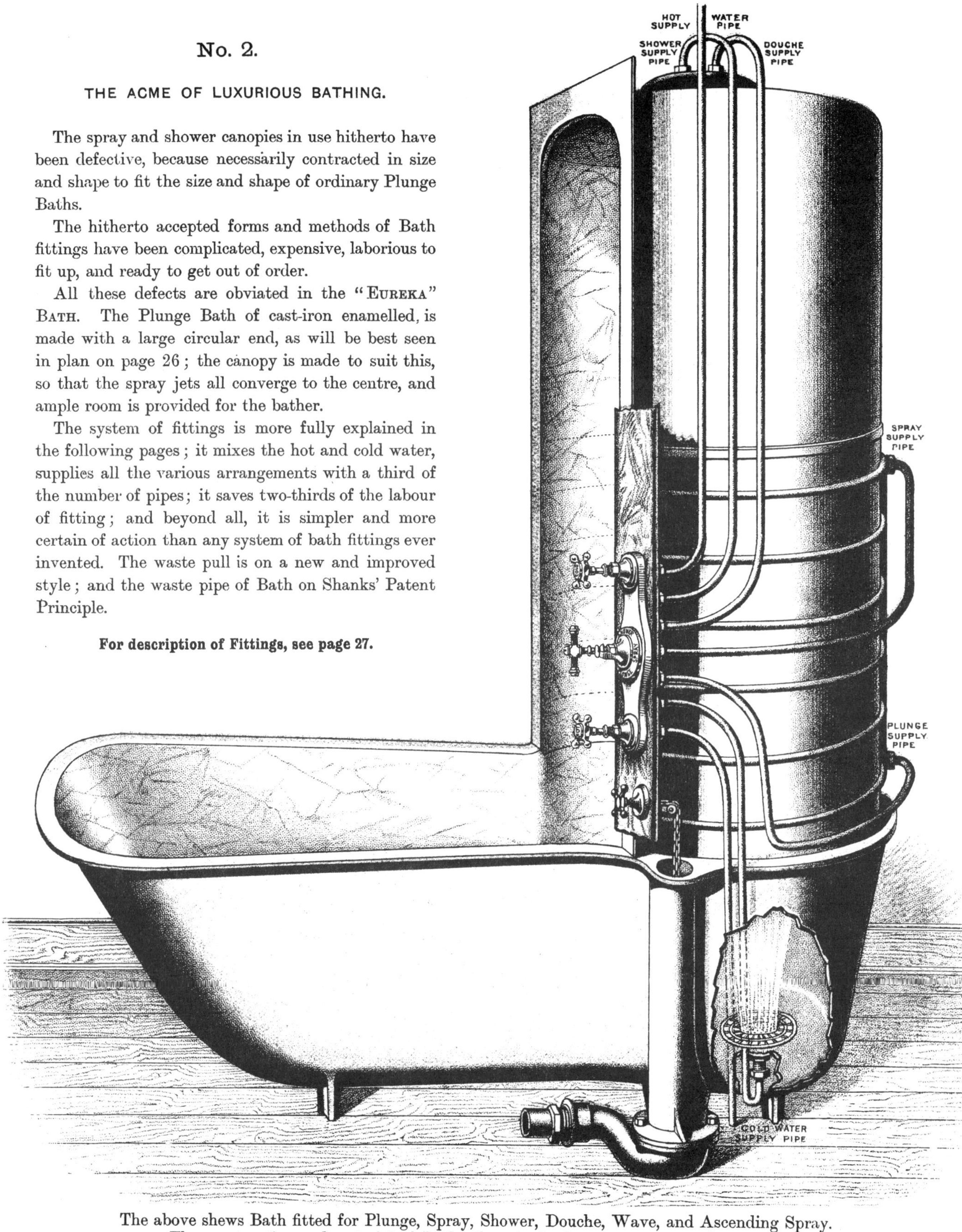

The above shews Bath fitted for Plunge, Spray, Shower, Douche, Wave, and Ascending Spray.
The construction and material of Bath otherwise is the same as on previous page.

SHANKS' SPRAY, SHOWER, WAVE, AND PLUNGE BATHS.

In view of the increasing and very wise desire to abandon the usual covering up of pipes and sanitary appliances with wood linings and casings, we have introduced this very fine arrangement.

This is an illustration of a Bath constructed entirely of Copper and Brass. The Rolled Edge is of Brass Nickel-plated, the Plunge is of Copper Enamelled, and the Spray and Shower are of Copper Nickel-plated. The Spray is surrounded by a Waterproof Curtain.

It is fitted with Copper Standing Waste Pipe, and the Patent "Eureka" Fittings for Plunge, Spray, Shower, and Wave, are all connected by N.-P. Copper Pipes. The arrangement is thus very complete, requiring no woodwork.

A cheaper arrangement of equal utility can easily be supplied.

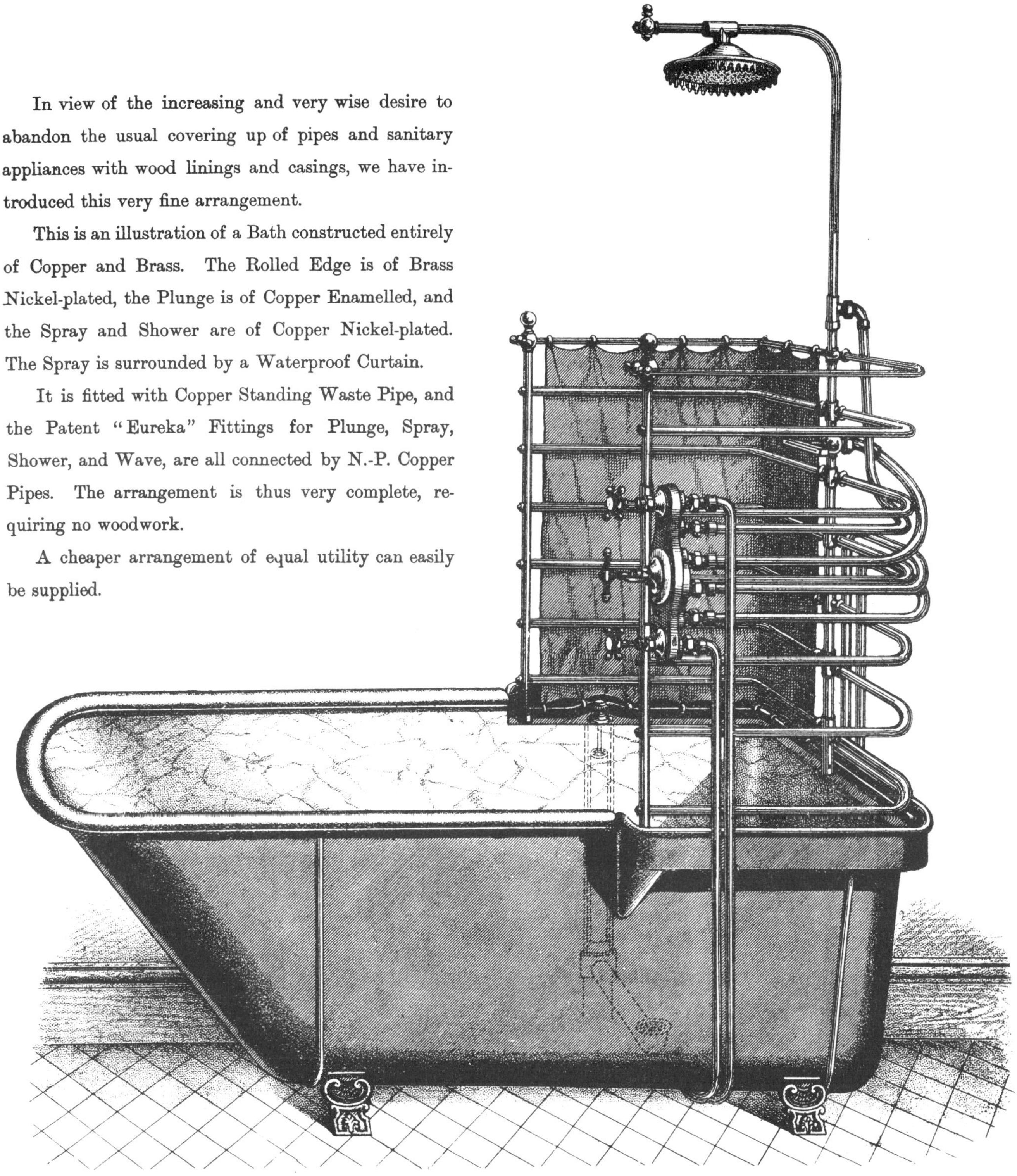

No. 14.

A really splendid Bath. Prices on application.

DOULTON'S IMPROVED HOODED BATHS.

No. 379.

THE Apparatus consists of a Recessed Cast-Iron Plunge Bath with Flange, 1st class Enamelled inside, with strong Copper Hood Enamelled the same colour as Bath. Fitted with Shower, Spray, and Plunge, Brass Plate for Valves and Pull-up Waste.

The temperature of the water may be regulated by the Hot and Cold Valves, and the centre valve on plate enables you to connect the water to any fitting required by turning the pointer to where it is marked on the plate.

PRICES.

		£	s.	d.
No. 379.	—6 ft. Cast-Iron Recessed Bath and Copper Hood with Brass Fittings for Shower, Spray, and Plunge, 1st class Enamelled,	£22	15	0
No. 379A.	—Do., do., but with 5 ft. 6 in. Bath,	22	5	0
No. 379B.	—Do., do., but with 6 ft. Bath and Zinc Hood, - - - - - - -	17	10	0
No. 379C.	—Do., do., but with 5 ft. 6 in. Bath and Zinc Hood, - - - - - -	17	0	0
No. 379D.	—Strong 6 ft. Copper Recessed Bath and Hood with Brass Fittings for Shower, Spray, and Plunge, 1st class Enamelled,	32	10	0
No. 379E.	—Do., do., but with 5 ft. 6 in. Bath and Zinc Hood, - - - - - -	31	10	0
	Wave Fittings, - - - - - - extra,	1	2	0
	Douche Fittings, - - - - - ,,	0	15	0
	Plated Fittings, - - - - - ,,	0	10	0

Measurements—5′6″ Bath; Length over all, 5′8½″; Height, 7′10″

Rising Spray and Jet may be had if required.

The Interior can be Enamelled any colour that may be desired.

For designs and particulars of Enclosures see pages 95, 96, 97.

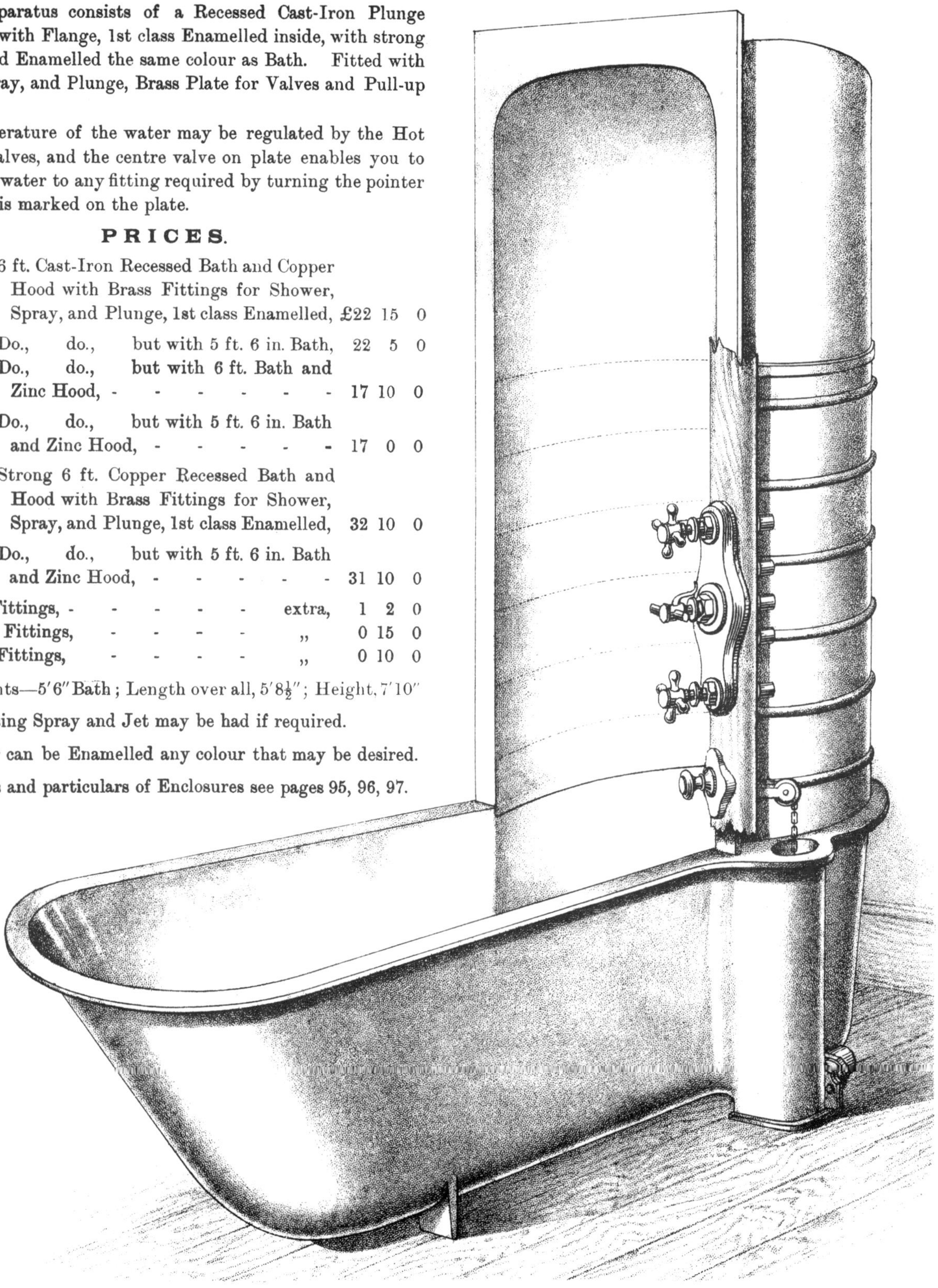

☞ These Baths are entirely Manufactured at our Paisley Works and Foundries.

For Designs of Tiling, see pages 4, 6, 38, 57, 58, 59, 60, 61, 157, 158.

DOULTON'S IMPROVED HOODED BATHS AND ENCLOSURES.

No. 222.

Prices of Enclosures only, without Bath and Fittings.

	£	s.	d.
No. 222.—In Polished Columbia Pine, with Carving, Bevelled Mirror, and Door, and Hand Painted Tile Skirting, - - -	£46	10	0
In Mahogany or Walnut,	50	0	0
In Oak, - - -	51	0	0
With St. Anne's Marble Top, extra,	4	15	0
Do. Rouge Royal do., ,,	5	0	0

For prices of Baths see pages 89, 90.

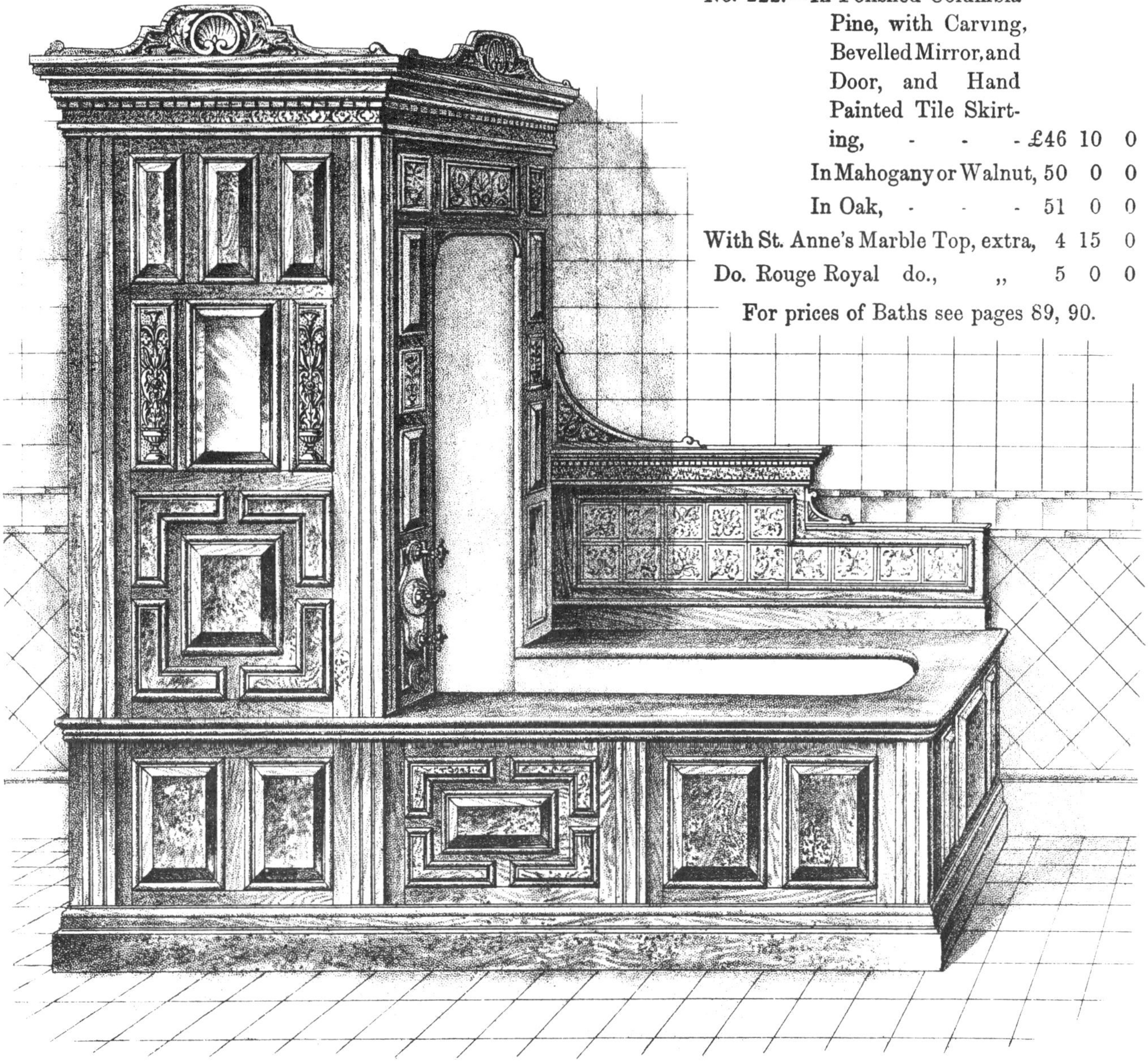

THIS Illustration shows a design of Bath Enclosure specially suited for Private Houses. It may be had in various woods to accord with the surroundings, or the design can be modified to suit architect's requirements.

For Designs of Tiling see pages 4, 6, 38, 57, 58, 59, 60, 61, 157, 158.

DOULTON'S IMPROVED HOODED BATHS AND ENCLOSURES.

No. 222B.

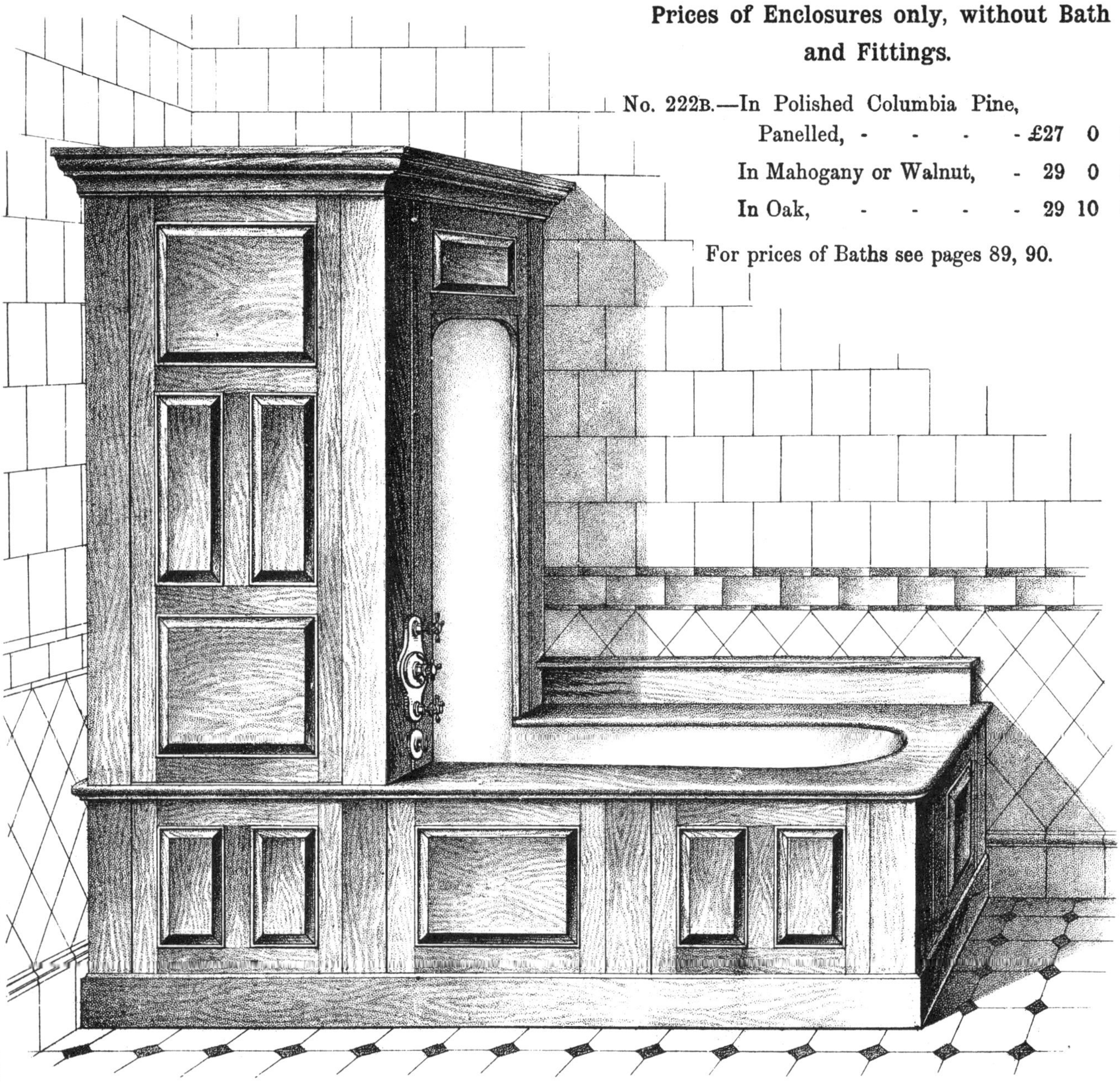

Prices of Enclosures only, without Bath and Fittings.

No. 222B.—In Polished Columbia Pine, Panelled, - - - -	£27	0	0
In Mahogany or Walnut, -	29	0	0
In Oak, - - - - -	29	10	0

For prices of Baths see pages 89, 90.

THIS Enclosure is strong and well finished, though plainer in design than those shown on previous pages.

For Designs of Tiling see pages 4, 6, 38, 57, 58, 59, 60, 61, 157, 158.

IMPROVED PATENT SPRAY, SHOWER, AND RECLINING BATHS.

MADE IN CAST-IRON, WITH ZINC OR COPPER SPRAY ENCLOSURE, AND ENAMEL PAINTED.

No. 57.—Spray and Shower Bath, Spray Enclosure made in Sheet Zinc, with 6′ 0″ Parallel-sided Cast-iron Reclining Bath, combined Hot and Cold $\frac{3}{4}$″ Taps, and Mixing Box with Controlling Taps for Spray, Shower and Reclining Baths; Lift-up Waste Arrangement with Reversible Trap, and all piping between Mixing Box and each way. Enamel Painted 1st Class Inside, and 2nd Class Outside, Decorated ... ... Price, £24 17 6

No. 58.—Do. do. with Copper Spray Enclosure instead of Sheet Zinc ... ... Price, £28 17 6

No. 146.—Bath and Mahogany or Walnut Enclosure with Tiled Skirting. This Bath is made with Sheet Zinc Spray Enclosure, and all Piping as No. 57, but prepared for Wood Enclosure ... ... Price, £34 8 6

No. 147.—Do. do. but Spray Enclosure in Copper ... ... Price, £37 8 6

No. 148.—Mahogany or Walnut Enclosure with Tiled Skirting, but without Bath and Fittings ... ... Price, £14 9 6

NICKEL-PLATING FITTINGS,

10/- extra.

Decoration Design No. 143.

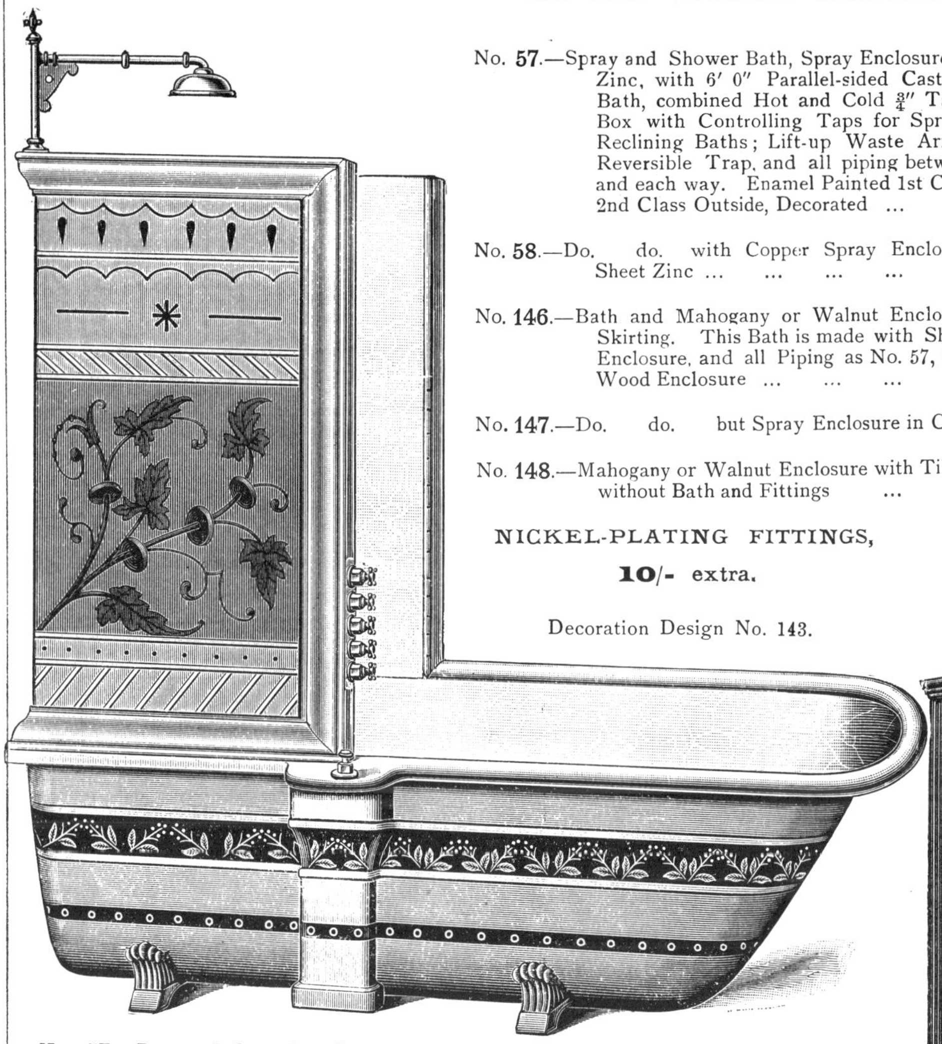

No. 57.—Patent Independent Spray Bath, Sheet Zinc Spray Enclosure.

No. 58.—Do. do. do. Copper Enclosure.

These Baths, if made without Shower and Fittings, and piping for same, **35/-** less.

NOTE.—The Nos. 57 and 146 Baths are made with Copper Spray Tubes.

Baths are made either hand. No. 57 is shewn left-hand and No. 146 right-hand.

No. 57 Bath, when packed for Shipment, requires 2 packages measuring respectively 6′ 7″ × 2′ 9″ × 2′ 4″ and 5′ 6″ × 3′ 0″ × 3′ 0″; gross weight of Bath (both), 9cwt. 2qrs. 14lbs.

Packing Charged 32/6 Nett.

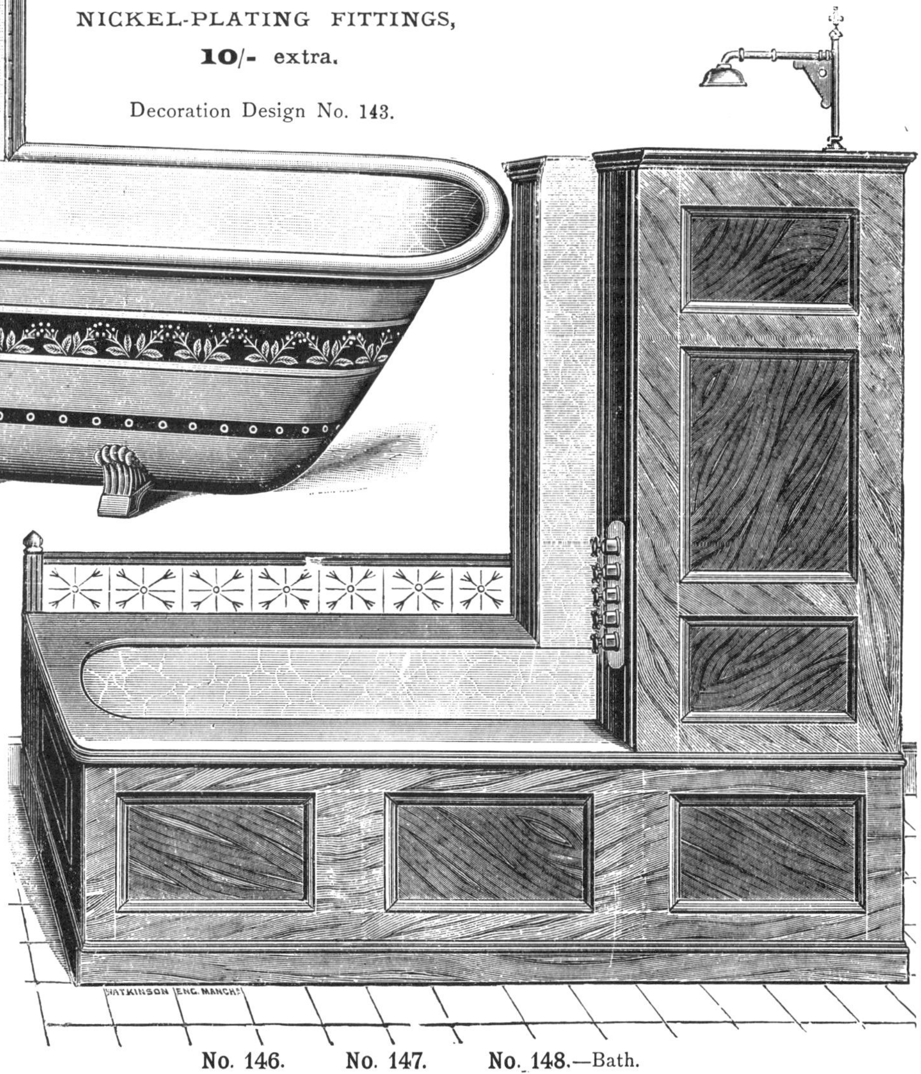

No. 146. No. 147. No. 148.—Bath.

PATENT ORIENTAL SPRAY BATH, WITH FURNITURE.

LUXURIOUS BATHING.

No. 122.—Bath.
„ 123.— „
„ 124.— „

No. 122.—Bath Enclosure, made in best manner, of Mahogany or Walnut, with Hand-painted Tiled Back Skirting, including No. 112 Bath and Fittings; no connecting Lead Piping ... ... Price **£65 16/-**

No. 123.—Bath do. do., but with No. 115 Bath and Fittings; no connecting Lead Piping ... Price **£97 6/-**

No. 124.—Bath Enclosure only, in Walnut or Mahogany, and Tiled Skirting; no Bath or Fittings ... ... Price **£37 10/-**

WHITE HYGEIA METAL OR NICKEL-PLATED FITTINGS, 10/- EXTRA.

When Ordering, please say if required Right or Left-hand; Bath Shewn is Left-hand.

Bath Furniture made in our own Workshops to Special Designs. ***Estimates on Application.***

PATENT ORIENTAL SELF-SETTING SPRAY BATH.

REFRESHING BATHING.

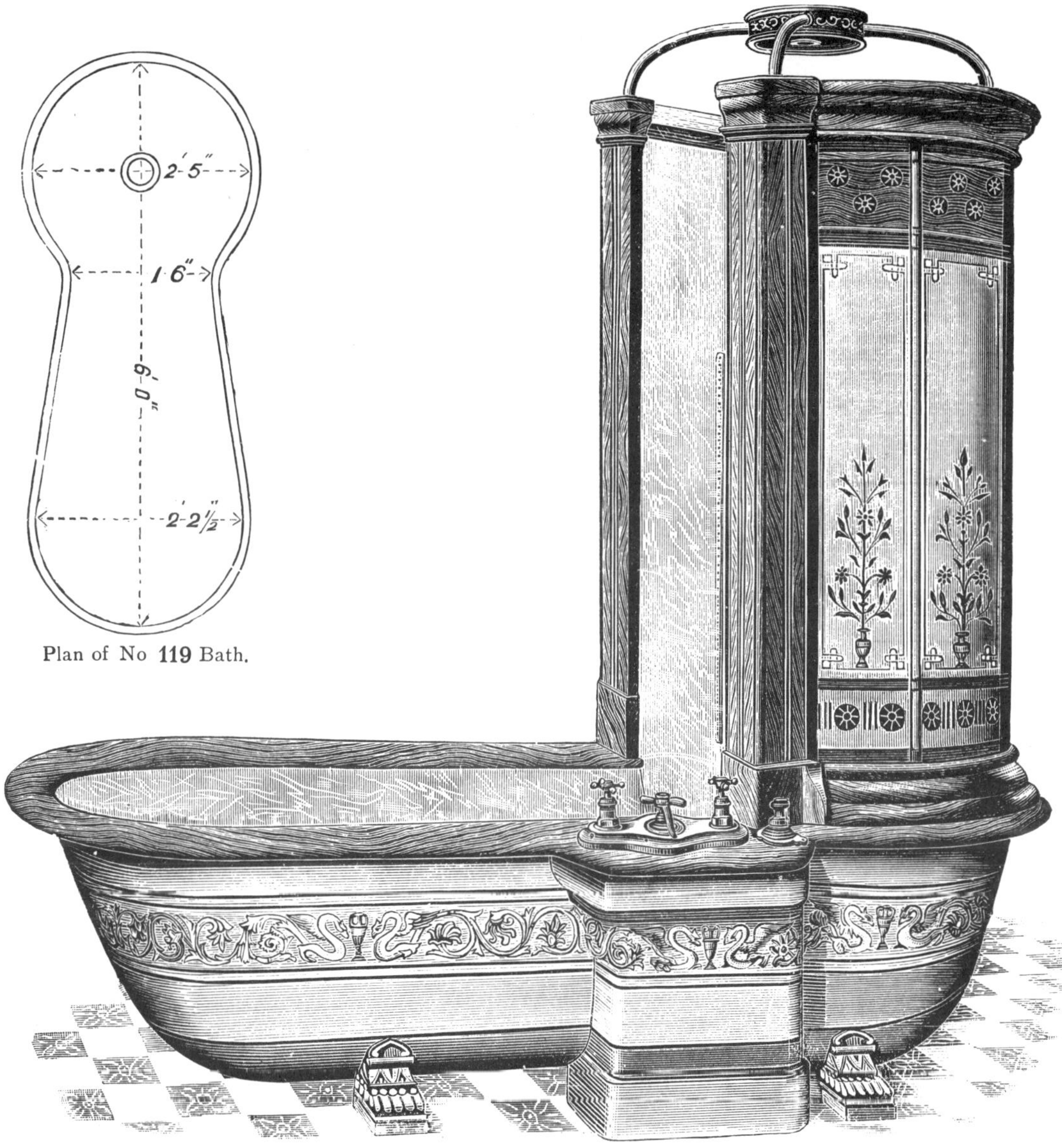

Plan of No 119 Bath.

Decorative Design No. 144.

No. 119.—Bath.
„ 120.— „
„ 121. – „

No. 119 Bath.—The unique Bath here shewn is made with 1″ Combined Hot and Cold Taps, Mixing Box and Dividing Arrangement, and Connecting Piping from same to Shower, Douche, Spray and Reclining Baths. The Reclining Bath is made of Cast Iron, and the Spray Enclosure of Plate Zinc; the interior is Enamel Painted 1st Class, and 2nd Class outside decorated. The Bath is finished in a superior manner with Walnut or Mahogany Capping, Pilasters, and bold circular Mouldings ... ... Price **£42 0 0**

No. 120.—Bath as above, but Reclining and Spray Baths are made of **Cast-brass** ... ... Price **£95 18 0**

No. 121.—Bath as No. 119, but Spray Enclosure made in Hammered Copper ... ... Price **£50 12 6**

IF WITHOUT DOUCHE AND CONNECTING FITTINGS, **22/6** Less.

These Baths, if made with Uprising Douche or Spray instead of descending Douche, same Price.

WHITE HYGEIA METAL OR NICKEL-PLATED FITTINGS, **10/-** Extra.

Baths are made either right or left hand. Bath shewn is right-hand.

SHANKS' SUPERIOR BATH CABINETS.

These are made in our own Cabinet Factory, and being fitted to the Baths with which they are supplied, a most satisfactory job is ensured.

MADE IN MAHOGANY, WALNUT OR OTHER FANCY WOODS.

Bath Cabinet, No. 968.

Bath Cabinet, No. 1017.

The above Cabinets may be fitted to any of Shanks' Plunge Baths.

Hundreds of most elaborate Cabinets have been supplied by S. & Co.

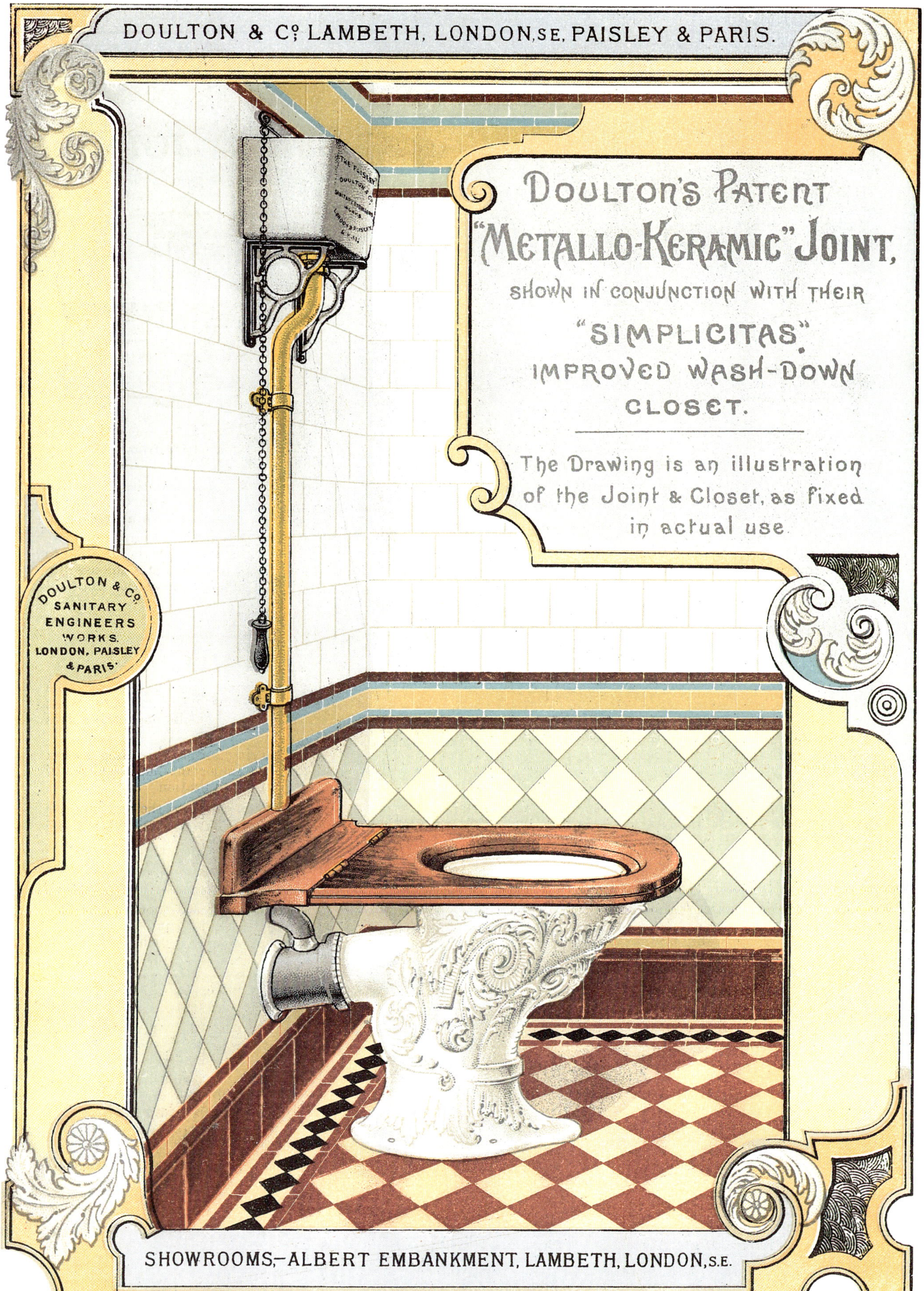

Floor Tile Design, No. 226a.—Dado, No. 230a.—Upper Wall Pattern, No. 229a.

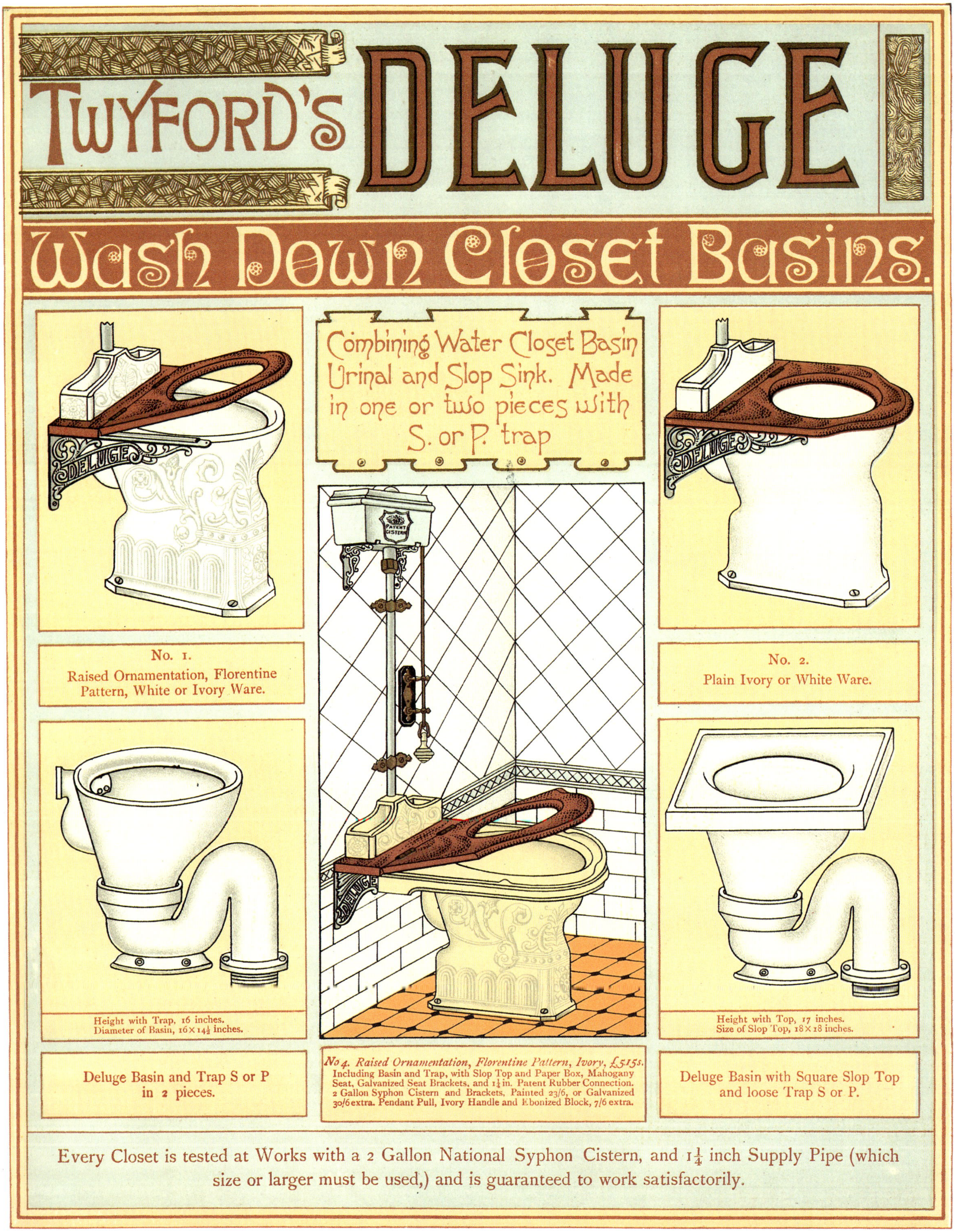
TWYFORD'S
DELUGE
Wash Down Closet Basins.
Combining Water Closet Basin Urinal and Slop Sink. Made in one or two pieces with S. or P. trap
DELUGE
No. 1.
Raised Ornamentation, Florentine Pattern, White or Ivory Ware.
No. 2.
Plain Ivory or White Ware.
PATENT CISTERN
Height with Trap, 16 inches.
Diameter of Basin, 16 × 14½ inches.
Deluge Basin and Trap S or P in 2 pieces.
No 4. Raised Ornamentation, Florentine Pattern, Ivory, £5 15s.
Including Basin and Trap, with Slop Top and Paper Box, Mahogany Seat, Galvanized Seat Brackets, and 1¼ in. Patent Rubber Connection. 2 Gallon Syphon Cistern and Brackets, Painted 23/6, or Galvanized 30/6 extra. Pendant Pull, Ivory Handle and Ebonized Block, 7/6 extra.
Height with Top, 17 inches.
Size of Slop Top, 18 × 18 inches.
Deluge Basin with Square Slop Top and loose Trap S or P.
Every Closet is tested at Works with a 2 Gallon National Syphon Cistern, and 1¼ inch Supply Pipe (which size or larger must be used,) and is guaranteed to work satisfactorily.

Combining Water Closet Basin

"UNITAS"

Also Urinal & Slop Sink

DIMENSIONS WITH SEAT.

Back to Front,	28 in.
Across,	20 ,,
Height,	19 ,,
Wall Line to Centre of Outlet, S Trap,	13¾ ,,

No. 4—" UNITAS,"—[No. 1 Florentine Pattern, Ivory, Raised Ornamentation and Slop Top], with After Flush and Paper Box—No. 2 Mahogany Seat, with Hinged Cover—Brass Seat Brackets—No. 1 Mahogany Cistern, with Hand-Carved Panels, fitted with either Copper or Earthenware Lining, including Fittings—Brass Cistern Brackets—Brass Flushing Pipe and Clips—Pendant Pull—and Brass Supply Connection, £13 5 0.

No. 8. "Dahlia" Pattern,
Blue Print on White Ware.

No. 9. "Florentine" Pattern,
Brown Print on Ivory Ware.

No. 10. "Florentine" Pattern,
Blue Print on White Ware.

Combining Water Closet Basin

"UNITAS"

Also Urinal & Slop Sink

No. 11. "Florentine" Pattern,
Blue and Gold on White Ware.

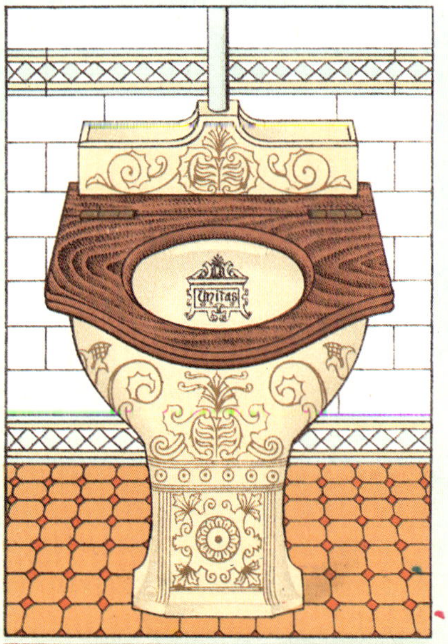

No. 12. Raised Ornamentation,
"Florentine" Pattern, Traced in Gold, Ivory Ware.

Traced in Blue is No. 14.

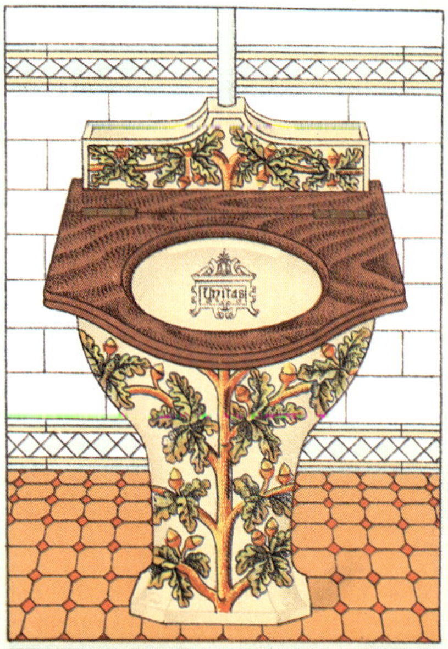

No. 13. Raised Ornamentation,
"Oak" Pattern, Coloured, White or Ivory Ware.

OKEANOS CLOSETS. PATENT WASH DOWN.

MADE OF FINEST IVORY OR WHITE WARE PORCELAIN.

No. 211.—Okeanos Closet Suite.

No. 212.—Embossed. No. 213.—Plain.

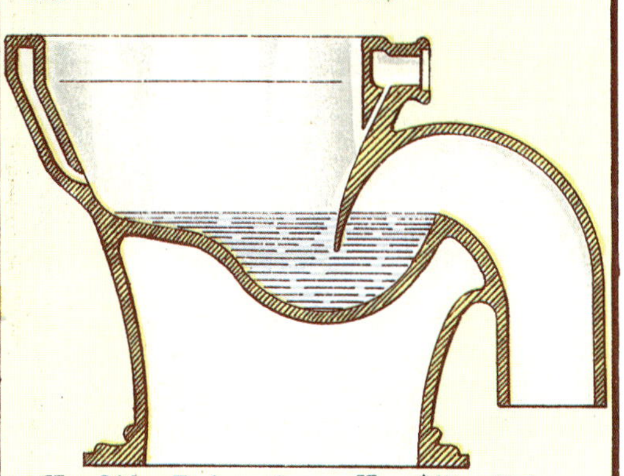

No. 214.—Embossed. No. 215.—Plain.

No. 213.—Closet printed and picked out in colors.

The Okeanos Closet is similar in principle to the Triton Closet shewn on page 144, save that the water area is slightly more. The outgo of Trap is arranged to connect with Earthenware or Brass Soil Pipe, either to go through floor or wall, as drawn. Attention is directed to our system of placing cistern away from window, and bringing straight flushing pipe down corner without the usual swan-necks.

Decorated in one color	10/-	Printed in one color	5/- extra.
Decorated in colors ...	13/6	Printed and picked out in colors...	13/6 „
Decorated in colors and picked out in best gold	47/6	Printed and picked out in colors and best gold	47/6 „

Reversible Ferrule Bend in Cast Gun Metal ... ... 9/4 „

No. 211.—Patent Okeanos Closet Suite consists of—

	£	s.	d.
No. 137, 3 gallons Flush, Mahogany or Walnut Cistern, Copper Lined	2	15	0
„ 138, Brackets, Enamel Painted, Decorated	0	5	4
„ 216, Copper Flushing Pipe, Enamel Painted	1	2	4
„ 134, Bracket Pull...	0	8	3
„ 217, Combined Cabinet Paper Box and Shelf	0	10	0
„ 218, Mahogany or Walnut Seat and Brackets	1	16	0
„ 214, Closet in Ivoryware ...	2	2	0
Price of complete Suite ...	£8	18	11

Okeanos Closets in Ivoryware, S or P Trap.

Nos.	212	213	214	215
	42/-	40/-	42/-	40/-

JOHN HEYWOOD, CHROMO LITHO. MANCHESTER, LONDON, BRISTOL, LIVERPOOL.

PLUG BASINS, DECORATED.

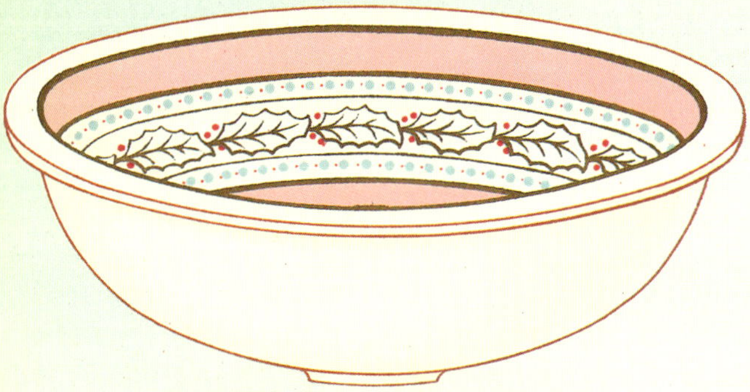

PLUG BASIN, decoration No. 19.

PLUG BASIN, decoration No. 20.

PLUG BASIN, decoration No. 21.

PLUG BASIN, decoration No. 22.

PLUG BASIN, decoration No. 23.

PLUG BASIN, decoration No. 24.

PLUG BASIN, decoration No. 25.

PLUG BASIN, decoration No. 26.

PLUG BASINS, PRINTED.

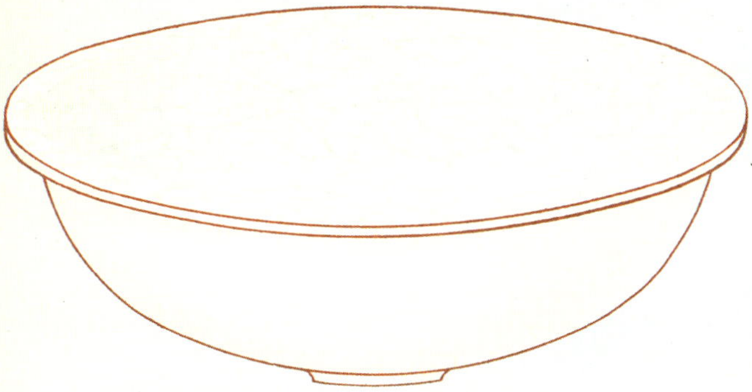

PLUG BASIN, printed marble, pattern No. 35.

PLUG BASIN, printed, pattern No. 36.

PLUG BASIN, printed, pattern No. 37.

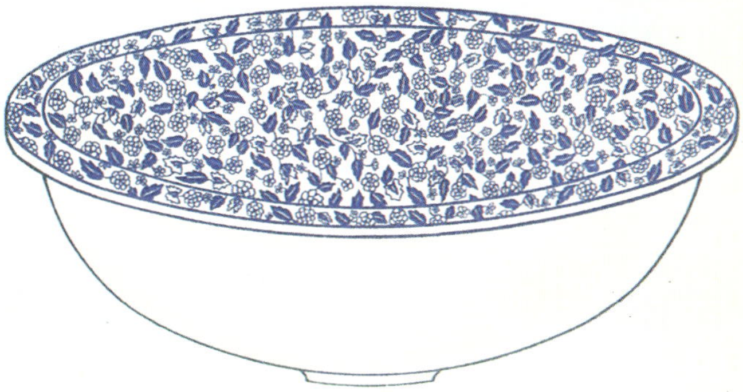

PLUG BASIN, printed, pattern No. 38.

PLUG BASIN, printed, pattern No. 39.

PLUG BASIN, printed, pattern No. 40.

PLUG BASIN, printed, pattern No. 41.

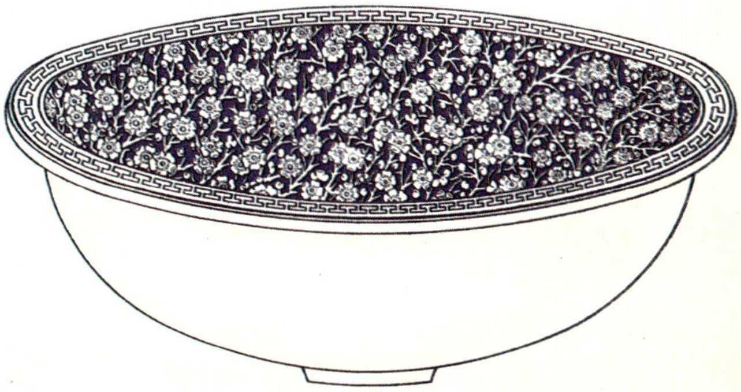

PLUG BASIN, printed, pattern No. 42.

DECORATED LAVATORIES.

Decoration No. 170.
Lavatory No. 35.

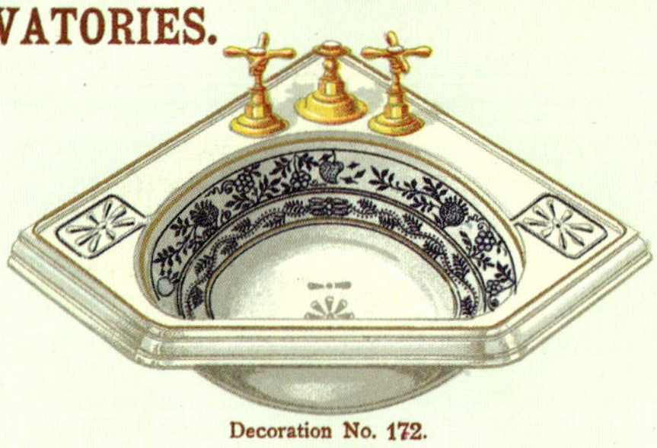

Decoration No. 172.
Lavatory No. 39.

When ordering Decorated Lavatories, for quick delivery, please give 2nd choice of decoration.

Decoration No. 171.
Lavatory No. 151.

Decoration No. 173.
Lavatory No. 36.

Patent Lavatory in Ivoryware, with Hot, Cold and Waste Fittings complete ...			No. 35	36			No. 39	151
Decorated as shewn			No. 170	173			No. 172 and Gold.	171 and Gold
	Size Outside.	Bowl Inside.			Size.	Bowl.		
	18″ × 18″	14″	55/6	66/9				
	22″ × 18″	16″	69/-	85/6	22″ × 18″	13″ × 10″	108/-	95/3
	27″ × 20″	18″	80/3	99/-	27″ × 20″	16½″ × 12″	121/6	109/6
	30″ × 22″	20″	99/-	126/-	30″ × 22″	17″ × 13″	145/6	125/3

HYGEIA WHITE METAL OR NICKEL-PLATING FITTINGS, 3/5 Extra. TRAP, 4/6 Extra.

These Decorations are Transferable. Prices on Application.

DECORATED LAVATORY BOWLS.

Decoration No. 160.
Lavatory No. 66.

Decoration No. 162. Lavatory No. 154.

Decoration No. 163.
Lavatory No. 66.

When ordering Decorated Lavatories, for quick delivery, please give 2nd choice of decoration.

Decoration No. 161.
Lavatory No. 64.

Decoration No. 165.
Lavatory No. 66.

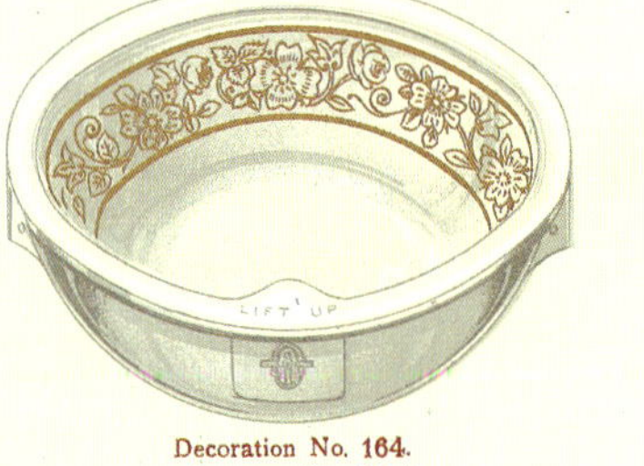

Decoration No. 164.
Lavatory No. 65.

No.		Size outside.	Size inside.	Ivory or White Ware.	Printed underglaze in 1 color.	Printed underglaze in colors.	Decorated in colors and gold. No. 160.	161.	162.	163.	164.	165.
64	D Tip-up Bowl. Price for Decoration only	17″	—	—	3/-	9/-	27/-	21/-	22/6	39/-	33/-	23/3
		20″	—	—	3/6	11/3	31/6	24/-	27/-	42/6	36/-	27/9
65	Round Tip-up Bowl. Price for Decoration only	12″	—	—	2/-	4/-	16/-	12/-	13/-	27/-	25/-	—
		14″	—	—	2/6	5/-	18/-	14/-	15/-	29/-	27/-	16/6
		16″	—	—	3/-	6/9	21/-	16/-	18/-	34/-	30/-	19/6
		18″	—	—	3/6	9/-	27/-	21/-	22/6	39/-	33/-	23/3
66	D Bowl with Brass Waste Arrangement	—	14″	26/-	28/6	31/3	44/-	40/3	41/-	56/-	53/-	42/6
		—	16″	28/-	30/6	34/9	49/9	44/6	46/9	64/-	58/-	47/6
		—	18″	32/3	35/3	41/3	59/3	53/3	54/9	71/3	65/3	55/6
		—	20″	33/9	37/6	45/-	65/3	57/9	60/9	76/3	69/9	61/9
154	Patented and Registered Lavozonic, Embossed Exterior, Lever Handle Quarter-turn Taps, and Brass Waste Arrangement	22½″ × 20″	20″ × 14″	66/9	69/9	78/-	98/3	90/9	93/9	111/9	102/6	94/6
154A	Do. do. Plain Exterior, not Embossed... ...	22½″ × 20″	20″ × 14″	60/2	63/2	71/5	91/8	84/2	87/2	105/2	95/11	87/11

HYGEIA WHITE METAL OR NICKEL-PLATING WASTE HANDLE, 1/1 Extra. HYGEIA WHITE METAL OR NICKEL-PLATING TAPS AND WASTE HANDLE, 3/5 Extra.
1½″ BRASS TRAP, 4/6 Extra. GRINDING FLANGE OF BOWL, 3/9 Extra.

NOTE.—Nos. 154 and 154A. Decorated outside on front, extra in proportion. If with Spoke Head Screw-down Taps, 3/9 less. Also made with Overedge Taps at same Prices.

DRESSING ROOM CABINET LAVATORY.

PATENT LAVOZONIC.

No. 226.

No. 226.—The Dressing Room Cabinet Lavatory here shewn, is made and finished in the very best style. The Stand and Overmantel may be in Walnut or Spanish Mahogany. Convenient Cupboards and Drawers of various sizes are provided, whilst the Overmantel is fitted with Bevelled Edge Mirrors, Hand Painted Tiles, and Bracket Shelves for the display of bric-a-brac, &c.

The Bowl is No. 154a Decorated Lavozonic, 20″ inside, with Quarter or Half Turn Hot and Cold Steamless and Noiseless Supply, and Quick Waste, carefully fitted to the 1¼″ Marble Slab (4′ 0″ × 2′ 0″), with Moulded Edges and Shaped Front ... ... Price complete, £37 17 6

NICKEL-PLATING OR HYGEIA WHITE METAL FITTINGS, 3/5 Extra.

ART POTTERY SHEWN NOT INCLUDED IN PRICE.

JOHN HEYWOOD, CHROMO LITHO, MANCHESTER, LONDON, BRISTOL, LIVERPOOL.

Morrison, Ingram & Co., Manchester.

No.		3rd Class in one color.	2nd Class in colors or bronzed	1st Class in various colors.
178	Lavatory Stand in Cast Iron, Mirror and Tile Back and Shelf; No. 158 Basin, 27″ × 19″, with Hot and Cold Taps and accessible jointed Waste Arrangement, and 1¼″ Outlet Union	109/1	130/-	139/5
203	Lavatory Stand as above, but with No. 200 Basin, 27″ × 19″, Taps, Plug and Chain, instead of No. 158 Basin	82/10	103/9	113/2
	If without Basin, Stand only	49/1	70/-	79/5
	Moveable Shield, each ... ... extra	5/9	8/-	9/-

BRASS TRAP, 4/6 Extra. **HYGEIA WHITE METAL OR NICKEL-PLATED FITTINGS, 3/5 Extra.**

The 3rd Class finish is Plain Painted one color, and the 2nd and 1st Class are Enamel Painted, and picked out in colors. The effect is very pleasing. These Stands are manufactured to occupy the least possible space when packed for shipment.

JOHN HEYWOOD CHROMO LITHO. MANCHESTER, LONDON, BRISTOL, LIVERPOOL.

DOULTON & CO., LAMBETH, LONDON S.E., PAISLEY & PARIS.

DOULTON'S IMPROVED HOODED BATHS.

TO STAND WITHOUT ENCLOSURE.

No. 377.

THE Apparatus consists of a recessed Cast-Iron Plunge Bath with wide Rolled Edge, 1st class Enamelled inside, with strong Copper Hood Enamelled same colour as Bath. Fitted with Shower, Spray, and Plunge, Brass Plate for Valves and Pull-up Waste. The Hood is protected by an outer casing of Zinc with hinged door to allow easy access to the pipes.

The temperature of the water may be regulated by the Hot and Cold Valves, and the centre valve on plate enables you to connect the water to any fitting required by turning the pointer to where it is marked on the plate.

The only Connections to be made are the Hot and Cold Water Supplies and Waste, three Joints in all.

PRICES.

No. 377. —6 ft. Cast-Iron Recessed Bath and Copper Hood with Brass Fittings for Shower, Spray, and Plunge, 1st class Enamelled,		£28	0	0
No. 377A.—Do., do., but with 5 ft. 6 in. Bath, - - - - - - - -		27	10	0
No. 377B.—Do., do., but with 6 ft. Bath and Zinc Hood, - - - - - -		23	0	0
No. 377C.—Do., do., but with 5 ft. 6 in. Bath and Zinc Hood, - - - - -		22	10	0
Wave Fittings, - - - - - -	extra,	1	3	0
Douche Fittings, - - - - - -	„	1	3	0
Plated Fittings, - - - - - -	„	0	15	0

Measurements.—5′ 6″ Bath; Length over all, 6′ 2″; Height, 7′ 9″.

Rising Spray and Jet may be had if required.

The Interior can be Enamelled any colour that may be desired.

The Exterior may also be varied.

For Designs of Tiling see pages 4, 6, 38, 57, 58, 59, 60, 61, 157, 158.

☞ These Baths are entirely manufactured at our Paisley Works and Foundries.

DESIGNS FOR BATH DECORATION.

THESE illustrations are chiefly for the purpose of showing exterior decoration, the interior may be any colour that is desired, excepting French Grey and Old Gold.

Decorations, I to P, 10/- extra.

I

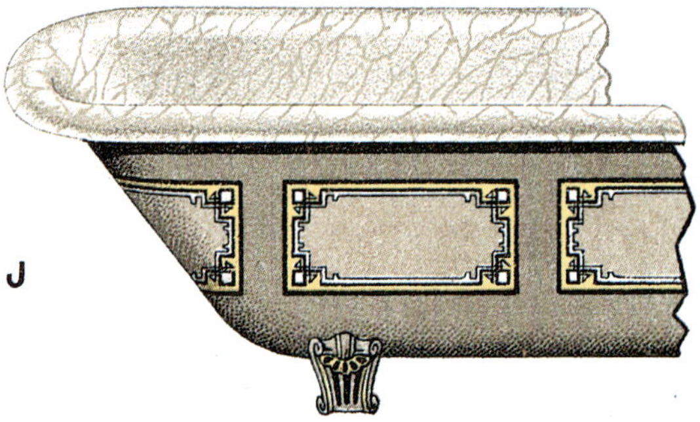

J

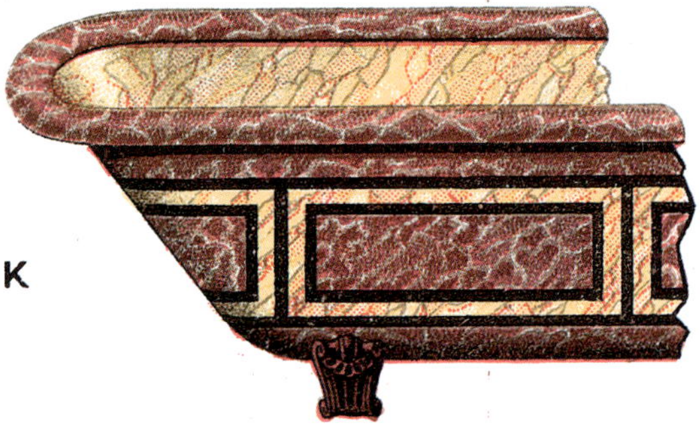

K

L

M

N

O

P

Imitation Mahogany, or Walnut, or Dark Marble Rolls, 5/- extra to prices quoted.

If special Roll not ordered the Baths will have it enamelled the same colour as the interior, which may be of any pattern shown except No. S, the Old Gold and French Grey, which are 5/- extra.

DESIGNS FOR BATH DECORATION.

THESE illustrations are chiefly for the purpose of showing exterior decoration, the interior may be any colour that is desired, excepting French Grey and Old Gold.

Decorations, Q to T, 15/- extra.

Q

R

S

T

Imitation Mahogany or Walnut Roll, 5/- extra to prices quoted.

If special Roll not ordered the Baths will have it enamelled the same colour as the interior, which may be of any pattern shown except letter. S, the Old Gold and French Grey, which are 5/- extra.

SPECIALLY DESIGNED BATH PLATES.

FOR PARALLEL BATHS. / **FOR TAPER BATHS.**

1. 

1A. 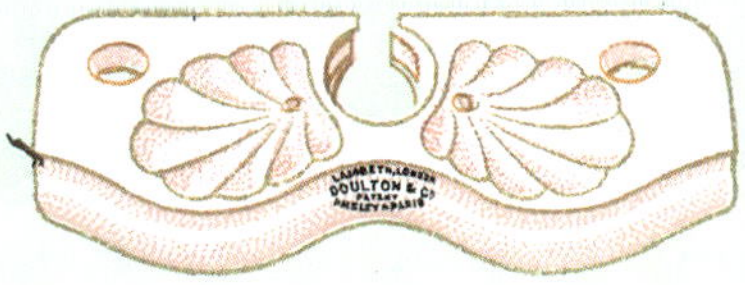

2. 

2A. 

3. 

3A. 

4. 

4A. 

5. 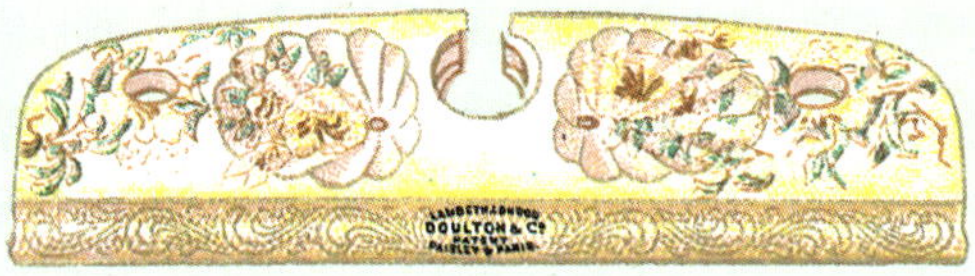

5A. 

These may be had with any Combined Baths in place of white at an extra cost of 15/- for Parallel, and 13/- for Taper.

Décor N° 6
ÉTABLISSEMENTS PORCHER
52, Rue d'Hauteville, PARIS
IMP. EUGÈNE VERNEAU. 108, R. FOLIE MERICOURT. _ PARIS

Installation de Salle de Bains (Modèle A)

1 **Baignoire modèle " ROMAINE "**, émail porcelaine blanc à l'intérieur et sur la gorge, extérieur laqué crème avec filets or, montée avec robinetterie extérieure eau chaude et froide, vidage perfectionné en cuivre nickelé formant trop-plein, avec siphon, douche en pluie et douche en jet et pluie interchangeables, cercle porte-rideau et rideau tissu caoutchouté. . . . . **Complète : 675** Frs

1 **Lavabo Louis XV** avec glace, monture fonte laquée crème et or, cuvette forme spéciale porcelaine crème et filets or avec vidage perfectionné formant trop-plein et robinets eau chaude et froide en cuivre nickelé . . . . **Complet : 375** »

1 **Bidet " PEDESTAL "** en une seule pièce de porcelaine crème avec filets or, robinetterie eau chaude et froide et vidage perfectionné formant trop-plein. . . . . **Complet : 200** »

(Les bords de ce bidet sont chauffés par l'arrivée d'eau chaude qui se fait tout autour de la gorge, ce qui évite à la personne qui s'en sert la sensation désagréable du froid de la porcelaine).

1 **Closet " LE PRIMO carré "**, appareil fonctionnant par aspiration avec siège double abattant acajou attenant à la cuvette; cuvette en une seule pièce de porcelaine crème et filets or; réservoir de chasse en porcelaine même décor, consoles, tuyau de descente et colliers en cuivre nickelé et tirage riche à glissière . . . . **Complet : 375** »

(Le closet de forme carrée a été créé de façon à pouvoir servir de tabouret ou siège dans la salle de bains).

1 **Porte-savon** en cuivre nickelé mobile s'adaptant sur la gorge de la baignoire . . . . **7** »

1 **Porte-éponge** cuivre nickelé . . . . **10** »

1 **Porte-serviettes n° 5**, cuivre nickelé . . . . **25** »

PRIX de l'Installation complète comme ci-dessus : 1667 Frs.

Ces Salles de Bains sont alimentées d'eau chaude par notre Chauffe-Bains à pression, page 36, ou par une circulation d'eau chaude sous pression.

ÉTABLISSEMENTS PORCHER

52, Rue d'Hauteville, PARIS

IMP. EUGENE VERNEAU, 108, R. FOLIE MERICOURT. – PARIS

JOHN HEYWOOD, CHROMO LITHO, MANCHESTER, LONDON, BRISTOL, LIVERPOOL.

SHOWER BATH

Plate 1090-B.

NICKEL-PLATED BRASS COMBINATION NEEDLE AND SHOWER with tubular head; curtain ring and white rubber curtain; check valves on supply pipes and china scalps marked "Hot," "Cold," "Shower" and "Spray" on valve handles; 42 inch enameled iron receptor with nickel-plated outlet strainer.

DIMENSIONS: Height, 94 inches; diameter of shower head, 10 inches; diameter of needle, 38 inches; distance from wall to centre of shower, 21 inches.

Price as described $175.00

Add if with exterior finish on receptor $5.00

Add if with 42 x 42 inch "Empress" porcelain-ware receptor (Plate 1104-B) Class "A" 13.00

Deduct if with 42 x 42 inch "Empress" porcelain-ware receptor (Plate 1104-B) Class "B" 4.00

IMPROVED NEEDLE BATH,

Made in Strong Solid Drawn Polished Copper Tube, and Gun Metal Mountings.

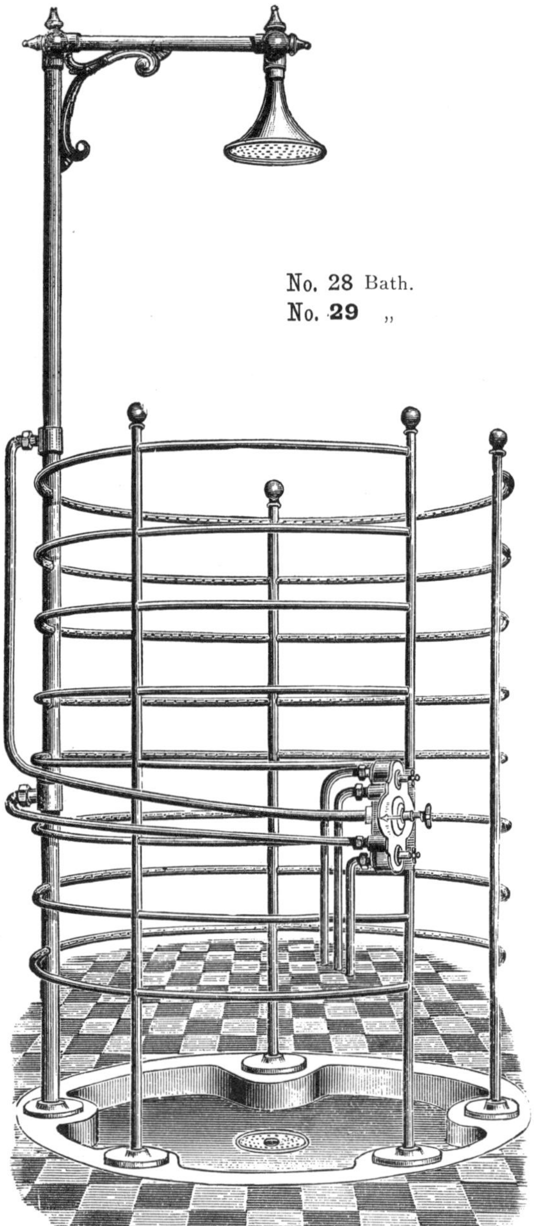

No. 28 Bath.
No. **29** „

No. 28 Needle Bath is made as follows:—The Back Vertical Tube is $1\frac{1}{2}''$ diameter, and the four others are $1\frac{1}{4}''$, whilst the eight Horizontal Tubes are $\frac{5}{8}''$ diameter. The Horizontal Spray Tubes pass through a nipple (not shewn on diagram) which is secured to each side of the Vertical Tubes. The sizes are—Height to top of Shower, 7′ 6″; to uppermost Spray Tube, 5′ 0″; diameter, 2′ 9″; and opening, 1′ $9\frac{1}{2}''$. The Bath is fitted with our Oriental Combined Hot and Cold Taps, Mixing Box, and dividing arrangement for Shower and Spray, with Connecting Copper Pipes to each way ... ... Price **£22 13 9.**

No. 29 Needle Bath is the same as No. 28 above described, with the addition of Dished Buff-glazed Fire-clay Soleplate in one piece, Uprising Douche and Spray, and Combined Waste Arrangement ... ... Price **£26 18 0.**

Back wave to No. 29 Bath may be supplied in lieu of Uprising Douche or Uprising Spray, at same price.

Trellis Wooden Grating to stand upon, extra to order.

NICKEL-PLATING, No. 28 BATH, **63**/-; No. 29, **74/3** Extra.

Considerable experience in the manufacture of Needle Baths enables us to turn them out in a strong and workmanlike manner. In point of quality and price they cannot be excelled.

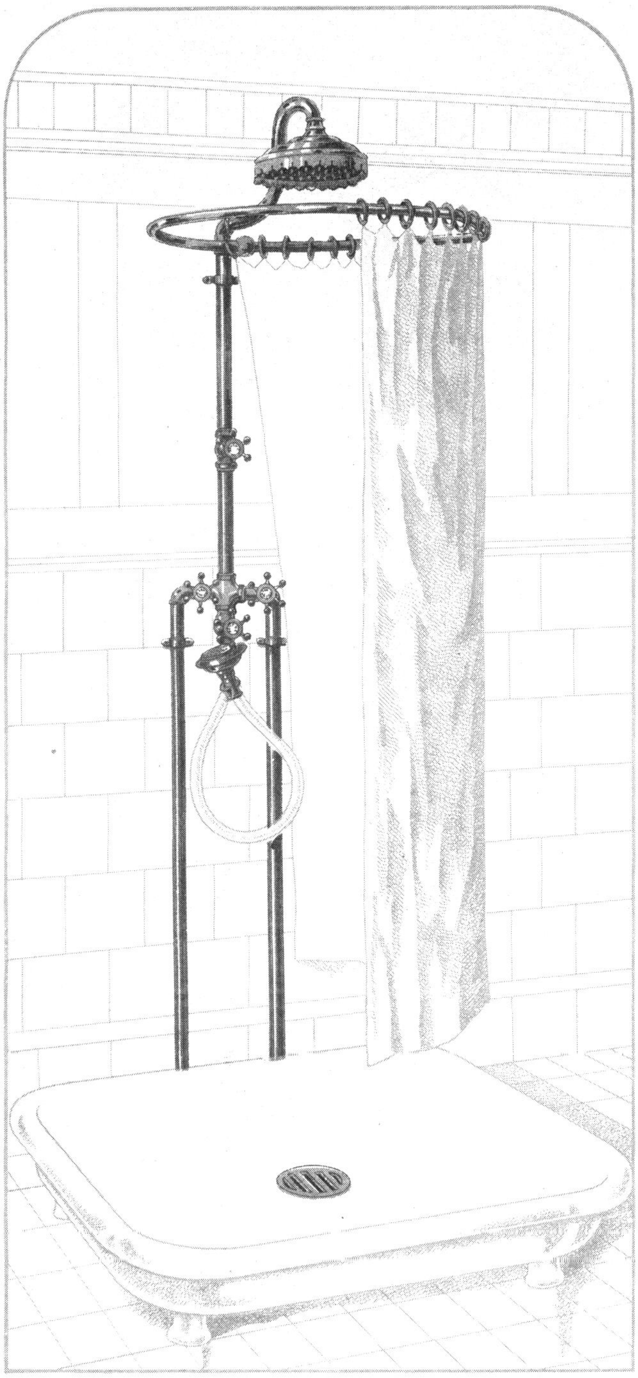

N° 227 bis

PRIX A PARIS :

Complète avec douche en pluie et douche en jet, pour eau chaude et froide, avec rideau caoutchouc et cercle porte-rideau.

En cuivre nickelé ou en cuivre rouge poli **250** fr.

La même sans rideau caoutchouc, ni cercle porte-rideau.

En cuivre nickelé ou en cuivre rouge poli. **200** fr.

Tub en fonte émaillée avec grille de vidage, cuivre nickelé . . . . En plus **75** fr.

N° 226 bis

Complète, avec douche en pluie et douches en cercle, pour eau chaude et eau froide avec rideaux caoutchouc et cercle porte-rideaux. Tub en fonte émaillée

Avec quatre cercles en cuivre nickelé ou en cuivre rouge poli . . . . **600** fr.

La même, sans rideaux caoutchouc . **520** »

Les mêmes, pour eau froide seulement
En moins . . . . **50.** »

Sans le **Tub** en fonte émaillée avec grille de vidage en cuivre nickelé, en moins . . . . **75** »

Chaque cercle en plus . . . . **40.** »

La même, avec robinet de commande à chaque cercle. En plus par robinet . . . . **20.** »

SHOWER BATHS

Plate 1076-B.

NICKEL-PLATED BRASS SHOWER with tubular head, curtain ring and white rubber curtain; check valves on supply pipes.

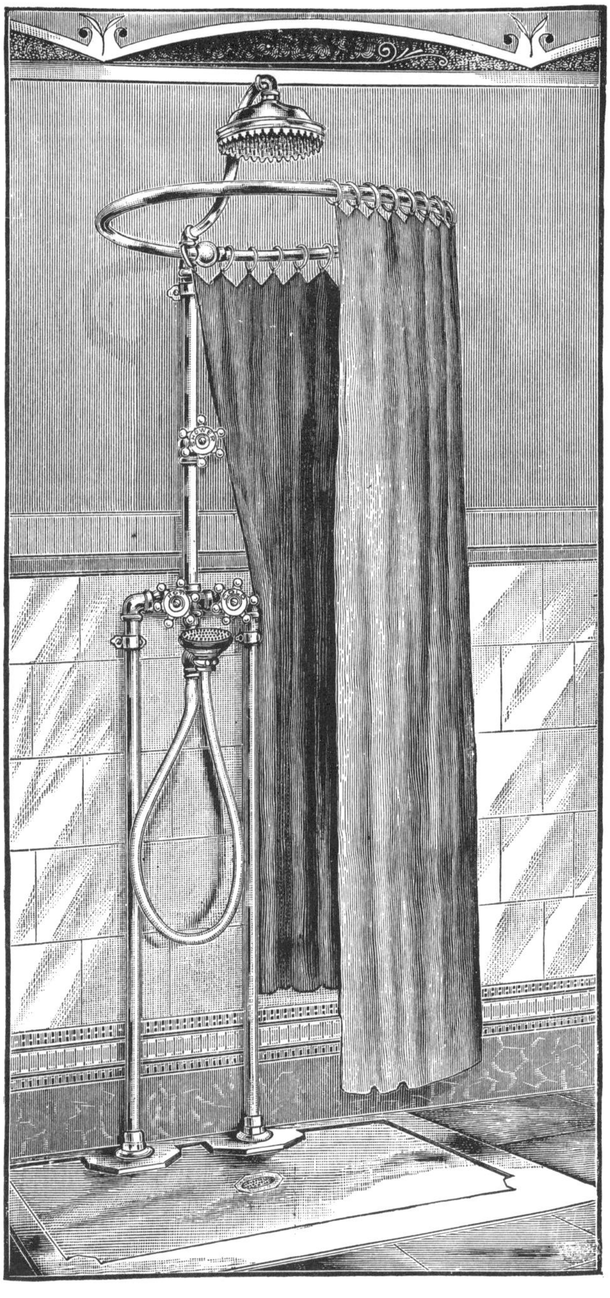

Plate 1078-B.

NICKEL-PLATED BRASS SHOWER with tubular head, rubber ring sprinkler and tube with yoke handle valve; curtain ring and white rubber curtain; check valves on supply pipes.

DIMENSIONS: Height, 93 inches; diameter of shower head, 8½ inches; diameter of curtain ring, 27 inches; distance from wall to centre of shower, 20 inches; centre to centre of supply pipes, 9 inches.

Plate 1076-B:

Price as described...$33.50
Price with ½ inch I. S. supplies, ¾ inch I. S. mixing column and marked china scalps on handles......... 38.50

Plate 1078-B:

Price as described...$38.50
Price with ½ inch I. S. supplies, ¾ inch I. S. mixing column and marked china scalps on handles......... 43.50

Add if with nickel-plated thermometer...$5.00
Add if with mixing chamber... 4.00

Add for 27 x 27 inch countersunk marble floor slab with nickel-plated strainer (Plate 1106-B).......................$12.00
Add for 36 x 36 inch enameled iron receptor (Plate 1102-B)... 42.00
Add for 36 x 36 inch "Empress" porcelain-ware receptor (Plate 1104-B) Class A......$55.00 Class B............ 38.00

SHOWER BATHS

Plate 1082-B.

NICKEL-PLATED BRASS NEEDLE SHOWER with tubular head; check valves on supplies.

DIMENSIONS: Diameter of shower head, 8½ inches; distance from wall to centre of shower, 18 inches.

Price as described...$40.00

Plate 1084-B.

NICKEL-PLATED BRASS NEEDLE AND RING SHOWER with tubular head; check valves on supplies.

DIMENSIONS: Diameter of shower head, 8½ inches; diameter of shower ring, 20 inches; distance from wall to centre of shower, 18 inches.

Price as described...$50.00

Add for 27 x 27 inch countersunk marble floor slab with nickel plated strainer (Plate 1106-B).........................$12.00

SHANKS' PATENT SITZ BATHS,

WITH PATENT "EUREKA" HOT AND COLD SUPPLY FITTINGS.

No. 1.

No. 1 Sitz Bath may be made of Copper or Zinc. It is beautifully enamelled inside, and is fitted with Hot and Cold Bottom Spray, Bottom or Ascending Douche, Back Spray and Back Wave, and with Shanks' Standing Waste and Overflow. The Fittings are more easily manipulated than any system yet applied to Sitz Baths, and more efficient in action.

The Fittings are Shanks' Patent "Eureka" Fittings, and either of the four arrangements may be had by simply turning the centre handle. Shanks & Co. have no hesitation in claiming that this Sitz Bath is the most complete, the most comfortable, and the most convenient Sitz Bath in the market. Woodwork may be made in any style, and to any design. Prices on application.

No. 2.

No. 2 is exactly the same as No. 1, with the difference that it is finished to fix up without any woodwork. It is equally efficient and satisfactory in action.

No. 3.

No. 3 is a Sitz Bath in strong Fireclay, white enamelled inside, with Fittings, &c., complete, as Nos. 1 and 2.

ENAMELED IRON SITZ BATHS

WHITE ENAMELED SITZ BATH with 3 inch roll-rim and extensions on sides; nickel-plated combined waste and five valve fittings including bell supply, liver spray and bidet; china scalps on handles marked "Waste," "Hot," "Cold," "Spray," and "Bidet."

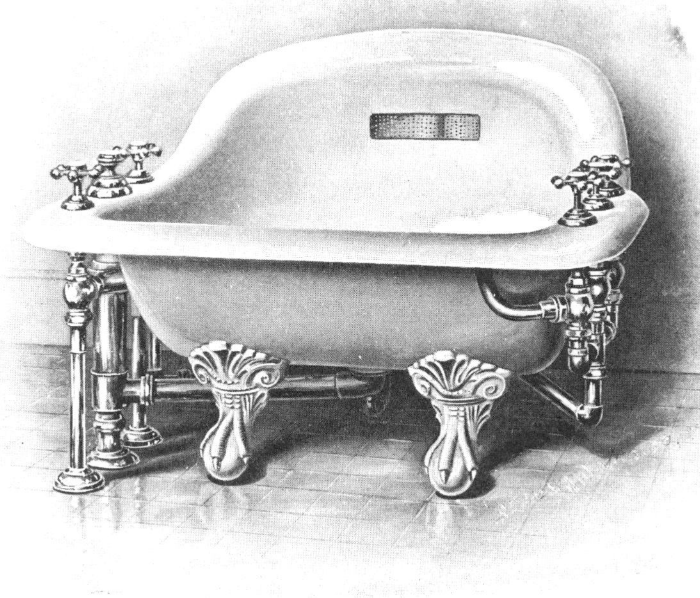

Plate 1008-B.

Price as described..$97.00

Add if with "A" grade exterior finish..$10.00
Add if with "B" grade exterior finish.. 6.00
Add (to price of finish) if with gold lines.. 2.00

WHITE ENAMELED SITZ BATH with 3 inch roll-rim and extensions on sides; "Princeton" nickel-plated combined waste and bell supply with handles through tub rim; china scalps on handles marked "Hot," "Cold," and "Waste."

Plate 1009-B.

Price as described..$62.00

Add if with "A" grade exterior finish..$10.00
Add if with "B" grade exterior finish.. 6.00
Add (to price of finish) if with gold lines.. 2.00
Add if with "Star" combined waste and bell supply with marked china scalps on handles......... 9.50

SHANKS' PATENT WASH-DOWN CLOSET, THE "CITIZEN,"

No. 77, IN WHITE ENAMELLED STRONG FIRECLAY, WITH SHANKS' PATENT "IMPROVED RELIABLE" CISTERN No. 16.

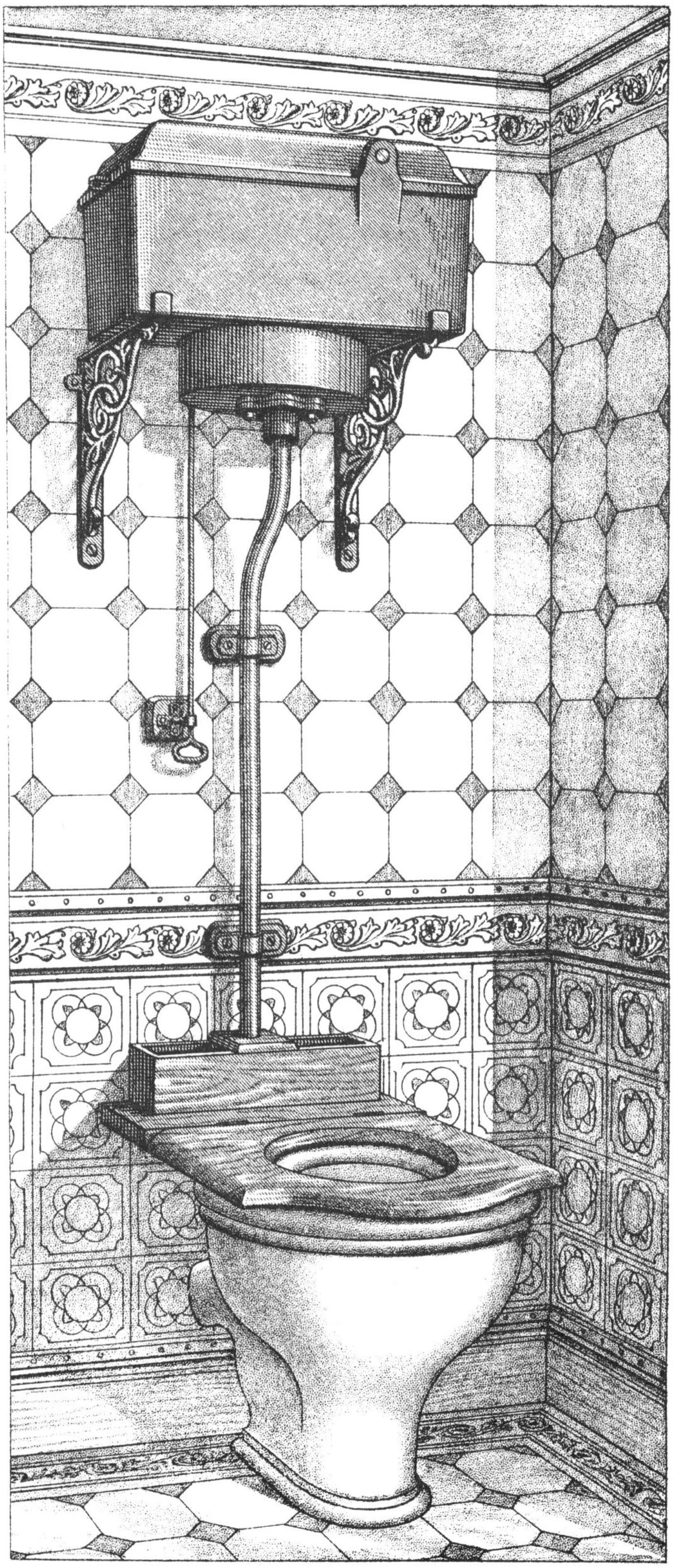

No. 77A "Citizen" Closet,
In strong Fireclay, with Raised Ornament, White Enamelled inside and outside.

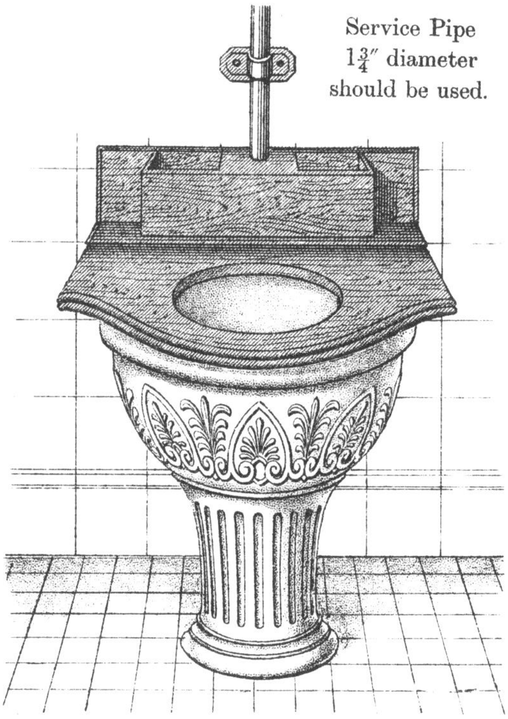

Large numbers of these have been fixed, and are working splendidly.

SECTION OF "CITIZEN" CLOSET.

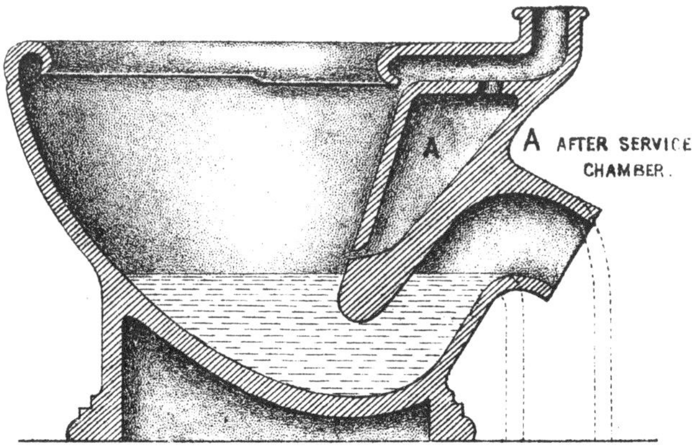

CHAPTER TWO

CLOSETS

The ancestor of the modern water closet was a modified close stool invented by Sir John Harington in 1596. The first valve WC, activated by a handle so that the contents descended directly into a syphon trap, was patented by Alexander Cummings in 1775. Three years later, Joseph Bramah developed a different form, which emptied and flushed the pan simultaneously. By 1797, Bramah claimed to have made 6,000 closets: an impressive achievement, but still not a revolution in the hygiene of the British nation as a whole. It was the experiments and modifications introduced by sanitary engineers during the nineteenth century that led to the evolution of the modern flush closet.

Victorian water closets can be classified into three main types. The pan closet kept the water in the pan before discharging it into a container and from there into a D-trap. This type could rapidly become unhygienic; the interior soon became fouled and if the water in the pan evaporated, the contents of the container were left open to the room. The wash-out closet, which left water as a seal in an S-trap after each flush, was the precursor of the modern closet. In the 1880s, the wash-down closet, of which there were many variants developed by pioneers like Twyford, Doulton and Humpherson, superseded all other types. The pedestal closet, such as Twyford's 'Unitas', in which the S-bend curves up behind the pan, supporting it and obviating the need for a boxed-in seat, was a further improvement. By doing away with dirt-harbouring wooden casing, it made it possible to wash the floor right up to the base of the closet.

Early closets were plumbed into a supply of running water, which was stopped on its way to the pan by a simple valve. The flush was achieved simply by opening the valve and allowing the water to flow on uninterrupted – something that might happen anyway if the valve was faulty or if the user failed to shut off the flow before leaving. As more and more closets were installed, it became essential to devise a method of controlling the amount of water used at each flush. The engineer Thomas Crapper perfected the Water Waste Preventer – a cistern that is still the model for all modern cisterns. Crapper's name, cast into the front panel of every cistern produced at his London works for export throughout Britain and the Empire, became inextricably associated with the WC. In America, the sanitary ware industry developed from 1847, but was at first overshadowed by exports from British firms. The period between the 1870s and 1910 witnessed a rapid expansion of the American industry, with the foundation of ten major manufacturers of sanitary ware. Despite this, most of the Webb Manufacturing Co.'s closets in 1900 were made of iron rather than ceramic.

Names were an important aspect of the marketing of closets. The 'Maelstrom', 'Deluge', 'Rapido', 'Zambesi' and 'Niagara' suggested a powerful flush action, while the durability of the appliance was conveyed by names such as the 'Rock' and the 'Adamant'. Thomas Crapper chose the names of the streets surrounding his Chelsea works, thereby giving his closets the second-hand cachet of the landowners who developed the West End, including 'Cadogan' and 'Sloane'. Shanks of Barrhead offered the reasonably priced 'Citizen', while Morrison, Ingram and Co.'s 'Triton' and 'Hygeia' recalled the classical antecedents of the modern bathroom.

SHANKS' PATENT No. 64 VALVE CLOSET,

TRAPPED ABOVE FLOOR-LINE, WITH OBLONG OUTLET-VALVE AND REGULATING SUPPLY-VALVE.

The oblong shape of the Outlet-Valve keeps the Valve working free of the water in the Trap, and gives space for the entire Trap above floor-line without increasing the height of the Closet.

This Closet is made with Flushing-Rim Basin of White or Printed Earthenware. The Trap is of Cast-Iron, Galvanized or Painted. The Valve is carefully fitted to a Rubber-Seating, to secure an absolutely tight job.

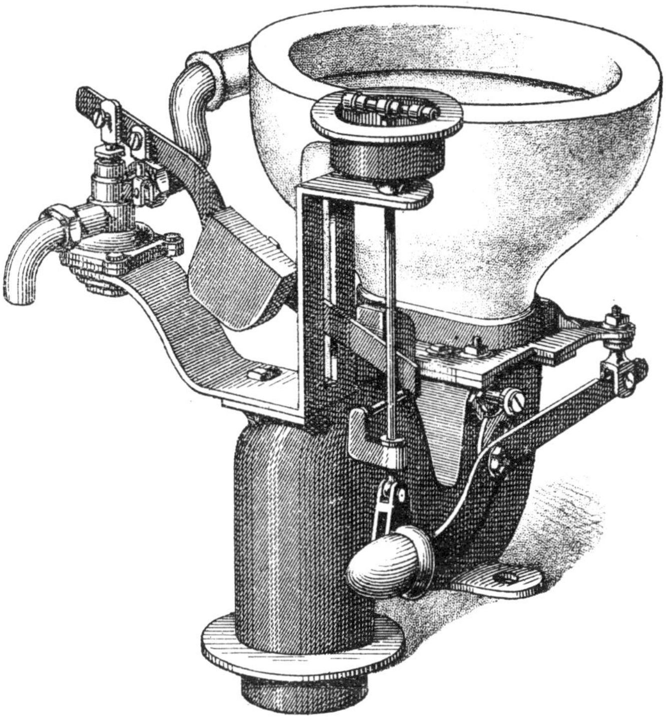

The Valve is regulated to give a limited quantity of water after the handle is dropped, for the purpose of filling up the Basin.

S. & Co. believe the improvements in construction to be quite novel, and that thereby the Valve Closet is rendered a more Sanitary apparatus than it ever has been.

No. 64A. Closet.

Same as above, but with P or Shoot-out Trap.

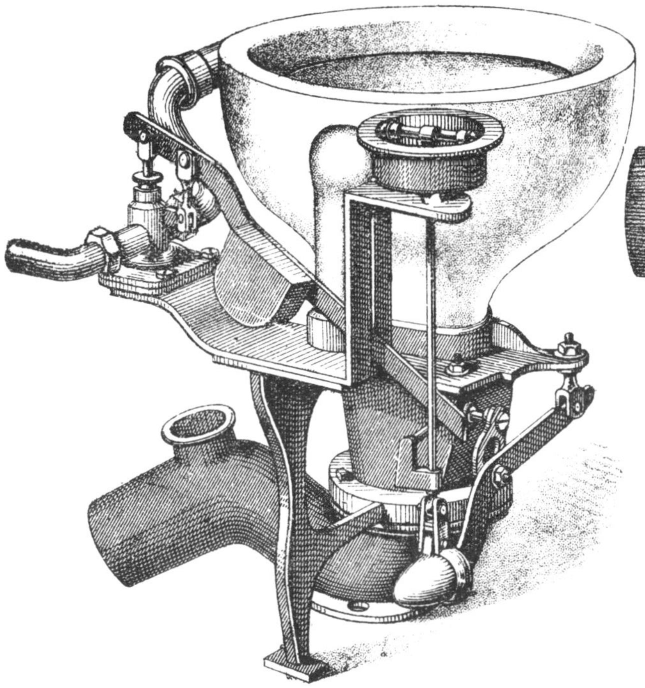

Plan of Closet shewing the space it occupies, and shewing the shape of Outlet-Valve.

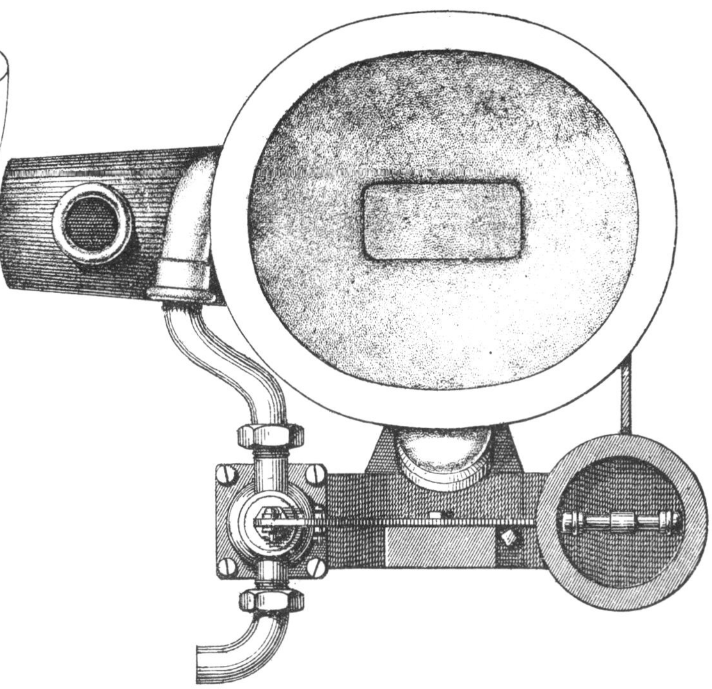

SHANKS' PATENT PEDESTAL VALVE CLOSET,

IN STRONG FIRECLAY, ENAMELLED.

No. 108.

SECTION.

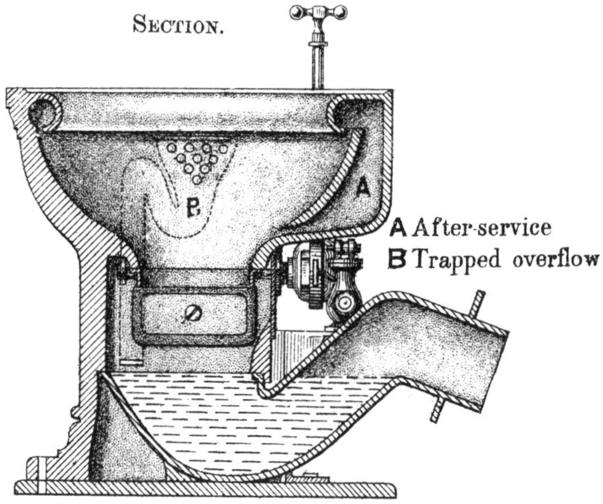

MADE ALSO WITHOUT TRAP

This is made on similar lines to No. 64A on preceding page, but the Basin, the Pedestal Flushing-Rim, and Top, are in one solid piece of strong Fireclay, Enamelled White. The Valve is oblong in shape, as No. 64A; and the Trap is of Cast-Iron, Galvanized or Enamelled. It is made with Regulating Valve of "Reliable" construction; and, as a whole, is a splendid Closet, both in appearance and working parts.

SHANKS' VALVE CLOSET,

FOR PRISON CELLS.

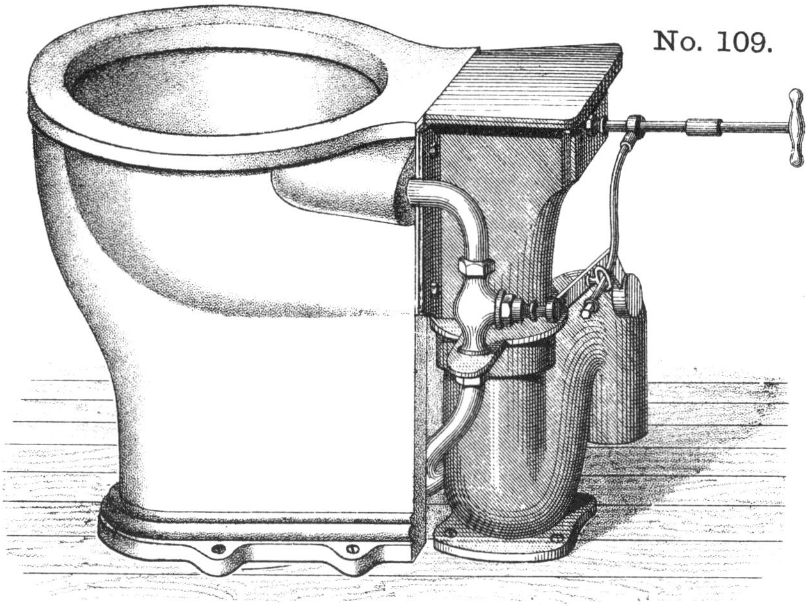

No. 109.

The Basin and Pedestal of this Closet is made in one solid piece of strong Enamelled Fireclay; the other parts being of Cast-Iron, with the exception of the working parts, which are Brass. It is a combination of the Wash-out, with the Valve principle. The Valve closing the Outlet from Basin cannot be kicked open from the inside; and the turning of the key by gaoler, outside the cell, opens simultaneously the Flushing-Valve and the Outlet-Valve, so that the Basin is thoroughly cleansed.

IMPROVED EARTHENWARE VALVE CLOSET,

WITH BASIN AND TRAP IN ONE PIECE, AND WITH DOULTON'S PATENT REGULATING SUPPLY VALVE.

LARGELY USED ON THE CONTINENT.

No. 109.

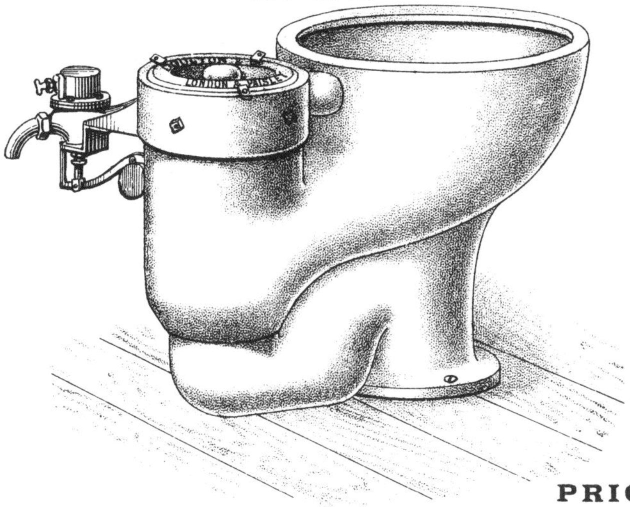

THIS Closet is constructed in one piece of superior Earthenware, and has a pottery sunk dish and handle, which add to its general cleanliness. It is provided with a hollow galvanized iron discharge Valve, also serving as a trapped overflow, and the seating of the Valve is formed of conical India Rubber which readily drops into the seat constructed in the earthen-ware to receive it.

PRICES.

No. 109.—Improved Earthenware Valve Closet, with White Basin and 1 in. Regulating Supply Valve,	£3	13	0
If $1\frac{1}{4}$ in. Valve,	extra, 0	3	0
If Printed Basin,	,, 0	7	6
If Gold Scroll Basin,	,, 0	15	0

In fixing this Closet the Bore of the Supply Pipe must equal the size of the Valve.

For Plan of Closet showing position of Outlet of Trap, see page 45.

IMPROVED VALVE CLOSET, WITH GALVANIZED IRON TRAP,

FITTED WITH DOULTON'S PATENT REGULATING SUPPLY VALVE.

No. 330.

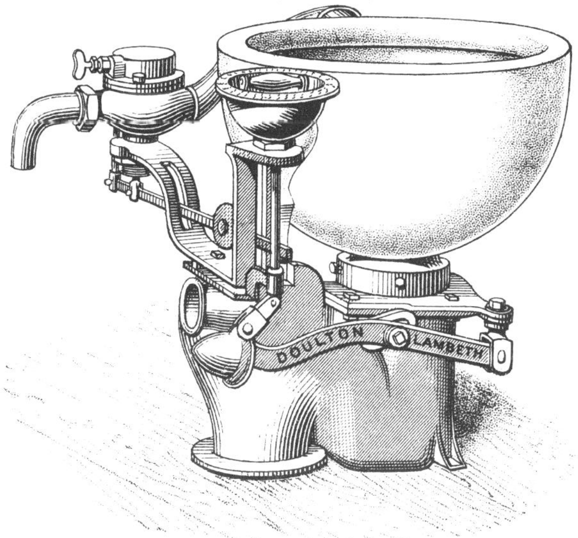

No. 330.—Improved Valve Closet, with Cast-Iron Galvanized Trap above Floor, White Basin, Doulton's Patent 1 in. Regulating Supply Valve with Ventilating Socket to Trap,	£3	10	0
No. 330.—Do. with $1\frac{1}{4}$ in. Regulating Supply Valve,	extra, 0	3	0

In fixing these Closets the Bore of Supply-Pipe should equal size of Valve.

For Designs of Tiling, see Pages 4, 6, 38, 57, 58, 59, 60, 61, 157, 158.

TRAPS, PANS, &c.

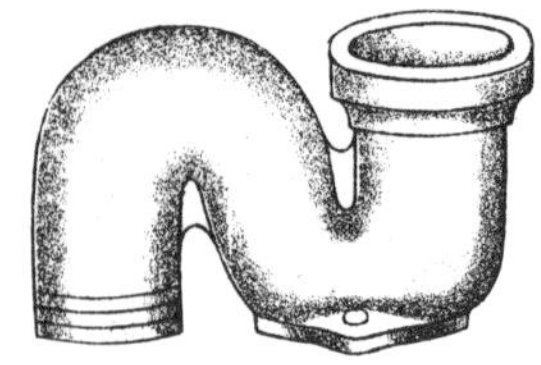

No. 526—S.

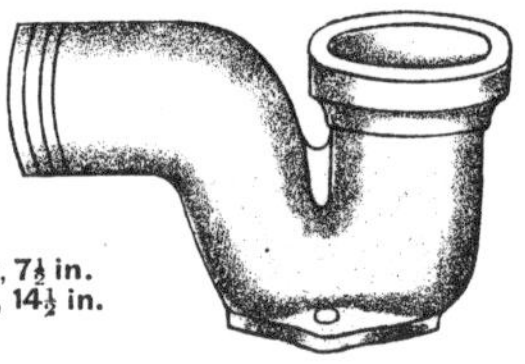

Height, 7½ in.
Length, 14½ in.

No. 526—P.

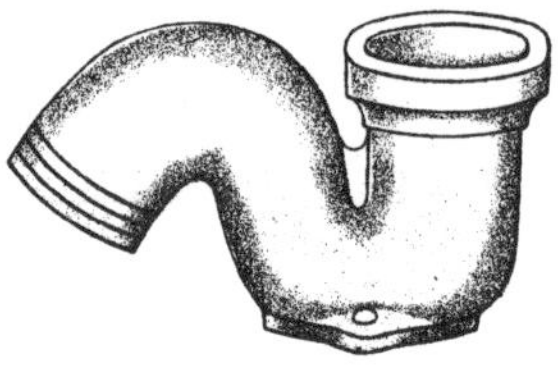

No. 526—Q.

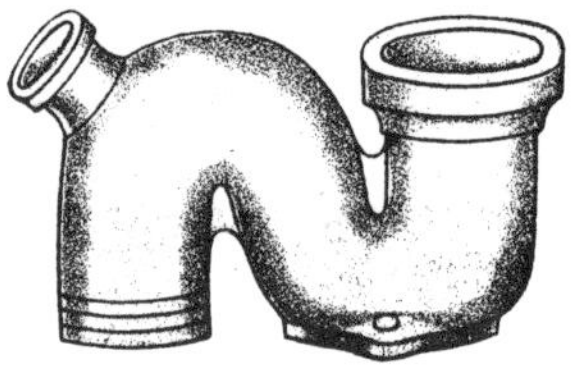

No. 526—S. Ventd.

These Traps suit Basins No. 510, 511, 514, 516, 518, 518a, 519, 576, & 635.

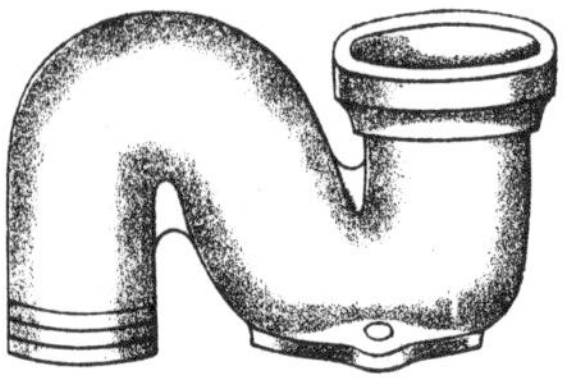

No. 528—S.

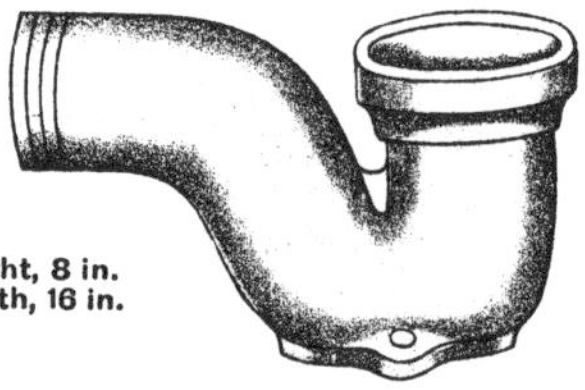

Height, 8 in.
Length, 16 in.

No. 528—P.

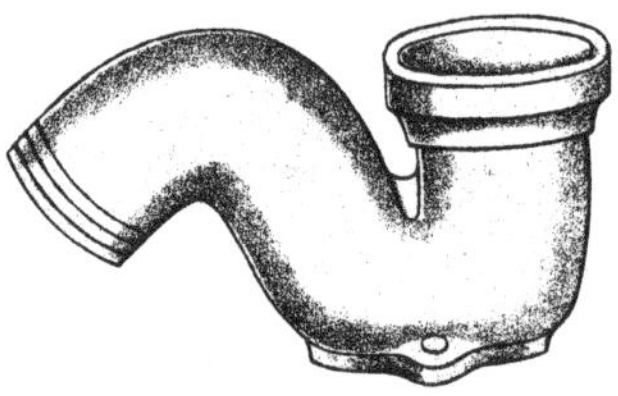

No. 528—Q.

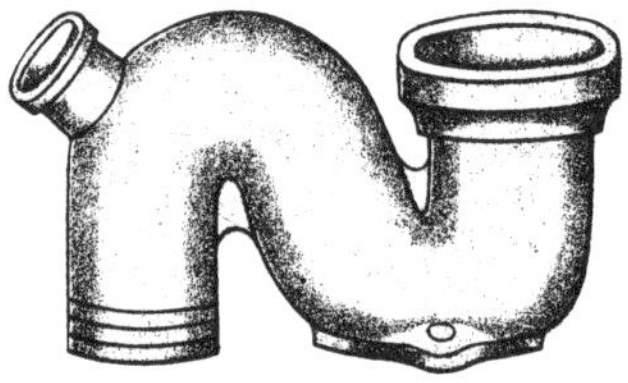

No. 528—P. Ventd.

These Traps Suit Basins No. 517, 520, & 638.

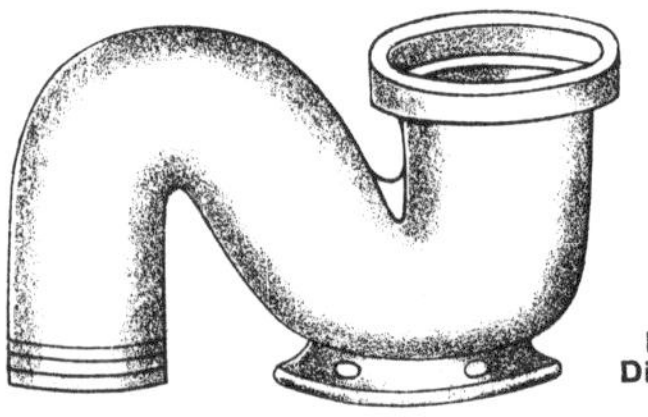

No. 530—S.

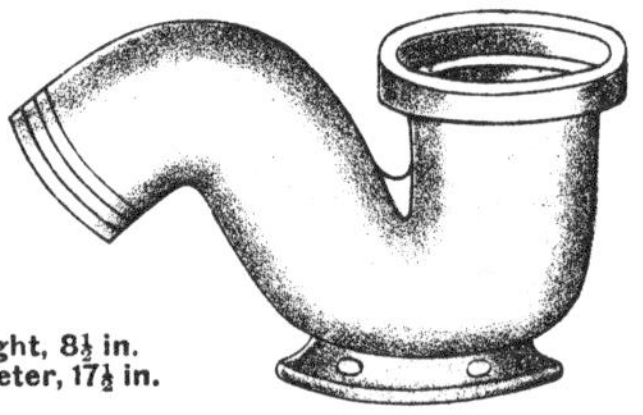

Height, 8½ in.
Diameter, 17½ in.

No. 530—P. or Q.

These Traps Suit Basin No. 516.

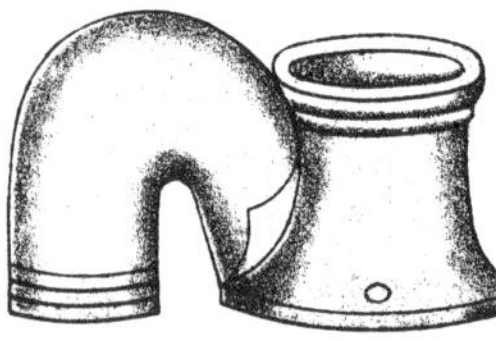

No. 531—S.

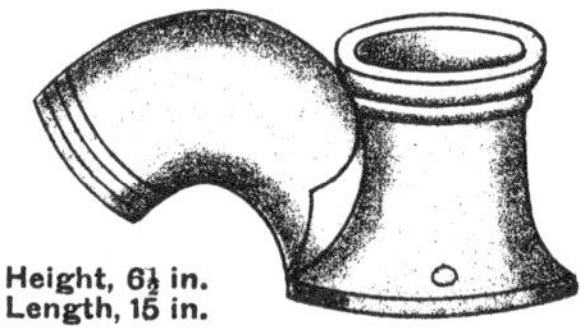

Height, 6½ in.
Length, 15 in.

No. 531—P. or Q.

Suit Basins Nos. 510, 511, 514, 516, 518, 518a, 519, 576, & 635.

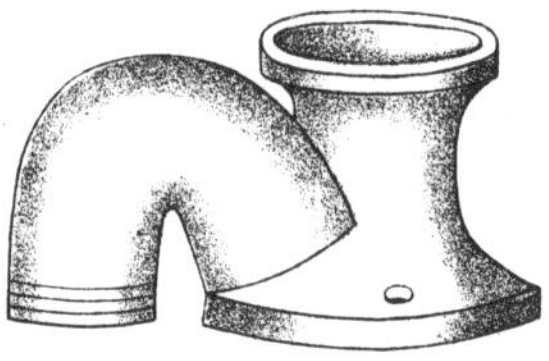

No. 532—S.

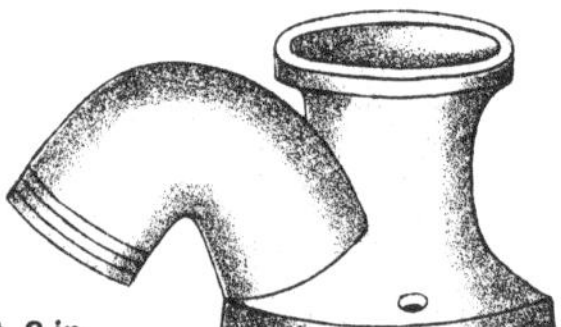

Height, 8 in.
Length, 16½ in.

No. 532—P. or Q.

These Traps suit Basins No. 517, 520, & 638.

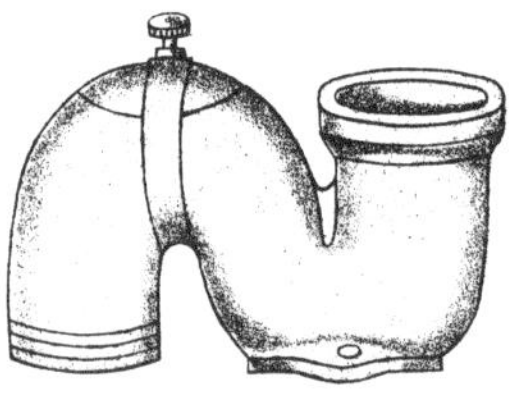

No. 527—S. with Loose Cap.

No. 529—S. with Vent. on Top.

Suit Basins Nos. 510, 511, 514, 516, 518, 518a, 519, 576, & 635.

Above Traps are also made in White Earthenware.

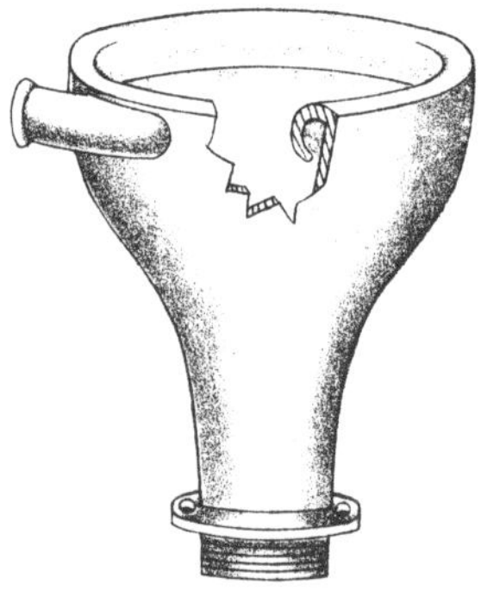

No. 580.—PHILADELPHIA HOPPER.
Diameter, 14 in., do. over Bottom, 4 in.
Height Over All, 16½ in.,
Height, from Flange, 14½ in.

No. 581—SWISS PANS [Round.]
Diameter, 14½ in.; Height, 11½ in.
LARGE. MEDIUM. SMALL.
3 Sizes. Dia. over Bottom, 9 in. 7 in. 6 in.

No. 582—SWISS PANS [Oval.]
Diameter, 15×13½ in.; Height, 12 in.
LARGE. SMALL.
Two Sizes. Dia. over Bottom, 7 in. 6 in.

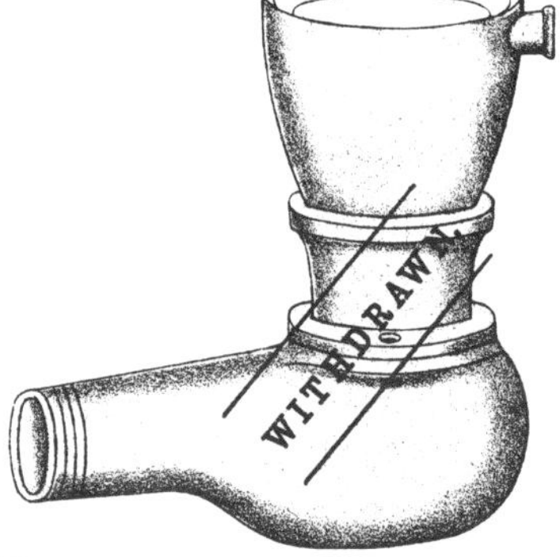

No. 535—PRISON CLOSET.

THE "TORNADO" PATENT.

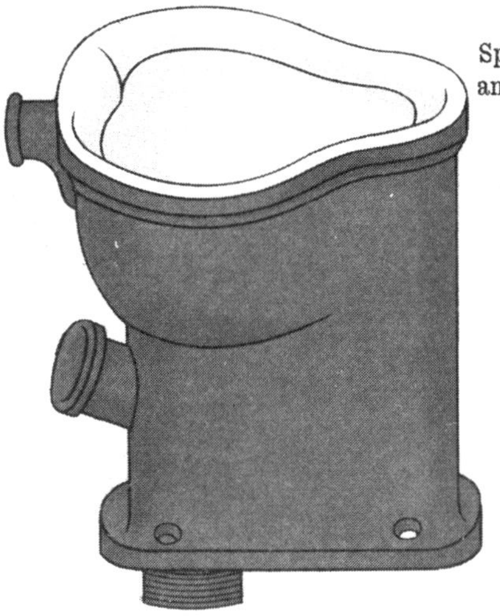

FIRE CLAY, White Enamelled.
Diameter, 15¾×14¼ in.
Height, 16 in.

Specially introduced to provide a STRONG, CHEAP and RELIABLE Pedestal W.C. Basin, suitable for Artizans' dwellings.

When fixed in conjunction with the "Tornado" 2 Gallon Flushing Cistern, it is guaranteed to be perfectly efficient.

Also made in White Earthenware, and can be supplied Printed Inside Only, Outside Only, or Inside and Outside. See Price List.

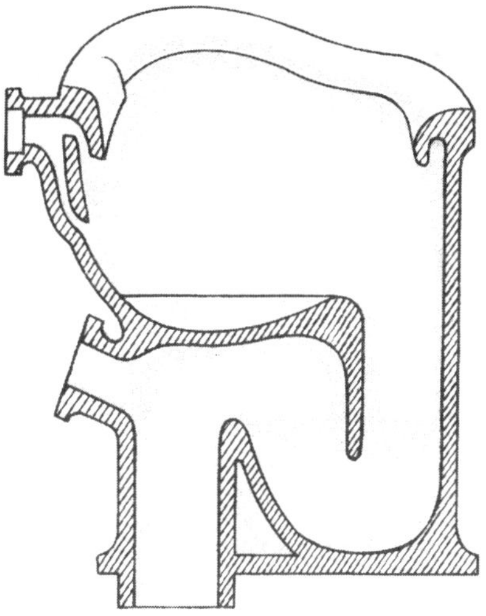

SECTION.
Dimensions with Seat,
Back to Front, 22½ in.; Across, 18 in.;
Height, 17½ in.

THE "TORNADO" PATENT—Strong Fire Clay—White Enamelled Inside, with Deal Seat.
"TORNADO" CISTERN AND BRACKETS, Painted, and BRASS CHAIN PULL.
PRICE £2 16 0 complete, Galvanized Flushing Pipe 13/6 extra. 1¼ in. Patent Rubber Connection 1/6 extra.

SHANKS' PATENT WASH-DOWN CLOSET, "THE CITIZEN."

No. 76, in Cast-Iron, Enamelled.

As supplied for the Rothschild Industrial Dwellings, with Shanks' Patent "Improved Reliable" Cistern No. 16.

The directness of the flush in a Wash-down Closet has always been an acknowledged advantage; but it has been impossible to get a sufficient surface of water in the Basin without raising the Trap so high, and so increasing the depth of water, that it could not be cleaned with the usual flush of water. Another difficulty was the danger of syphoning the Trap and opening a connection with the drain.

These defects are all obviated in Shanks' Patent "Citizen." The Basin and Trap are so constructed that a large surface of water is secured in the Basin, with an amply sufficient depth of water in the Trap. The special formation and sweep of the Trap render it easily washed out by the flush of water, which, by means of the improved Spreader or Fan, washes the Basin thoroughly, and falls with force in the centre.

To prevent emptying of Trap by syphonage, a Service-Box, **A**, is constructed, which catches part of the flush, and allows its contents to percolate through the little hole, **B**, after flush is past.

The Closet is supplied, complete, with Cistern, Brackets, Pull-Handle, Iron Down-Pipe, &c., so that it may be fixed with least possible labour.

Other combinations
with Self-acting Seat arrangement, &c.

Prices on application.

SECTION.

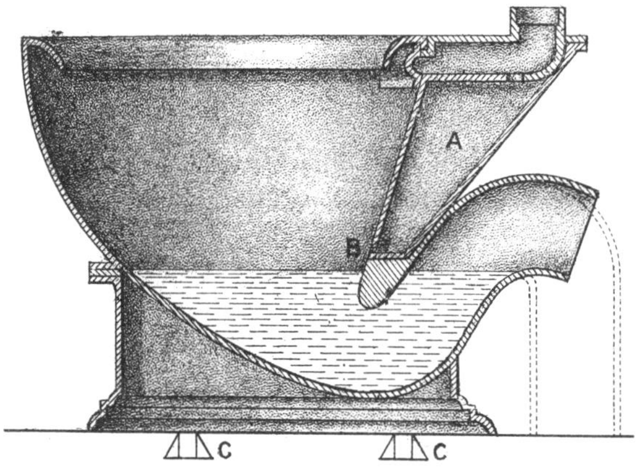

CC Snugs, for fixing in Cement Floor.

SHANKS' PATENT CLOSETS,

WITH SELF-RAISING SEAT, AND WITH SELF-FLUSHING ARRANGEMENT.

No. 1 "Tubal" Closet and Cistern,

With No. 6 Self-raising Seat.

The Seat is weighted, so that after being released it gently rises to an upright position, as shewn. This ensures the Seat always being kept clean when Closet is used as Urinal or Slop Sink.

No. 1 "Tubal" Closet,

With No. 7 Seat, with attachment for Automatic Flushing of Closet.

When the person rises from Seat, the arrangement is such that the Syphon Cistern No. 16 Special is discharged, and flushes the Closet.

These arrangements may be fitted to any of S. & Co.'s Closets.

SHANKS' PATENT "TUBAL" CLOSETS,

WITH AUTOMATIC FLUSHING ARRANGEMENT AND SELF-RAISING SEAT.

The Seat of No. 110, when not in use, is kept in an upright position by means of balance weights; and the flush is obtained by means of a Self-closing and Regulating Supply-Valve. When the Seat is pressed down it puts the Lever of Valve in position for opening; and when the Seat is released and rises it opens the Flushing-Valve, which may be regulated to give a measured quantity of water. Otherwise the Closet is just the No. 1 "Tubal" in strong Fireclay.

No. 110. With Self-acting Valve.

No. 111. With Pull-up Valve.

No. 111 has Valve at back like No. 110, but it is Pull-up and not Self-acting.

The Closet Seat may be made of various Woods; and the Closets may be made decorated in the various styles of Shanks' No. 2A "Tubal" Closets.

SHANKS' PATENT "TUBAL" CLOSETS.

PATENTED COMBINATION OF BOTTOM-FLUSH, AFTER-SERVICE AND UPRIGHT INLET-HORN.

No. 5 "Tubal" Closet. Made in one solid piece.

With No. 16A "Reliable" Cistern, and Hinged Mahogany Seat.

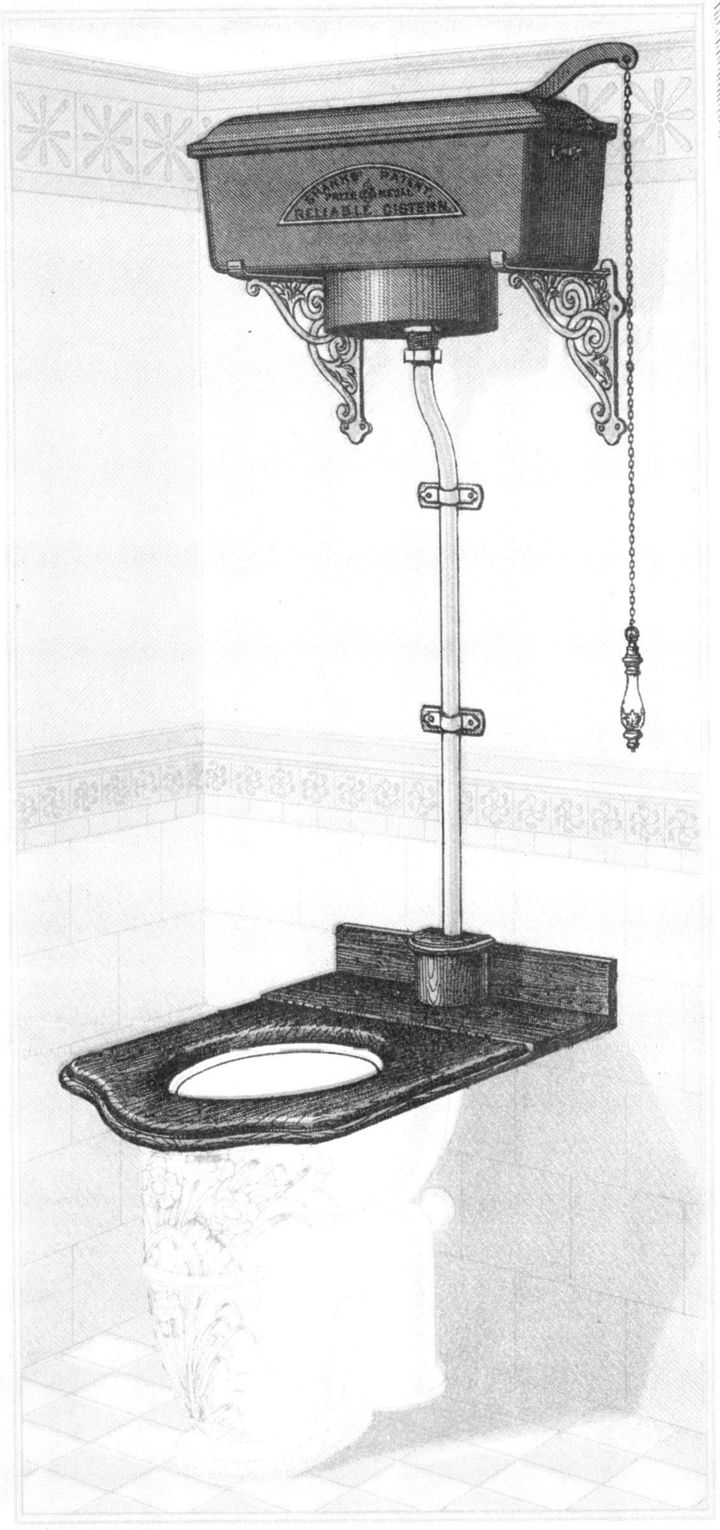

SECTION OF No. 5 CLOSET.

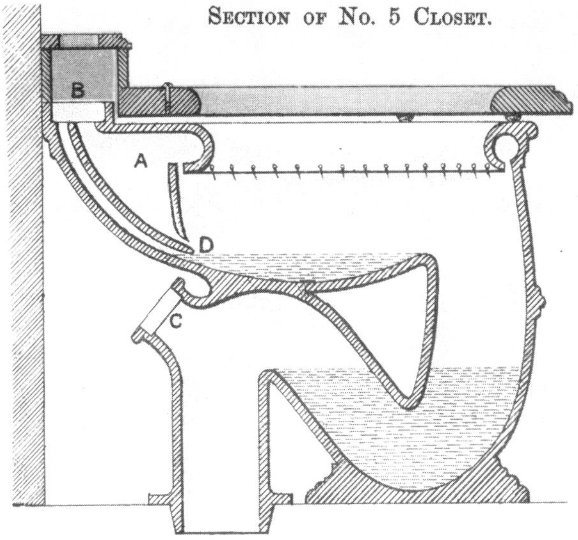

A After-service Chamber.
B Upright Inlet-horn.
C Ventilating Horn.
D Bottom Stream.

No. 3 "Tubal" Closet. Made in two pieces.

Exactly similar in internal construction to No. 5 "Tubal" Closet.

Made with Cane and White Basin, or White Earthenware Basin, either of which may be printed inside, and with S or P Caneware Trap.

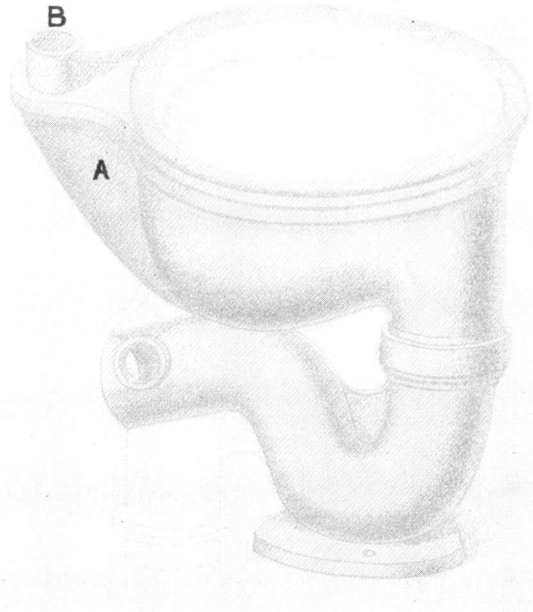

No. 5 "Tubal" is made in the following styles:—In Cane and White Earthenware; in White Earthenware, plain or printed, as shewn. Either of above may be printed inside.

PATENT WASH-DOWN TRITON CLOSET.

MADE IN FINEST IVORY OR WHITEWARE PORCELAIN.

This ideal Closet possesses the advantages of the Valve Closet without its disadvantages.

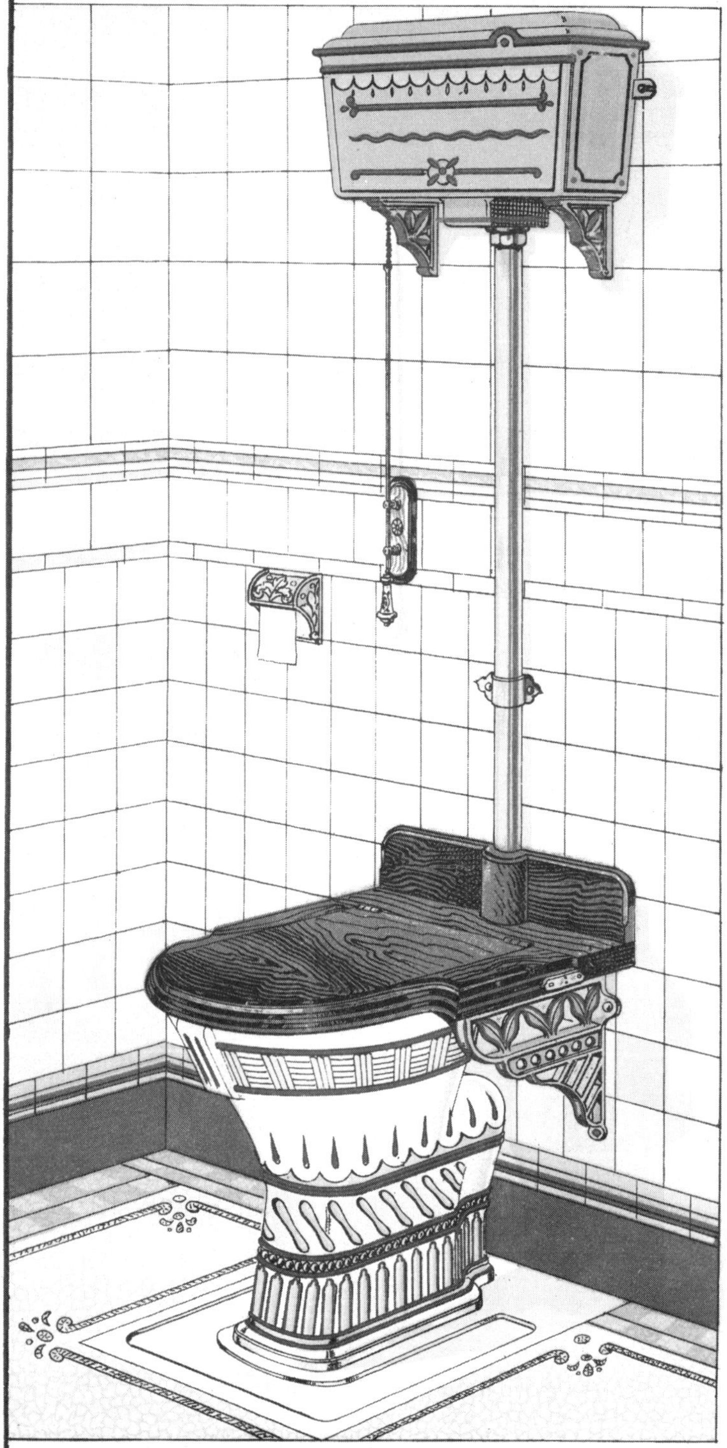

No. 145.—Triton Closet Suite.

Attention is called to the unique form of the Improved Triton Closet, affording such great water area, and yet capable of being successfully cleansed by a 3 gallons flush. The Patent Drip Soleplate has been designed to enable the plumber to make a reliable gas-tight joint, especially with the S Trap Closet. This system, which overcomes well-known objections, is of high sanitary value, and has met with considerable approval.

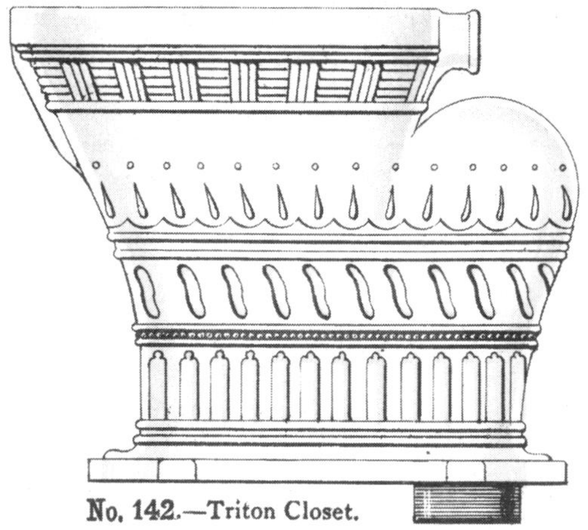

No. 142.—Triton Closet.

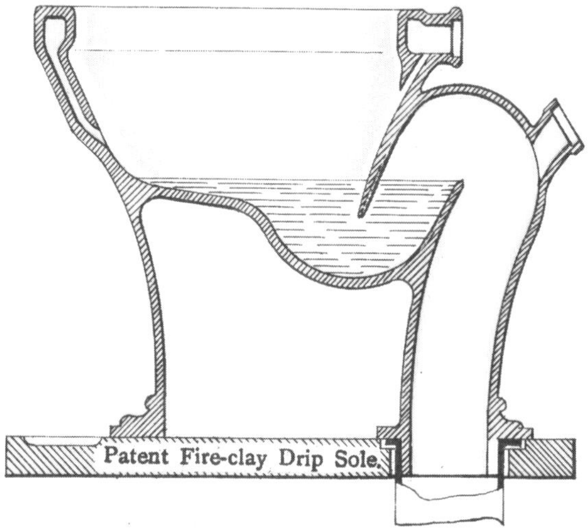

No. 145.—Patent Triton Closet Suite comprises—

	£	s.	d.
No. 8, Enamel Painted 3 gallons Cistern ...	1	10	6
,, 198, Cistern Brackets, Decorated... ...	0	2	6
,, 147, Bracket Pull and Chain	0	4	8
,, 139, Polished Copper Pipe...	0	16	8
,, 146, Walnut Seat	1	12	6
,, 141, Seat Brackets, Decorated	0	8	0
,, 142A, Ivoryware Closet, Decorated and best gilt	4	7	6
,, 143, Patent Drip Sole, fitted	0	17	6
,, 210, Paper Case, Embossed Brass ...	0	10	6
Price of Suite as shewn... ...	£10	10	4

No. 142.—Triton Closet in Finest Ivoryware, S or P Trap, and with or without Vent ... 40/-

,, 142B.—Do. do. Decorated in colors ... 53/6

,, 142A.—Do. do. do. do. and picked out in best gold 87/6

,, 146A.—If with Polished Copper Buffer Plate fitted under front of seat to prevent urine trickling down front of Closet... 2/4 extra.

JOHN HEYWOOD, CHROMO LITHO. MANCHESTER, LONDON, BRISTOL, LIVERPOOL.

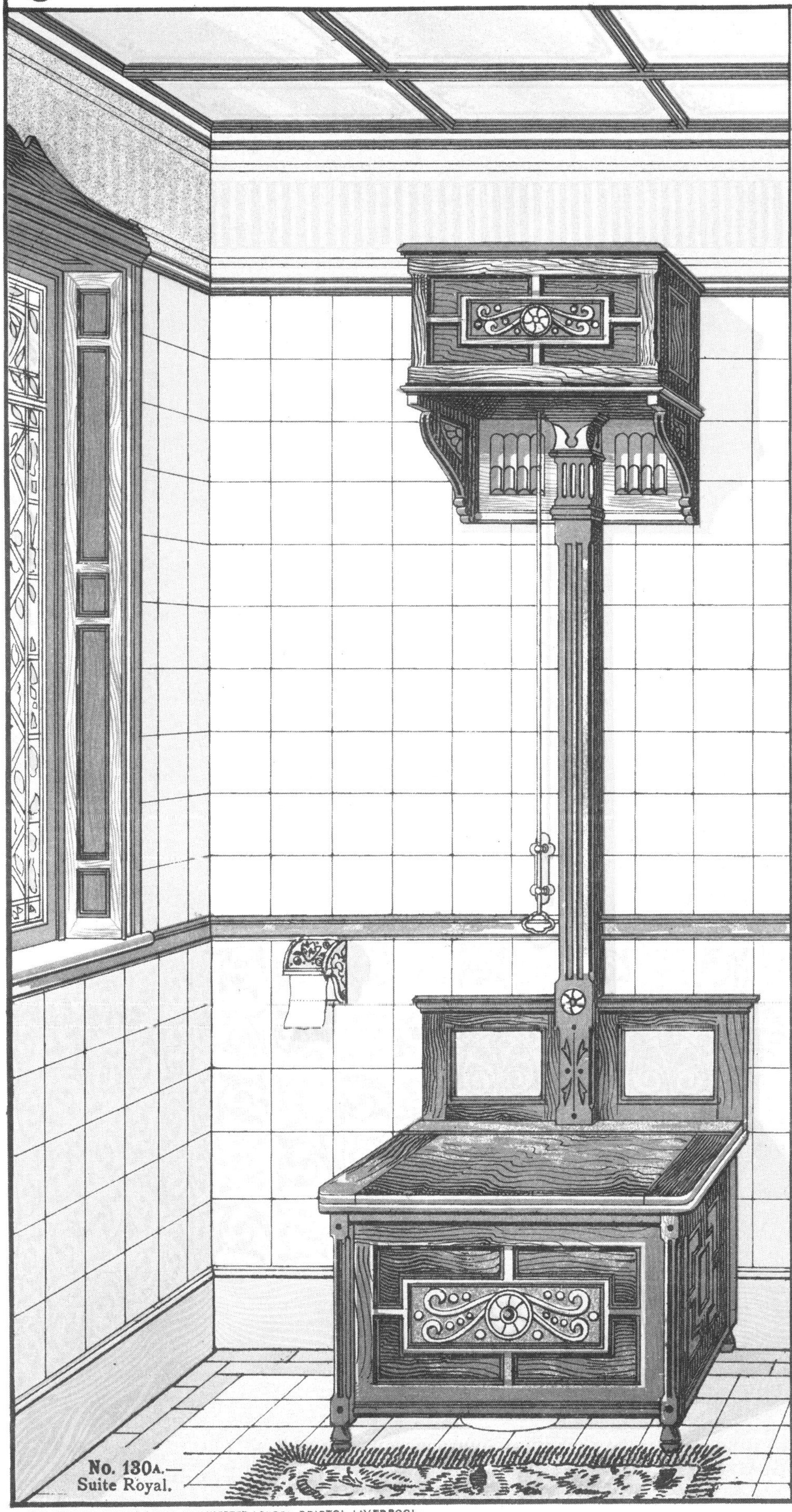

No. 130A.—
Suite Royal.

THE SUITE ROYAL CABINET CLOSET.

Objections have been urged against the naked appearance of some modern Closets, of which our Hygeia Closet may be regarded as the pioneer, but the "sanitary reform" which now obtains is almost universally approved. Recognising, however, that a Cabinet Closet is required, we have produced the Suite Royal. It is constructed upon sound sanitary lines, and represents favourably the Cabinet Makers' art.

The Closet Pan is of our Triton type, whilst the cabinet front and side are made so that even the housemaid may unhook the cabin hooks and remove the framing, for the necessary periodic washing. It will be observable that the framing is designed not to reach the floor. This affords ventilation and cleansing space.

No. 130A Suite Royal is made in high-class cabinet work, Spanish Mahogany or Walnut, richly carved, including 4 gallons Copper-lined Cistern and Cover, 1½" Brass Valve Syphon, Concealed Inlet and Overflow Unions, Pipe Casing, Tile Back, Bracket Pull and Embossed Brass Paper Case.

Price complete ... £22 10.

If with Polished Brass Swivel Arms, Handsomely Upholstered in Best Morocco Leather ... 80/- extra.

JOHN HEYWOOD, CHROMO LITHO. MANCHESTER, LONDON, BRISTOL, LIVERPOOL.

THE LAMBETH
PATENT PEDESTAL "COMBINATION" CLOSET.

No. 118B.

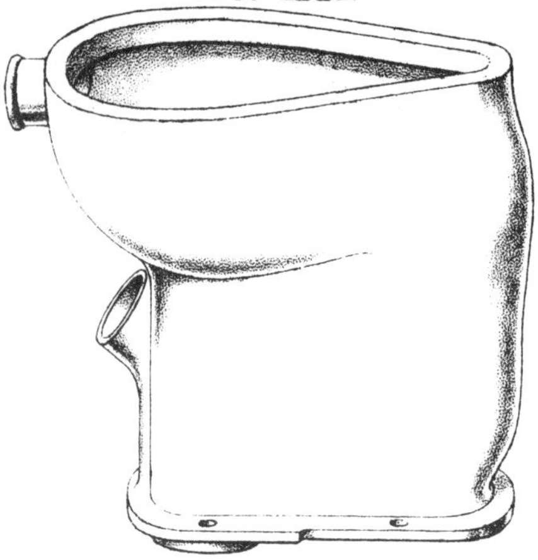

No. 118D.

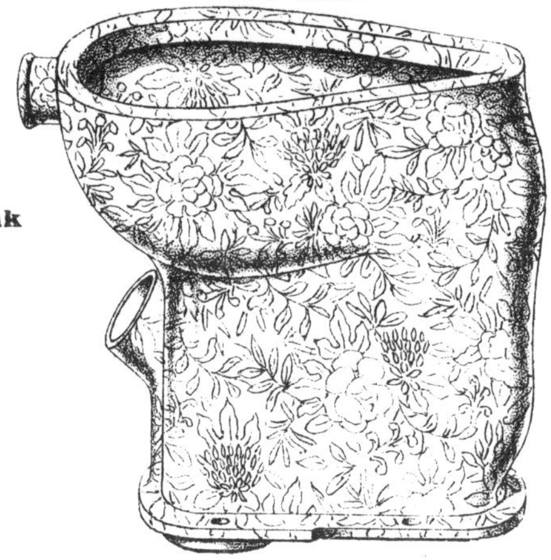

N.B.—In connecting Tank to Closet, 1¼ inch Pipe must be used.

No. 118E.

No 118X.

For Section showing Distance of Outlet from Wall, see page 20.

PRICES
OF PEDESTAL "COMBINATION" CLOSET, Complete.

It can be supplied with Turn-down (S) Trap as shown, or Shoot-out (P) Trap.

No. 118B.—Plain Queensware Basin and Trap, in one piece, White or Ivory, with polished Mahogany Seat, No. 162 2-gallon Paisley Cistern, painted Brackets, and No. 153B Brass Chain and Doultonware Handle, - - - - - - - - -	each,	£4	9	6
No. 118D.—Ditto, same as above, coloured surface, Blue Magnolia design, - - - - - -	,,	4	15	6
No. 118E.—Ditto, ditto, ditto, Blue Wild Rose design, - - - - - -	,,	4	18	6
No. 118H.—Decorated Queensware Basin and Trap, Raised Acanthus Pattern, White or Ivory, with Fittings the same as No. 118B, - - - - - - - - - - - -	,,	5	5	6
No. 118X.—Ditto, same as above, but with Decoration picked out in Blue, - - - - - -	,,	5	14	0
No. 118J.—Ditto, ditto, ditto, in Ruby Hispani, picked out in Gold, - -	,,	8	10	6
No. 118K.—Ditto, ditto, ditto, Old Ivory on dark ground, picked out in Gold,	,,	9	7	6

In all Cases turn-down (S) Traps are sent with Closets unless otherwise ordered.

PRICES for BASINS and TRAPS only.

No. 118B.—Plain Queensware Basin and Trap, in one piece, White or Ivory, - - - - -	each,	£2	2	0
No. 118D—Ditto, ditto, ditto, plain surface, Blue Magnolia design, -	,,	2	8	0
No. 118E.—Ditto, ditto, ditto, Blue Wild Rose design, - - - -	,,	2	11	0
No. 118H.—Queensware Basin and Trap, in one piece, with Raised Acanthus Pattern Decoration, White or Ivory, - - - - - - - - - - - - - - - - - -	,,	2	18	0
No. 118X.—Ditto, same as above, Decoration picked out in Blue, - - - - - - - -	,,	3	6	6
No. 118J.—Ditto, ditto, Decoration in Ruby Hispani, picked out in Gold, - - - -	,,	6	3	0
No. 118K.—Ditto, ditto, Decoration Old Ivory on dark ground, picked out in Gold, -	,,	7	0	0

N.B.—If Basins and Traps only are required this must be clearly specified, or Closets will be sent complete.

A cheaper Mahogany Seat as No. 151, in one thickness, can be supplied if wished at a reduction of 6/on above prices.

For Designs of Tiling, see pages 4, 6, 38, 57, 58, 59, 60, 61, 157, 158.

THE LAMBETH

PATENT PEDESTAL "COMBINATION" CLOSET.

No. 118 X.

ADVANTAGES.

Front of Basin Lipped to form Urinal and Slop Sink when the seat is raised.

A water area equal to size of hole in seat, reducing the possibility of soiling basin.

Can be readily fixed, either square or across the corner of a room.

Self-contained, and all parts open to inspection.

Depth of water retained in basin, 1½ ins.

It may be flushed by simple seat-action arrangement, or by a pull handle as shown.

THE LAMBETH PATENT PEDESTAL "COMBINATION" CLOSETS are made both in STONEWARE, WHITE QUEENSWARE, and STRONG GLAZED WARE.

The former being especially adapted for places where they are liable to rough usage, as, by reason of their great strength, they are not likely to be damaged.

THE WHITE QUEENSWARE are specially well finished and suitable for higher-class work.

These Closets are strongly recommended for HOSPITALS, ASYLUMS, PUBLIC INSTITUTIONS, FACTORIES, TENEMENTS, MODEL DWELLINGS, Also MANSIONS and PRIVATE HOUSES. They are made both PLAIN AND ORNAMENTAL, and can be supplied either with Turned-down (S) or Shoot-out (P) Traps.

THE WATER CLOSET, SLOP-SINK, AND URINAL COMBINED.

This Closet has been Designed by DOULTON & CO., and was awarded THE GOLD MEDAL at the HEALTH EXHIBITION.

For Prices and full particulars, see pages 13, 14, 15.

For Designs of Tiling, see pages 4, 6, 38, 57, 58, 59, 60, 61, 157, 158.

DOULTON'S PATENT SYPHONIC CLOSET.

No. 516.

Made in One Piece of Earthenware.

Simple in Action. Easily Fixed.

Cannot be syphoned out by slops or large body of water being poured into basin.

A perfect connection between Trap and Soil Pipe is made by means of Doulton's Patent "Metallo-Keramic" Joint.

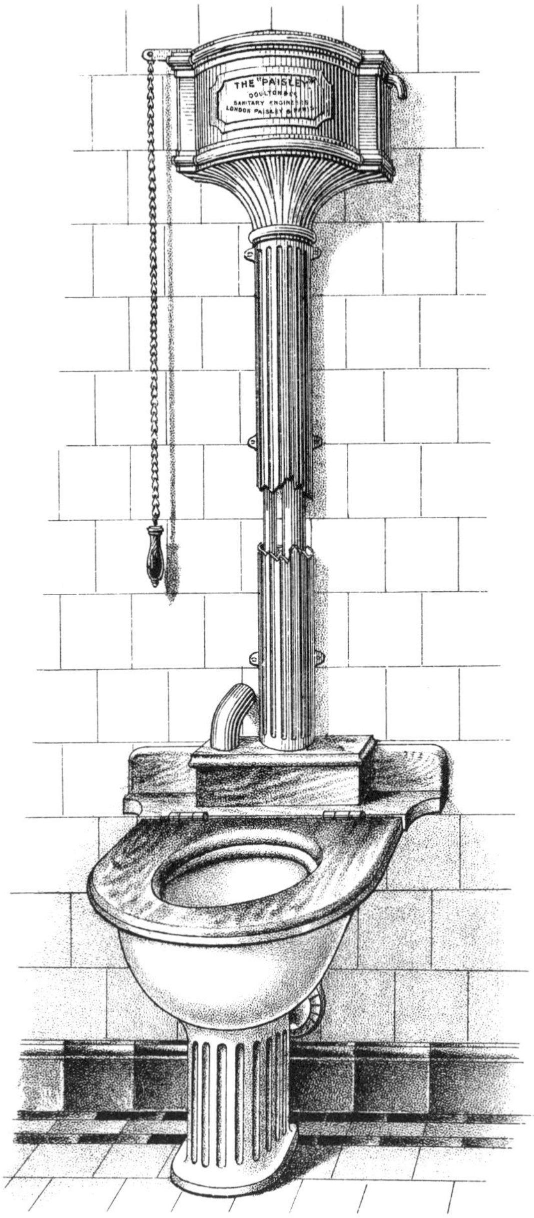

Large Water Area.

Perfect Flush, and all parts of the basin thoroughly cleansed.

Will work with 2 gallon Flush, though a 3 gallon is strongly advised where permitted by the Water Companies.

It is provided with an Air Pipe, so that the Syphon is perfectly ventilated.

PRICES.

No. 516. —White Earthenware Basin and Trap with "Metallo-Keramic" Joint, Cast-Iron Decorated Cistern, Brackets, Brass Chain and Pull with Ebonized Handle, and special made Mahogany Seat, - - - - - - - - - - - - -	£5	10	0
No. 516A.—Do., do., but with Blue Magnolia decoration, - - - - - - -	5	16	6
No. 516B.—Do., do., but with Wild Rose decoration, - - - - - - - -	6	0	6
No. 516C. —Do., do., but with White Pattern decoration, - - - - - - -	6	5	0
No. 516D.—Do., do., but with Blue and White decoration, - - - - - - -	6	15	0

Cast-Iron Cover for Pipes, 4 ft. 6 in. long, Painted, 5/-.

For designs of Tiling see pages 4, 6, 38, 57, 58, 59, 60, 61, 157, 158.

DOULTON'S SIMPLICITAS CLOSET.

WITH SPECIAL CISTERN FIXED JUST ABOVE SEAT.

No. 517.

No. 518.

No. 517.

UNDER some conditions, such as want of necessary height, etc., it is inconvenient to fix the ordinary tank. This Apparatus is designed to meet such requirements. The tank has a large outlet, and the closet is made with an increased inlet, so that a considerable quantity of water is discharged into the basin.

PRICES.

No. 517. —Strong Glazed Ware Closet, White inside, Brown out, with Polished Pine Seat and Cistern Lead-lined, and Brackets,	£4	11	0
No. 517A.—Do., do., do., but with Mahogany Seat and Cistern,	4	17	6
No. 517B.—Strong Glazed Ware Closet, White inside and out, with Polished Pine Seat and Cistern Lead-lined, and Brackets,	4	17	6
No. 517C.—Do., do., do., but with Mahogany Seat and Cistern,	5	4	0

No. 518.

This Closet is the same as No. 517, with the exception of the cistern being in decorated cast iron in place of wood lead-lined.

No. 518. —Strong Glazed Ware Closet, White inside, Brown out, with Polished Pine Seat, Decorated Cast-Iron Cistern and Brackets,	£3	7	0
No. 518A.—Do., do., do., but with Mahogany Seat,	3	10	0
No 518B. —Strong Glazed Ware Closet, White inside and out, with Polished Pine Seat, Decorated Cast-Iron Cistern and Brackets,	3	13	6
No. 518C.—Do., do., do., but with Mahogany Seat,	3	16	6

Can be supplied with Turn-down (S) Trap or Shoot-out (P) Trap.

In all cases Turn-down (S) Traps are sent unless otherwise ordered.

For designs of Tiling see pages 4, 6, 38, 57, 58, 59, 60, 61, 157, 158.

"YUKON" CLOSET COMBINATION

Plate 210-B.

"YUKON" VITREOUS EMBOSSED TWIN JET SYPHON CLOSET with floor screws and nickel-plated washers; piano polish recessed low down tank, with special syphon refill valve; bottom supply Duplex ball cock and float; nickel-plated push button; 2 inch nickel-plated flushing connection to closet, and nickel-plated brass supply pipe; Style "C" piano polish seat and cover, with nickel-plated attachment to closet.

Price as described with woodwork in Light or Golden Oak, Light or Dark Cherry...$42.00

Add if with woodwork in Black Walnut or Mahogany...$5.00
Add if with Italian or Tennessee marble top on tank... 1.50
Add if with nickel-plated wheel handle stop on supply pipe... 1.50
Add if with nickel-plated local vent pipe and collar (2 inches)... 1.00
Add if with brass floor flange and bolts... 1.00
If with plain closet, deduct... 1.00

Tank with pull and chain may be substituted at same price.

* * *

Add for 24 x 30 inch countersunk Italian or Tennessee marble floor slab...$7.50

Roughing in Measurement, Plate 210-B, 13½ inches.

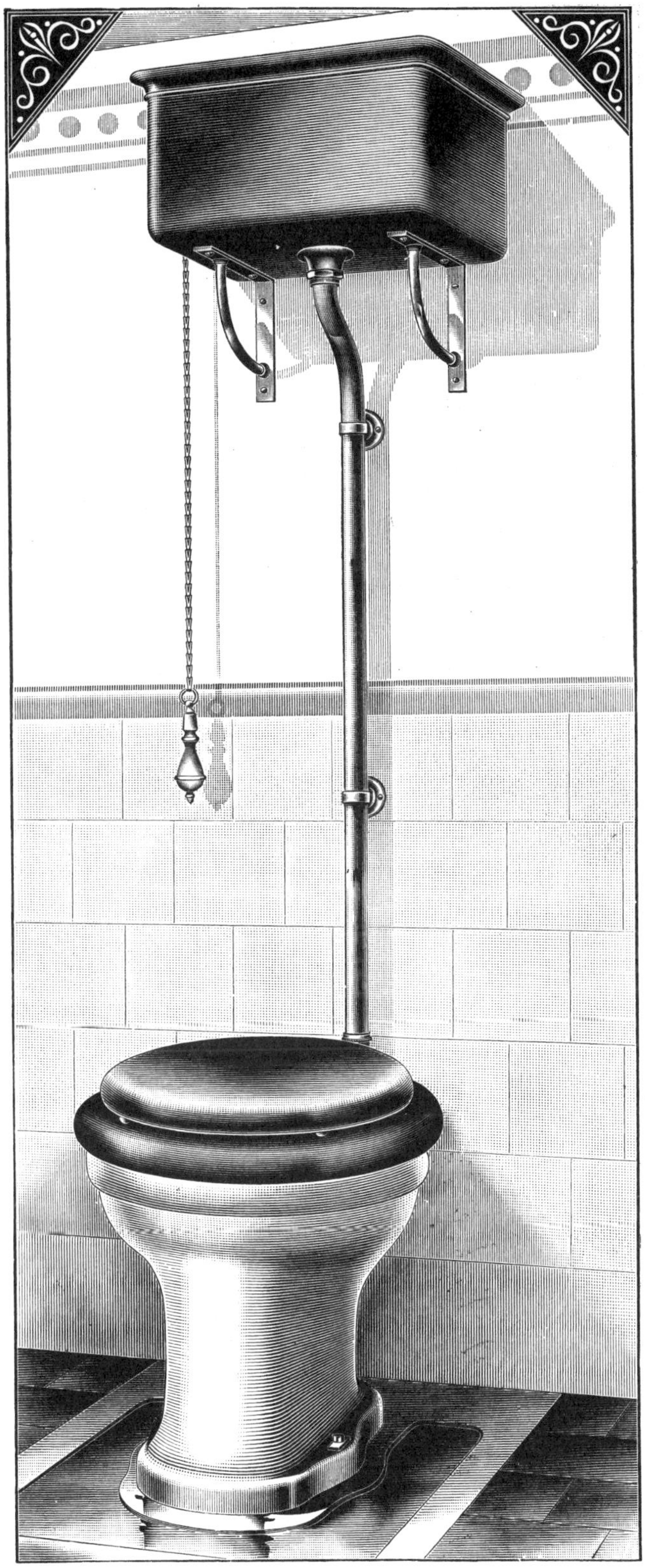

"ATLAS" CLOSET COMBINATION

Plate 212-B.

"ATLAS" VITREOUS PLAIN HEAVY PATTERN WASHDOWN CLOSET. Style "O" piano polish tank with "M" syphon valve; Duplex ball cock and float; nickel-plated brass brackets, pull and chain; 1½ inch nickel-plated brass flush pipe; adjustable holder and nickel-plated slip connection; Style "D" piano polish three-ply seat and cover, with nickel-plated relief hinge attachment to closet; brass floor flange and bolts with nickel-plated washers.

(Tank furnished with either top or bottom supply).

The "Atlas" is an extra heavy substantial closet (the walls being treble the thickness of those on an ordinary closet) and is designed for public places where subject to hard usage. The weight of the earthenware alone is 55 pounds.

Price as described with woodwork in Light or Golden Oak, Light or Dark Cherry.......................................$41.00

Add if with woodwork in Black Walnut or Mahogany....................$5.00
Add if with Style "E" seat and cover with friction hinges.................... 3.00
Add if with heavy nickel-plated brass supply pipe and holders.................... 4.00
Add if with nickel-plated local vent pipe and collar (2 inches).................... 1.00
Add if with 4 inch local vent on closet.................... 1.50
Add if with 4 inch nickel-plated local vent pipe and collar.................... 2.00
If with Style "C" seat and cover, deduct.................... 3.50

* * *

Add for 24 x 24 inch countersunk Italian or Tennessee marble floor slab....................$6.00

Roughing in Measurement, Plate 212-B, 14 inches.

SHANKS' PATENT PEDESTAL BIDET,

With Fittings for Hot and Cold Water, Ascending Spray, and Standing Waste and Overflow, complete.

No. 342.

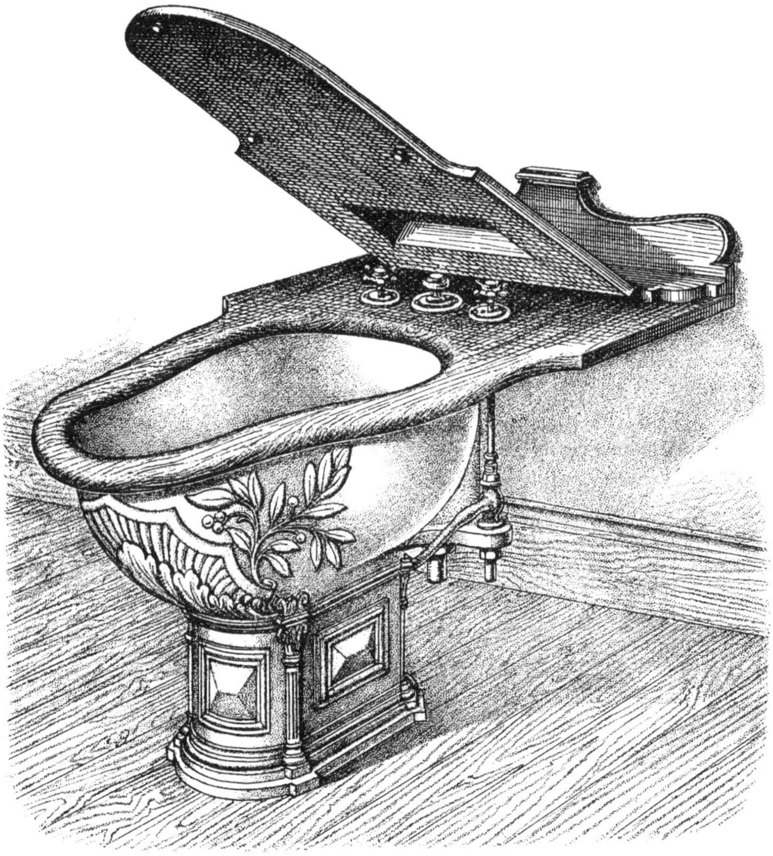

SECTION

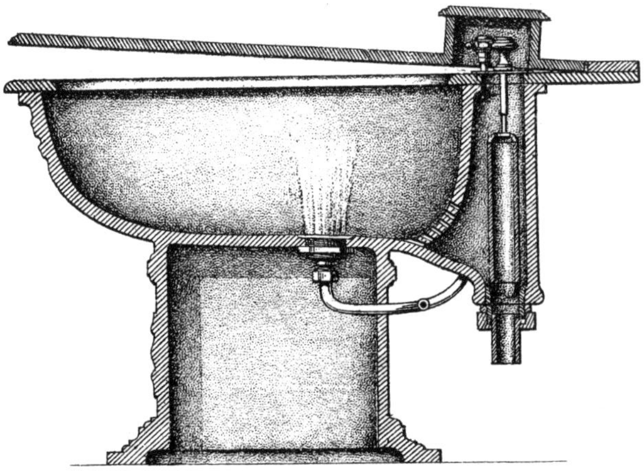

The Basin and Pedestal, with Waste Pipe and Ledges for fixing the Taps, are made in one solid piece of Porcelain of the very finest make, either Ivory White or decorated in Gold and Colours. The Taps are screw-down, and the Waste on Shanks' Patent principle. S. & Co. have confidence in recommending this as the most perfect appliance of its kind ever introduced. It is a very necessary appliance in a well-appointed Bath-room.

BIDET PEDESTAL N° 658

En une seule pièce de porcelaine avec robinetterie eau chaude et froide et vidage perfectionné formant trop-plein ; l'arrivée d'eau chaude se faisant par la gorge du bidet, dispense de tout siège et évite à la personne qui se sert de cet appareil la sensation désagréable du froid de la porcelaine.

PRIX A PARIS

Complet, avec cuvette blanche	. . . .	**135** fr.
— — décorée bleu Mulberry	. . . .	**150.** »
— — décorée riche de plusieurs couleurs	.	**165.** »

Longueur totale, 0m72, Grande largeur, 0m39. Petite largeur, 0m32

BIDET PEDESTAL N° 658 bis

En une seule pièce de porcelaine avec robinetterie eau chaude et froide, vidage perfectionné formant trop-plein et douche ascendante avec robinetterie spéciale.

Ce **bidet** offre les mêmes avantages que le bidet n° 658 ci-contre et en plus une douche ascendante.

PRIX A PARIS

Complet avec cuvette blanche	. . . .	**185** fr.
— — décorée bleu Mulberry	. . . .	**200.** »
— — décor riche de plusieurs couleurs	. . .	**215.** »

Longueur totale, 0m72. Grande largeur, 0m39. Petite largeur, 0m32.

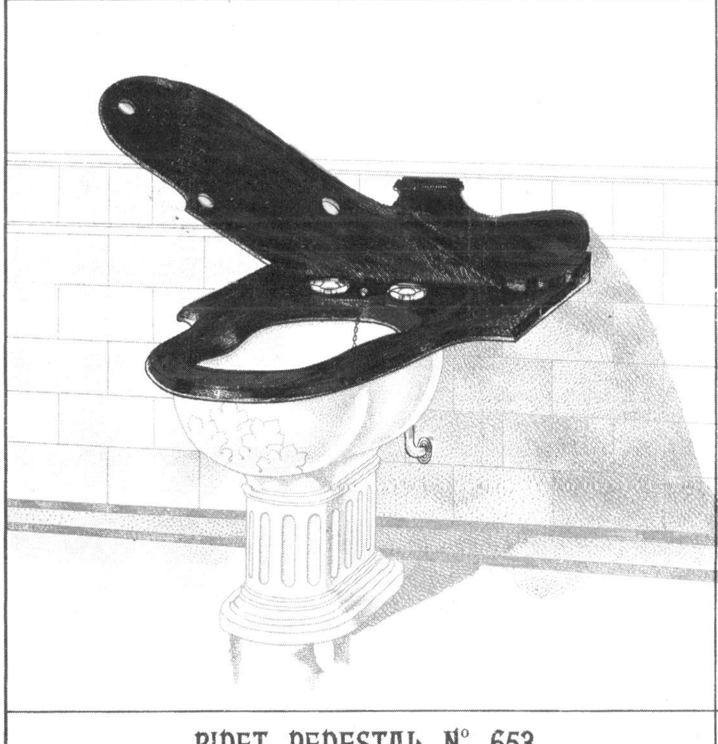

BIDET PEDESTAL N° 653

Ce bidet se fait dans tous nos principaux décors de façon à pouvoir l'assortir soit aux cuvettes de lavabos, soit au décor de nos closets dans le cas où ceux-ci doivent aller dans la même pièce.

PRIX A PARIS

Complet, avec siège acajou, noyer d'Amérique ou pitchpin et robinets eau chaude et froide, trop-plein et vidage.

Cuvette blanche	. . . .	**135** fr.
— décorée	. . . .	**150.** »
— décor riche de plusieurs couleurs	. . . .	**165.** »

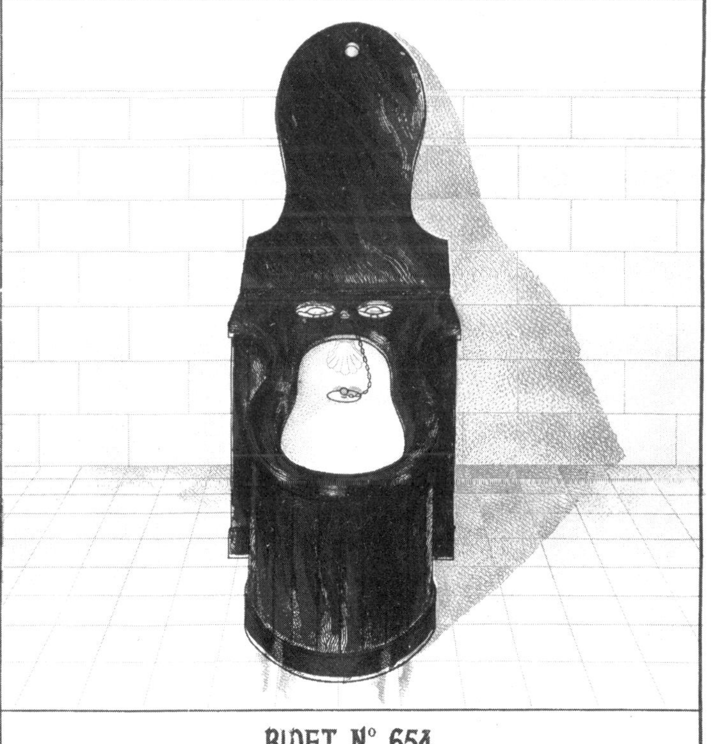

BIDET N° 654

Monté avec entourage acajou massif, noyer d'Amérique ou pitchpin.

Ce **Bidet** offre les mêmes avantages que le n° 653, c'est-à-dire arrivée d'eau froide et d'eau chaude, vidage et trop-plein.

La cuvette en porcelaine anglaise et la robinetterie en cuivre nickelé, sont entièrement dissimulées par la boiserie.

PRIX A PARIS

Complet . . . . **175** fr.

IMP. EUGÈNE VERNEAU, 108, R. FOLIE-MERICOURT, PARIS

PATENT LAVATORY ON CAST-IRON STAND.

No. 121.—Lavatory.

			Enamel Painted.		
		Size.	3rd Class in one color.	2nd Class in colors or bronzed	1st Class in various colors.
No. 121	Cast-iron Lavatory Stand, with Mirror and Tile Back, No. 35 Ivoryware D Lavatory, Hot and Cold Taps, Lift-up Waste Arrangement, and Moveable Shield	18″ × 18″	102/3	125/6	136/-
		22″ × 18″	115/9	139/-	149/6
		27″ × 20″	126/1	149/3	159/8
		30″ × 22″	147/10	172/-	183/5
	If without Moveable Shield ... ... less		5/9	8/-	9/-

HYGEIA WHITE METAL OR NICKEL-PLATED TAPS AND WASTE, 3/5 Extra. 1⅛″ BRASS TRAP, 4/6 Extra.

No. 22 Tcwel Rail, 99/-; Nickel-plating same, 18/- extra.

THESE STANDS MAY BE ENAMEL-PAINTED ANY COLOR TO ORDER.

The above Stand is also supplied with No. 200 Basin, with Overedge Taps, Plug and Chain. For Prices, see page 49. It is No. 123.

JOHN HEYWOOD, CHROMO LITHO. MANCHESTER, LONDON, BRISTOL, LIVERPOOL.

CHAPTER THREE

LAVATORIES

The development of the fixed and plumbed-in basin, or 'lavatory', was relatively straightforward, since the traditional wash-stand and basin offered models that could readily be adapted for fixed pipework. An intermediate design, the tip-up lavatory, was useful for situations where there was a good water supply but the drainage was more uncertain. The tip-up basin was swung on a pivot to drain into a hopper, which could feed into a drainpipe or a bucket. Tip-ups were much cheaper than plughole basins, since they did not have to be fitted with a brass waste arrangement or supplied with a plug and chain. However, the sheer convenience of a basin fitted with a plug (which could simply be removed to allow the dirty water to drain away down a fixed pipe) ensured the eventual disappearance of the tip-up type.

A tremendous variety of lavatory designs was available, and great ingenuity went into devising lavatories for every situation. No matter how awkward a corner or restricted a space, there was a lavatory that would fit. Integral to the design of most lavatories is a soap and brush dish, sometimes simply ribbed to hasten the flow of water to the basin, sometimes elaborately moulded into an acanthus leaf or scallop shell. Most ceramic basins were plain white glazed, but the makers took every opportunity to show what could be achieved in the way of decoration and the majority provided basins with coloured underglaze decoration. Unlike the decoration on the side of the bath or the closet, this would be seen at close range, and would have to stand up to more wear. Flowers, classical motifs and Oriental patterns were all popular, as were Rococo designs, many of them lavishly gilded.

The lavatory could be supported on metal brackets bolted into the wall or fitted into a wooden cabinet. The cabinetwork was directly descended from the free-standing wash-stand with its marble top, tiled splashback, and towel rail. What was originally the cupboard for the chamber pot was easily adapted to conceal the pipework. While the cabinet lavatory of the 1880s was as elaborate as any dining room sideboard, the more functional look of the bathroom at the turn of the century was achieved with nickel-plated stands which revealed the pipework, so that the up-to-date engineering of the appliance itself became a feature.

"IDEAL" PATENT LAVATORY BASINS.

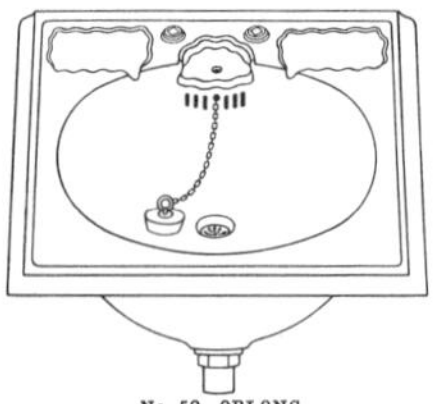

No. 50—OBLONG.
With "Ideal" Patent Overflow and Waste, Brass Waste Connection, and Rubber Plug with Chain.

	LARGE.	SMALL.
Two Sizes.	26½ × 20½ in.	22 × 18 in.
BASIN [oval],	21 × 15 ,,	17 × 13 ,,

SECTION SHEWING "IDEAL" PATENT OVERFLOW AND WASTE.

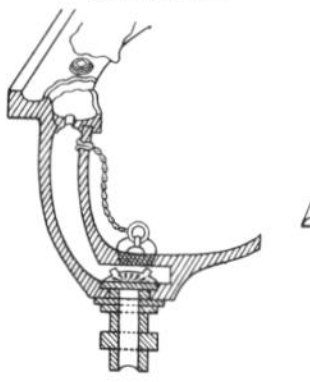

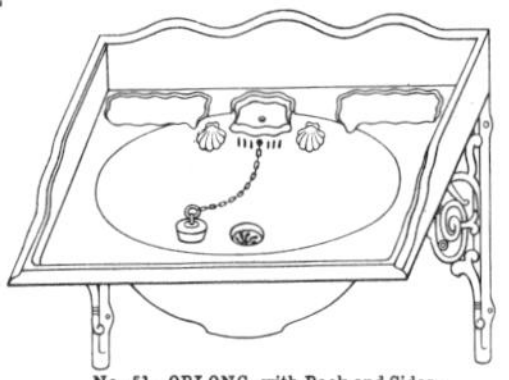

No. 51—OBLONG, with Back and Sides.
"Ideal" Patent Overflow and Waste, Brass Waste Connection, Rubber Plug with Chain, and Wall Brackets with Patent Fastenings.

	LARGE.	SMALL.
Two Sizes.	26½ × 20½ in.	22 × 18 in.
BASIN [oval],	21 × 15 ,,	17 × 13 ,,

Nos. 60, 61, 62, 63, WITHOUT PEDESTALS are Nos. 52, 53, 54, 55.

"IDEAL" PATENT LAVATORY BASINS WITH ORNAMENTAL PEDESTALS.

These Lavatory Basins are made with 2 Shell Supplies, or with 2 Holes for Pillar Cocks, No. 814 or 815, to deliver over the Basin. When ordering please specify which method is required. If not stated, will be sent as shewn.

The Ornamental Pedestals can be supplied with ordinary Lavatory Basins of corresponding sizes to those here described.

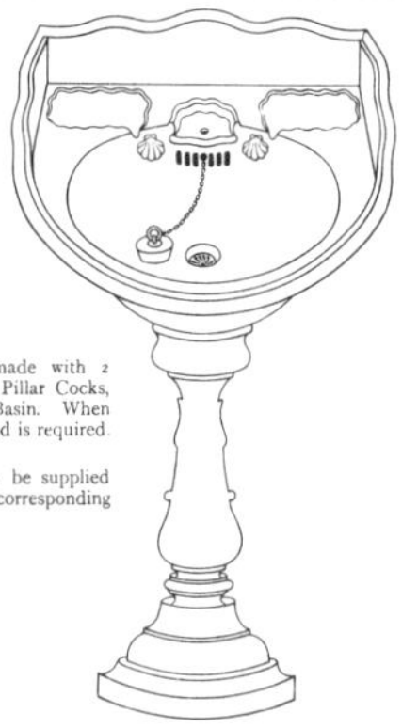

No. 60—ANGULAR, Square Front with Sides.
"Ideal" Patent Overflow and Waste, Brass Waste Connection, Rubber Plug with Chain, and Ornamental Pedestal.
Size, 26½ × 20½ in.; BASIN, [oval], 17 × 12 in.; Length of Side, 19 in.

No. 61—Same as No. 60 but without sides.

No. 62—ROUND FRONT, with Back and Sides.
"Ideal" Patent Overflow and Waste, Brass Waste Connection, Rubber Plug with Chain, and Ornamental Pedestal.
Size, 26½ × 20½ in.; BASIN [oval], 21 × 15 in.

No. 63—Same as No. 62 but without back and sides.

LAVATORY BASINS.

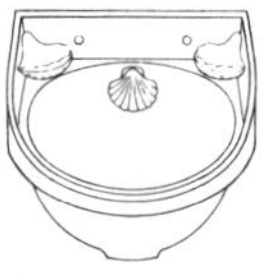

No. 130—FLAT WALL, with Back and Sides.
Two Sizes.

	LARGE.	SMALL.
	15½ × 15½ in.	13 × 13 in.
BASIN [round],	12½ ,,	11 ,,

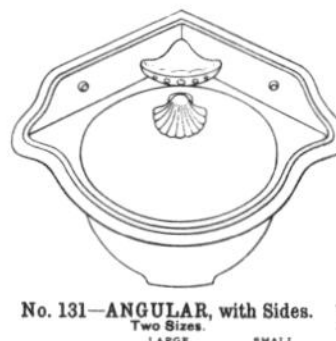

No. 131—ANGULAR, with Sides.
Two Sizes.

	LARGE.	SMALL.
	20 × 18 in.	16 × 15 in.
BASIN [round],	14 ,,	10 ,,
Length of side,	14½ ,,	12 ,,

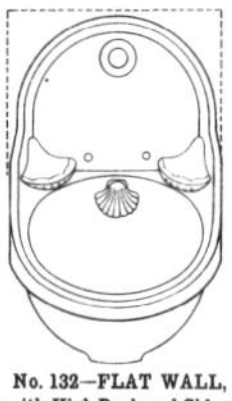

No. 132—FLAT WALL, with High Back and Sides.
12½ × 12½ in.; BASIN [round], 10½ in.
Full Height, 15 in.
Made with Square Back, as shown by dotted lines.

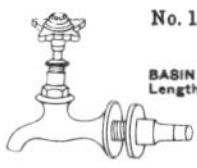

No. 804A.
With Tinned Ferrule, to suit Lavatory Basins Nos. 132 & 132a.

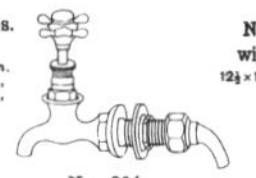

No. 804.
With Back Nut and Bent Union, to suit Lavatory Basins Nos. 132 & 132a.

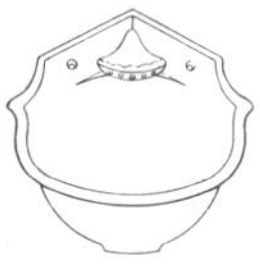

No. 133—ANGULAR.
14½ × 17 in.; BASIN [round], 13 in.
Length of Side, 10 in.

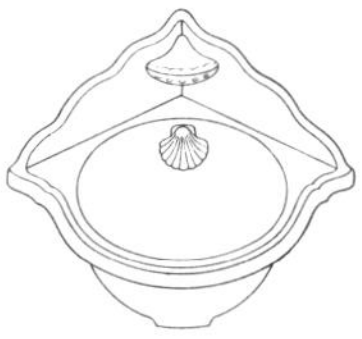

No. 134—ANGULAR, with Sides.
21½ × 20 in.; BASIN [round], 13 in.
Length of Side, 15 in.

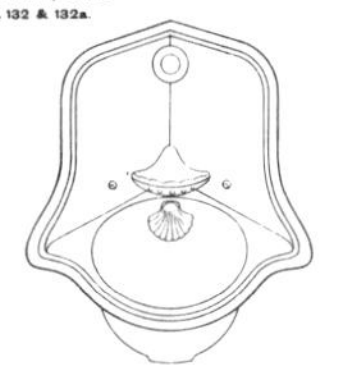

No. 132A—ANGULAR, with High Sides.
17 × 14 in.; BASIN, 10 in.; Length of Side, 12 in.
Full Height, 15 in.

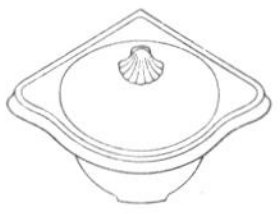

No. 135—ANGULAR,
Two Sizes.

	LARGE.	SMALL.
	20 × 18 in.	16 × 15 in.
BASIN [round],	14 ,,	10 ,,
Length of Side,	14½ ,,	12 ,,

No. 136—ANGULAR.
17 × 17 in.; BASIN [round], 11 in.
Length of Side, 12 in.

No. 137—FLAT WALL, with Back.
Two Sizes.

	LARGE.	SMALL.
	18 × 12 in.	12 × 9 in.
BASIN [oval],	15 × 11 ,,	10½ × 8 ,,

Lion Head can be made to order, in Place of Shell Supply and Overflow. When not specially ordered Shell will be understood.

LAVATORY BASINS.

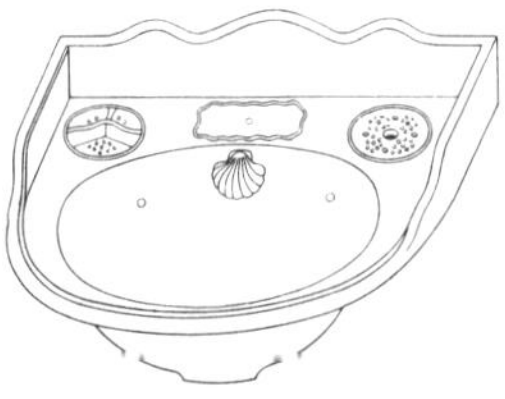

No. 168—ROUND FRONT, with Back and Sides.
28 × 22 in.; BASIN [oval], 20 × 14 in.

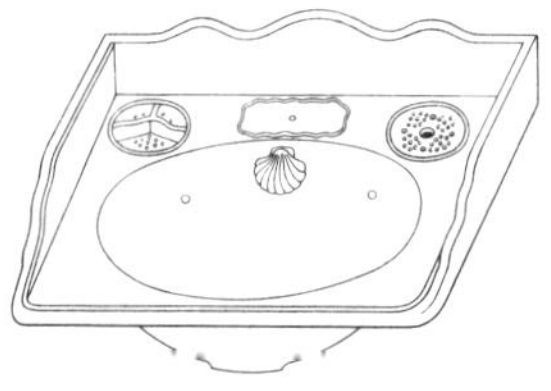

No. 169—OBLONG, with Back and Sides.
28 × 22 in.; BASIN [oval], 20 × 14 in.

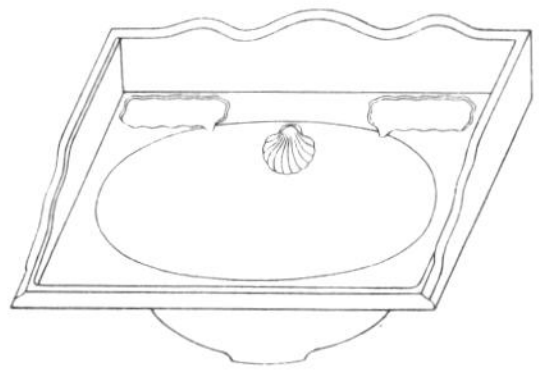

No. 170—OBLONG, with Back and Sides.
26½ × 20½ in.; BASIN [oval], 21 × 15 in.
Made also with Straight Back as No. 120 [page 8.]

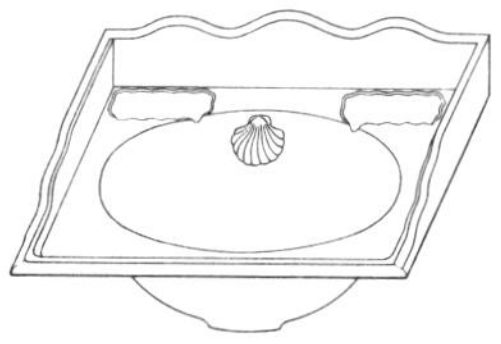

No. 171—OBLONG, with Back and Sides.
25 × 18 in.; BASIN [oval], 19 × 13 in.
Made also with Straight Back as No. 120 [page 8.]

RIGHT.

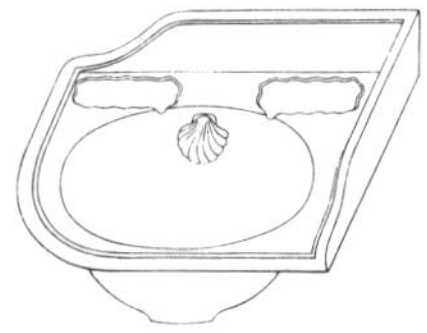

No. 172—CORNER, with Sides.
22 × 19 in.; BASIN [oval], 16 × 13 in.

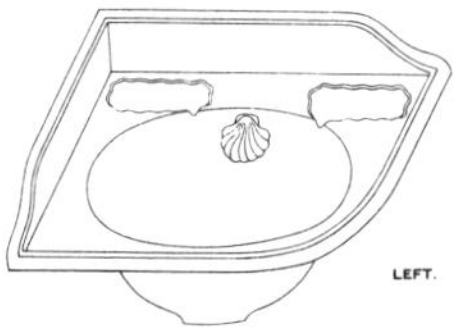

LEFT.

No. 173—CORNER, with Sides.
22 × 19 in.; BASIN [oval], 16 × 13 in.

Also made with 2 Tap Holes for Pillar Cocks [as shown page 5.] If not mentioned with Tap Holes, Shell Supply is understood. Can also be made to order with Lion Head, instead of Shell Supply and Overflow.

LAVATORY BASINS.

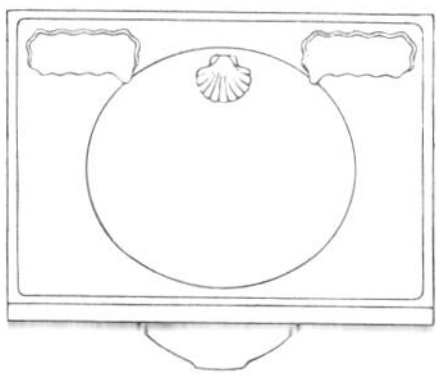

No 106—OBLONG.
26½ × 20½ in.; BASIN [round], 16 in.

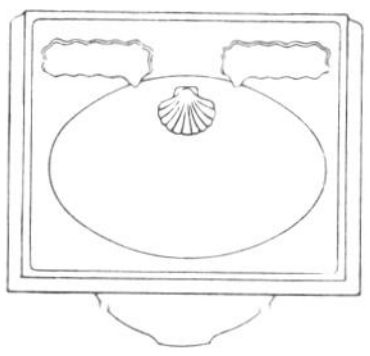

No. 107—OBLONG.
22 × 20 in.; BASIN [oval], 17 × 13 in.

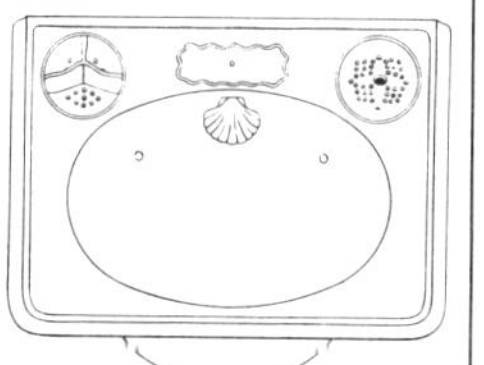

No. 108—OBLONG.
28 × 22 in.; BASIN [oval], 20 × 14 in.
Made also with Square Edge, as No. 106.

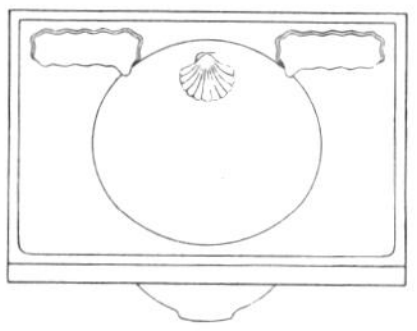

No. 109—OBLONG.
25 × 18 in.; BASIN [round], 14 in.

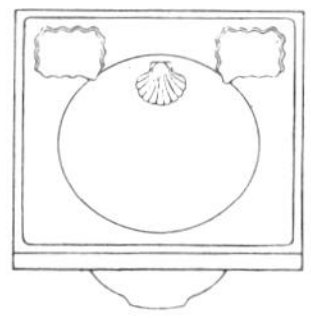

No. 110—SQUARE.
18 × 18 in.; BASIN [round], 13 in.

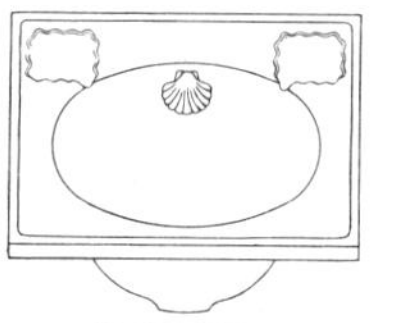

No. 112A—OBLONG.
22 × 17 in.; BASIN [oval], 17 × 11½ in.

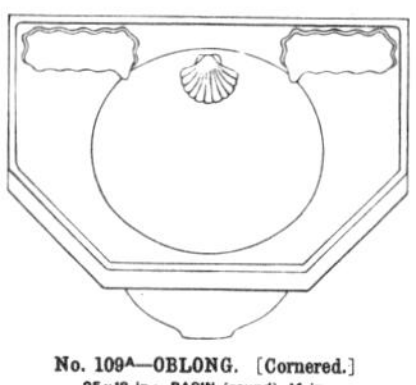

No. 109A—OBLONG. [Cornered.]
25 × 18 in.; BASIN [round], 14 in.

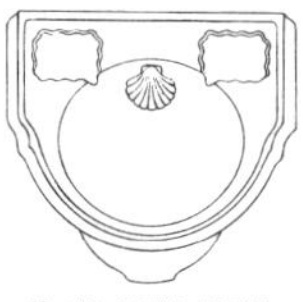

No. 113—ROUND FRONT.
18 × 17 in.; BASIN [round], 12 in.

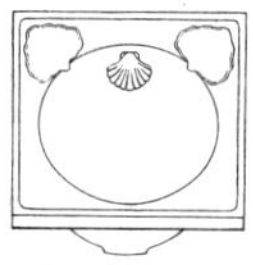

No. 114A—SQUARE.
14½ × 14½ in.; BASIN [round], 12 in.

Excepting Nos. 113 and 114A above are also made with 2 Tap Holes for Pillar Cocks [as shown page 5.] If not mentioned with Tap Holes, Shell Supply is understood. Can also be made to order, with Lion Head, instead of Shell Supply and Overflow.

PATENT D LAVATORIES, WITH UPRISING EYE-SPRAY.

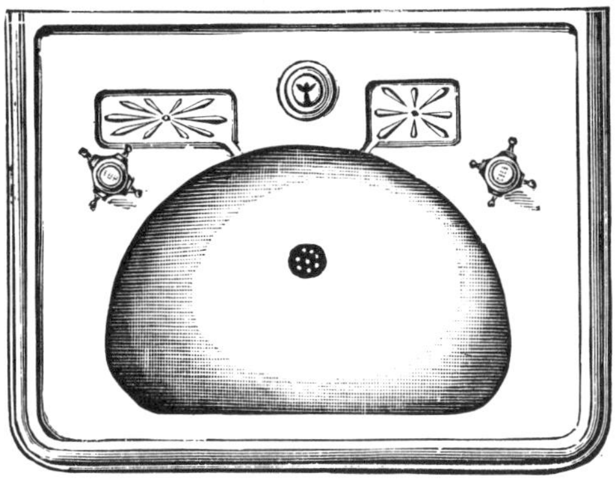

No. 74.

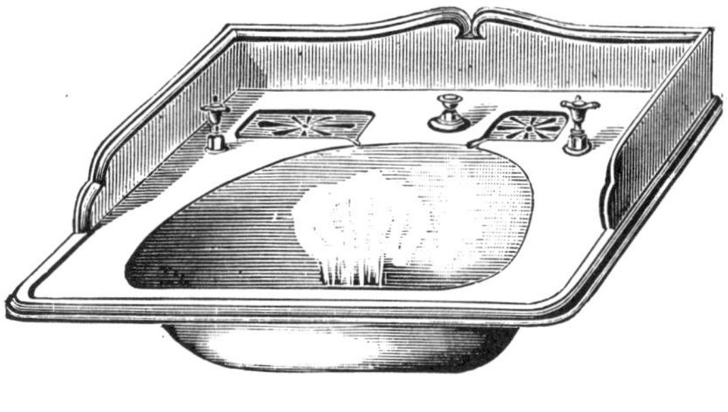

No. 75.

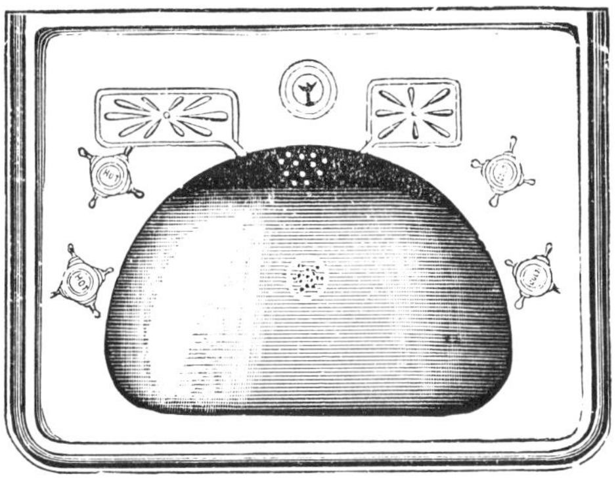

No. 37.

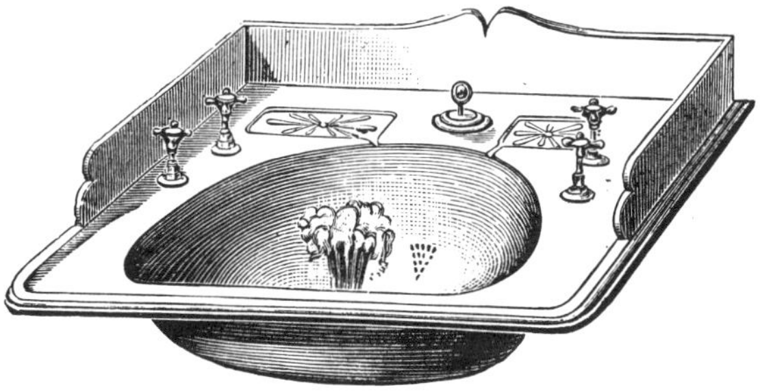

No. 38.

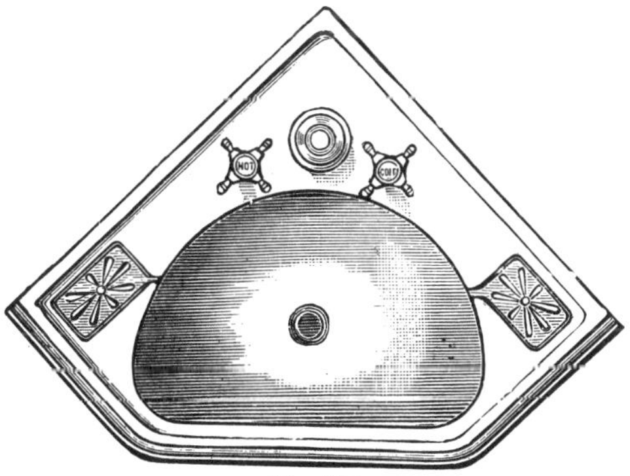

No. 76.

No. 77.

The Lavatories here shewn are made with Cold Tap to Lavatory and Cold Tap to Uprising Spray—see Diagrams Nos. 74, 75, 76 and 77. Also made with Hot and Cold Taps to Lavatory and Hot and Cold Taps to Uprising Spray, as Nos. 37 and 38. The Supply Tubes to Lavatory and Spray are made in one piece of Porcelain with Basin. Each Basin is complete with Quick Waste Arrangement.

FOR COLD WATER ONLY.

	Size—18″ × 18″	22″ × 18″	27″ × 20″	30″ × 22″
No. 74.	54/-	67/6	75/6	94/6
„ 75.	57/9	75/-	85/6	109/6
„ 76.	—	63/-	69/-	87/-
„ 77.	—	69/-	76/6	97/6

FOR HOT AND COLD WATER.

	Size—27″ × 20″	30″ × 22″
No. 37...	97/-	116/-
„ 38...	107/-	131/-

NICKEL-PLATING FITTINGS, 3/9 per Set .. .. 6/1 per Set.

These Lavatories afford a refreshing Spray, without any objectionable projecting parts.

PATENT STEAMLESS AND NOISELESS D LAVATORIES.

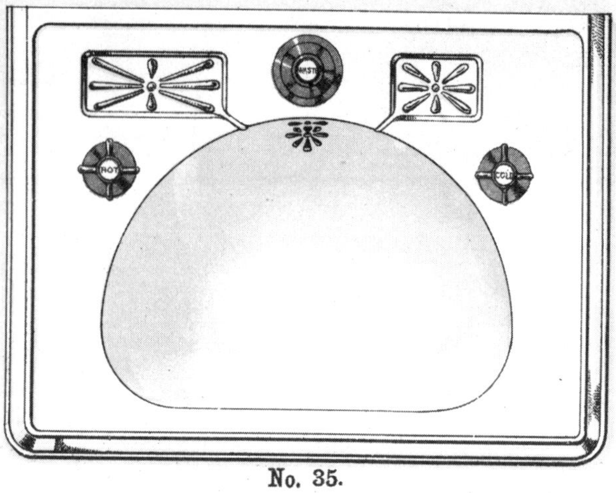

No. 35.

No. 36.

No. 40.

No. 39.

These Sanitary Lavatories are made in the finest Ivory or White Ware Porcelain, and the D Bowl is shaped so as to afford the greatest freedom to the user. No loose or projecting fittings are inside the Bowl. Each Lavatory is complete with Hot and Cold Taps, Quick Waste, 1½″ Central Tube Overflow, and 1½″ Outlet Union. As the Waste Pipe is made in strong copper and not earthenware, the risk of breakage is greatly lessened, and being circular in form, easy cleansing is ensured. There are thousands of these celebrated Lavatories in use all over the world.

PRICES COMPLETE.

	No. 35.				No. 36.				No. 39.			No. 40.		
Sizes outside	18″ × 18″	22″ × 18″	27″ × 20″	30″ × 22″	18″ × 18″	22″ × 18″	27″ × 20″	30″ × 22″	22″ × 18″	27″ × 20″	30″ × 22″	22″ × 18″	27″ × 20″	30″ × 22″
Size of Bowl ...	14″	16″	18″	20″	14″	16″	18″	20″	13″ × 10″	16½ × 12″	17″ × 13″	13″ × 10″	16½ × 12″	17″ × 13″
Ivory or White Ware	49/6	63/-	71/3	90/-	53/3	70/6	81/-	105/-	58/6	64/6	82/6	64/6	72/-	93/-
Do. Printed under glaze in 1 color as Decoration No. 177.	55/6	69/-	80/3	99/-	60/-	79/6	91/6	115/6	64/6	73/6	91/6	70/6	81/-	102/-
Do. Printed under glaze in colors as Decorations No. 167. 169. &c.	61/6	76/6	87/9	108/-	66/9	85/6	99/-	126/-	70/6	79/6	99/-	78/-	88/6	112/6

HYGEIA WHITE METAL OR NICKEL-PLATING FITTINGS, **3/5** **Extra.**

NOTE.—Ivoryware only kept in stock. Whiteware made to order.

A crate containing 6 No. 35 Lavatories, 27″ × 20″, measures 4′ 5″ × 2′ 8″ × 2′ 11″, and weighs about 3cwt. 2qrs. 6lbs. gross.

JOHN HEYWOOD, CHROMO LITHO. MANCHESTER, LONDON, BRISTOL, LIVERPOOL.

No. 120.—Lavatory.

PATENT D BOWL STEAMLESS AND NOISELESS SANITARY LAVATORIES.

These Lavatories have obtained considerable popularity, and are recommended for the sound principle upon which they are constructed, and the tasteful manner they can be placed upon the market. Attention is directed to the moveable Shield, which not only protects the Supply and Waste Pipes, but conceals their unsightly appearance.

The Dished Marble Soleplate is supplied to order.

PRICES.

No. 119.—Patent D Lavatory in Ivoryware, with Hot and Cold Taps and Waste Arrangement, Cast-iron Enamel Painted Frieze and Shield, picked out in colors.

Sizes	18″ × 18″	22″ × 18″	27″ × 20″	30″ × 22″
Price	84/10	104/3	117/-	143/3
No. 120.	Do.	do.	do.	
Price	—	89/3	99/5	122/6

Dished veined Marble Soleplate 2′ 6″ × 2′ 2″, 45/- Extra.

White Hygeia Metal or Nickel-plating Fittings, 3/5 Extra.

If with 1½″ Brass Trap, 4/6 Extra.

If without Shield, 9/- Less.

A crate containing 3 No. 119 Lavatories, 27″ × 20″, weighs about 4cwt. 2qrs. 14lbs. gross, and measures 4′ 5″ × 2′ 8″ × 2′ 11″.

No. 119.—Lavatory.

JOHN HEYWOOD, CHROMO LITHO. MANCHESTER, LONDON, BRISTOL, LIVERPOOL.

PATENT D LAVATORIES ON CAST IRON STANDS.

No 122

No. **122.**—Lavatory Stand, with No. 36 Patent Basin in finest Ivoryware, Hot and Cold Taps and Waste Arrangement; Stand and Shield in Cast Iron.

Size.	3rd Class in one color.	Enamel Painted. 2nd Class in colors.	1st Class in various colors
18″ x 18″	**81/11**	**91/7**	**101/3**
22″ x 18″	**99/2**	**108/10**	**118/6**
27″ x 20″	**111/-**	**120/9**	**130/5**
30″ x 22″	**135/9**	**146/6**	**157/6**
If without Shield, less	**5/9**	**8/-**	**9/-**

No. 204

No. **204.**—Lavatory Stand in Cast Iron, with Tile Back, and No. 35 Patent Basin in finest Ivoryware; Hot and Cold Taps and Quick Waste Arrangement.

Size.	3rd Class in one color.	Enamel Painted. 2nd Class in colors.	1st Class in various colors.
18″ x 18″	**81/9**	**93/-**	**100/6**
22″ x 18″	**95/3**	**106/6**	**114/-**
27″ x 20″	**103/6**	**116/3**	**123/9**
30″ x 22″	**125/-**	**136/-**	**143/6**

WHITE HYGEIA METAL OR NICKEL-PLATED FITTINGS, 3/5 Extra.

IF WITH POLISHED BRASS TRAP AND PIPE, 12/6; Nickel-Plating same, 3/9 Extra.

IF WITH BRASS TRAP, 4/6 Extra.

REGISTERED LOUIS XV. LAVATORIES.

ON CAST IRON STANDS.

No. 205.

No. 179.
„ 182.

No.		Size.	Enamel Painted. 3rd Class in one color.	2nd Class in colors.	1st Class in various colors.
179	Lavatory Stand, with No. 158 Basin in finest Porcelain, Hot and Cold Taps and easily removeable Waste, Cast Iron Stand and Tile Back, with Wood Fitting Strip under Basin	27″ × 19″	93/9	105/-	112/6
182	Lavatory Stand as above, but with No. 159 Basin, no Tile Back	27″ × 19″	93/3	101/3	109/5
	Moveable Shield, extra		5/9	8/-	9/-
205	Lavatory with Bracket Stand as No. 180, but with Basin No. 152, and Tile Back as No. 179 Stand, complete	27″ × 20″	80/-	92/2	94/7

BRASS TRAP, 4/6 EXTRA. POLISHED BRASS TRAP AND PIPE, 12/6; NICKEL-PLATING SAME, 3/9.
WHITE HYGEIA METAL OR NICKEL-PLATED BASIN FITTINGS 3/5 EXTRA.

SHANKS' PATENT LAVATORIES.

Shanks' Patent Sanitary Lavatory, No. 1, fixed on Cast-iron Frieze and Wrought-iron Brackets.

Design No. 306.

The above Stand is usually supplied nicely Japanned and picked out in Gold or Colours. It is cleanly and durable, and meets the most advanced Sanitary requirements.

SHANKS' PATENT LAVATORIES.

Shanks'
Improved Shampooing Fittings,
For Hot and Cold Water, with Screw-Down Cocks.
Specially suitable for Hairdressers.

Design No. 6.

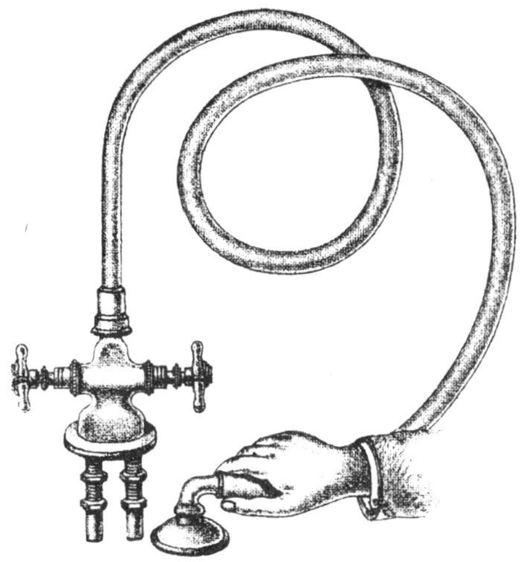

For durability and perfect mixing of Hot and Cold Water this fitting is unsurpassed.

Hairdresser's Lavatory, with No. 6 Shampooing Arrangement,
For Hot and Cold Water.

Design No. 304.

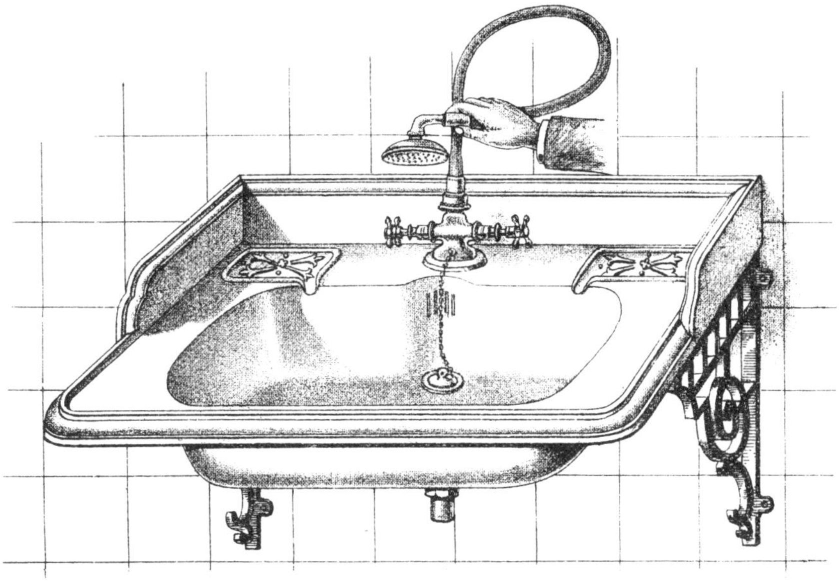

This Lavatory is made like "Citizen" Lavatories, with recess for Waste and Overflow, and I. R. Plug.

"Imperial" Lavatory, on Wooden Frieze, with Brass Brackets.

Design No. 305.

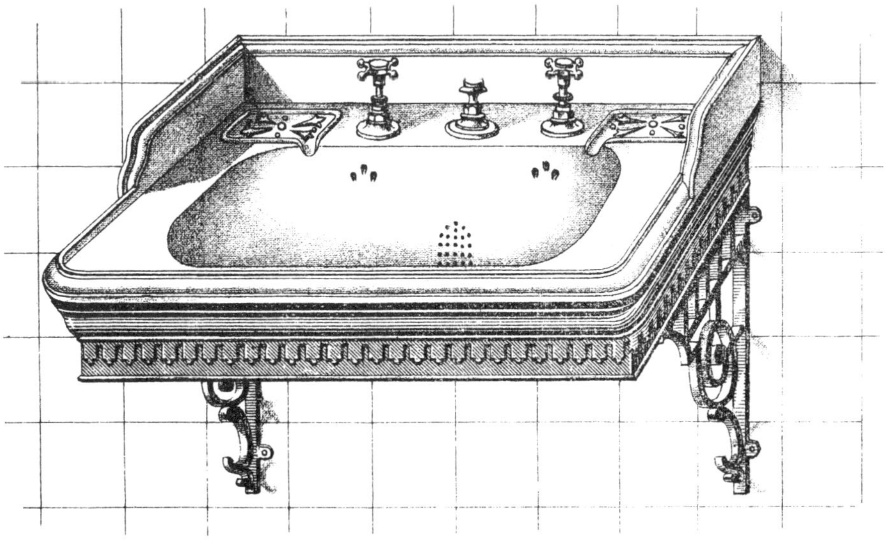

These Brackets may be made to fit any of our Lavatories; so that, in ordering, it will be necessary to give the size or the number of the Basin required.

DOULTON'S IMPROVED LAVATORIES.

WITH ENAMELLED IRON SKIRTING, FRIEZES, AND STANDARDS.

No. 432.

COMPLETE as illustration, including lavatory basin, enamelled slate or marble top, soap and brush trays, hot and cold valves, and 1½ in. plug, washer, and chain, with enamelled iron standards, frieze, and tiled skirting

PRICES.

	With Oval Basin. 17½ by 13½ in.	With Oblong Basin. 17 by 14 in.	With Straight-Fronted Basin. 16 by 14 in.
No. 432 .—In Enamelled Slate, - - - - - - -	£5 10 0	£5 12 0	£5 13 0
No. 432A.—In Veined Marble, - - - - - - -	6 7 6	6 10 6	6 11 6
No. 432B.—In St. Anne's Marble, - - - - - -	7 2 6	7 5 6	7 7 6
No. 432C.—In Rouge Royal Marble, - - - - - -	7 10 0	7 13 0	7 15 0

No. 433.

WITH PULL-UP WASTE.

No. 433 .—In Enamelled Slate, - - - - - - -	£6 18 0	£7 0 0	£7 1 0
No. 433A.—In Veined Marble, - - - - - - -	7 15 6	7 18 6	7 19 6
No. 433B.—In St. Anne's Marble, - - - - - -	8 10 6	8 13 6	8 15 6
No. 433C.—In Rouge Royal Marble, - - - - - -	8 18 0	9 1 0	9 3 0

With Brass Trap in place of Straight Union, 2/6 extra.

With Vulcanite Plug, 1/6 extra.

DOULTON'S IMPROVED LAVATORIES.

WITH ENAMELLED IRON BACK, FRIEZE, AND STANDARDS.

No. 430.

COMPLETE as illustration, including lavatory basin, enamelled slate or marble top, soap and brush trays, hot and cold valves, and 1½ in. plug, washer, and chain, with enamelled iron standards, frieze, and back, with looking-glass.

PRICES.

	With Oval Basin. 17½ by 13½ in.	With Oblong Basin. 17 by 14 in.	With Straight-Fronted Basin. 16 by 14 in.
No. 430 .—In Enamelled Slate,	£7 0 0	£7 2 0	£7 3 0
No. 430A.—In Veined Marble,	7 17 6	8 0 6	8 1 6
No. 430B.—In St. Anne's Marble,	8 12 6	8 15 6	8 17 6
No. 430C.—In Rouge Royal Marble,	9 0 0	9 3 0	9 5 0

No. 431.

WITH PULL-UP WASTE.

No. 431 .—In Enamelled Slate,	£8 8 0	£8 10 0	£8 11 0
No. 431A.—In Veined Marble,	9 5 6	9 8 6	9 9 6
No. 431B.—In St. Anne's Marble,	10 0 6	10 3 6	10 5 6
No. 431C.—In Rouge Royal Marble,	10 8 0	10 11 0	10 13 0

With Brass Trap in place of Straight Union, 2/6 extra.

With Vulcanite Plug, 1/6 extra.

SHANKS' CABINET LAVATORIES.

No. 2B. Cabinet Stand,
In Walnut or Mahogany, with No. 1 Basin and Fittings.

No. 79. Cabinet Stand,
In Walnut, Mahogany, or other Woods.

Above is shewn with Shanks' Patent No. 24 Lavatory, with Marble Slab. It may be supplied with any of Shanks & Co.'s Square-front Lavatories.

No. 81. Cabinet Stand.

Above is shewn with No. 121 "Citizen" Lavatory.

No. 80. Cabinet Stand.

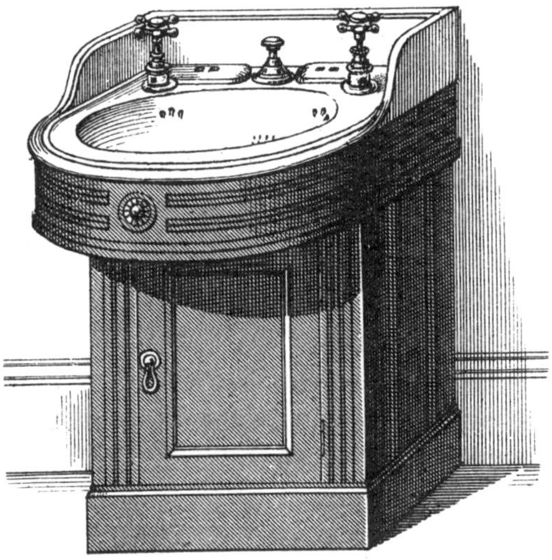

Above is shewn with No. 36 Basin and Fittings.

SHANKS' CABINET LAVATORIES.

No. 970. "The Langtry."

This Lavatory is shewn fitted with Shanks' Patent Sanitary Basin No. 24; Hot, Cold, and Waste Fittings; and "St. Ann's" Marble Slab Top. It may also be fitted with No. 96 Basin. The Cabinet is of best workmanship and materials and may be had in different Woods, according to order. The back is constructed with Jewel Drawers, Tiles, and Bevelled Plate-glass Mirrors.

Other varieties and styles on application.

SHANKS' CABINET LAVATORIES.

Design No. 833.

The above is shewn with Angle "Imperial" Lavatory, having Tile Back and Corner Shelf.

Design No. 5B.

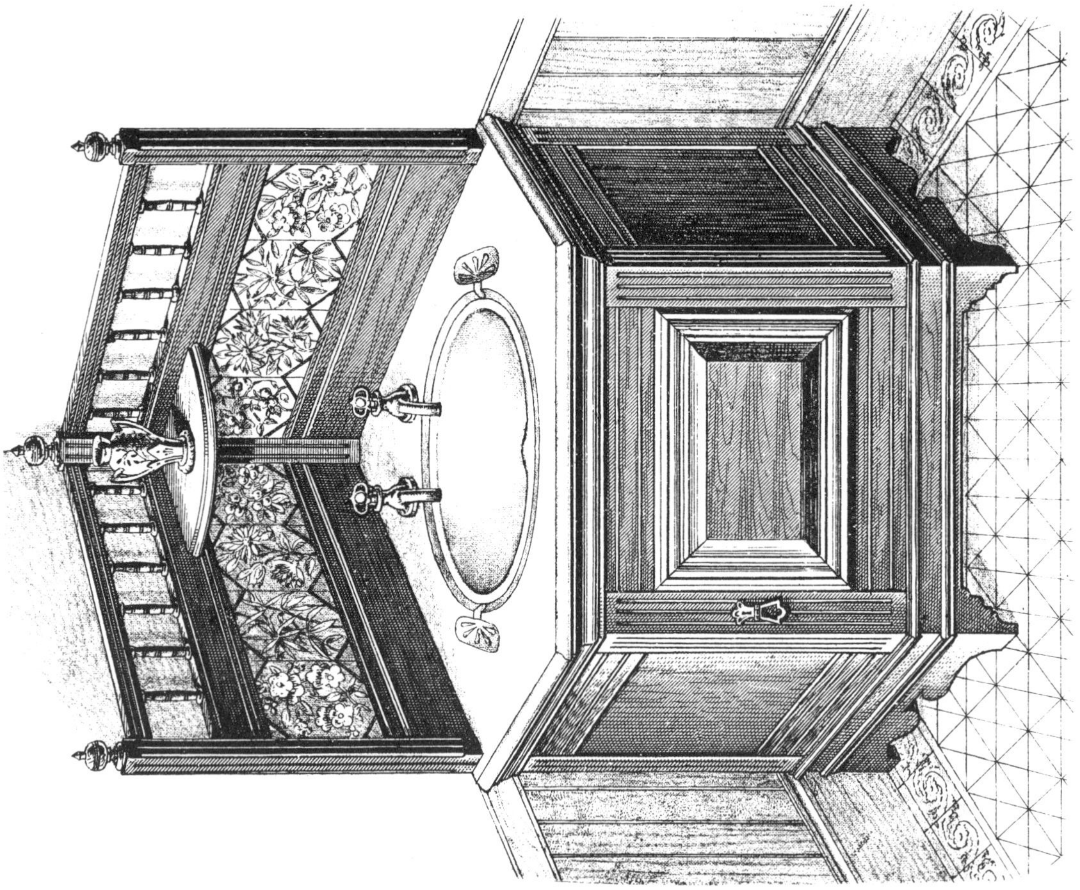

The above is specially suited for a Tip-up Basin and Marble Slab, as shewn.

CABINET LAVATORIES, WITH MARBLE SLABS.

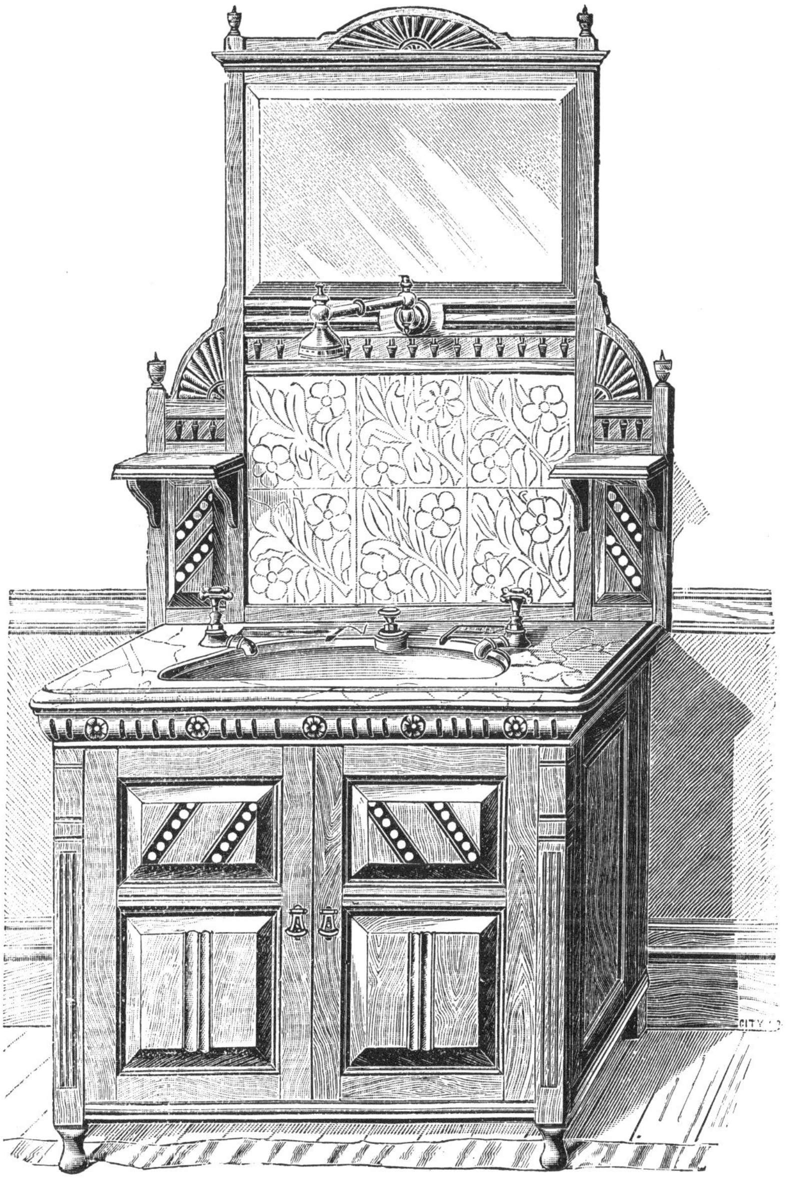

No. 70. No. 210.

No. 70. Lavatory Stand, made in Walnut or Mahogany, with High Back, Bevelled Edge Mirror, and Hand-painted 8″ Tiles St. Ann's or Best Dove 1¼″ Marble Top and Soap Sinkings, Moulded Edges; 20″ No. 66 D Bowl, with No. 61 Hot and Cold Taps* and Quick Waste complete.

Size of Slab	36″ × 24″
Price	£23 9 4

No. 210. The above Stand also made with No. 154a Lavozonic Bowl, Hot and Cold Quarter-turn Screw-down Lever Handle Taps, and Waste Arrangement, instead of No. 66 Bowl; no Soap Sinkings in Slab.

Size of Slab	42″ × 24″
Price...	£24 15 0

IF WITH NICKEL-PLATED FITTINGS 3/5 Extra. IF WITH No. 73 BRACKET SHOWER, 19/- Extra.

IF WITH 1½″ BRASS TRAP, 4/6 Extra. *IF WITH SWIVEL SHOWER AND EYE SPRAY, 45/- Extra.

For Decorated Bowls see page 7.

NOTE.—The Flange of Bowl in these Lavatories is ground, and Bowl is secured to underside of Marble Slab by means of Brass Bolts

PATENT CABINET LAVATORIES.

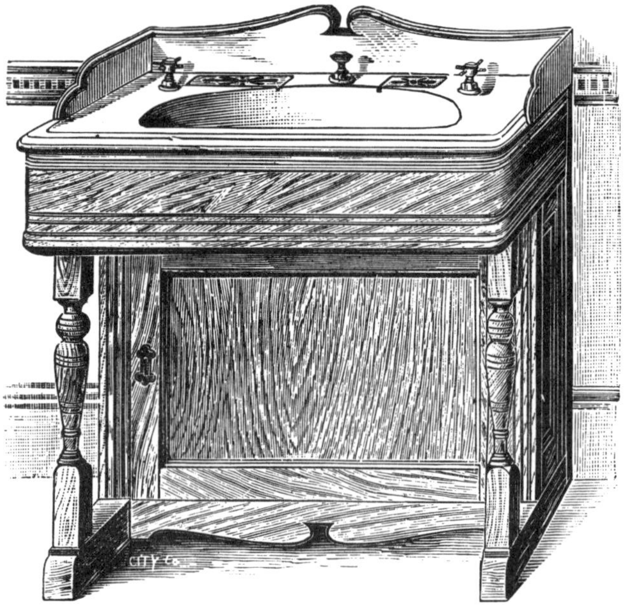

No. 48.

No. 31.

No. 48. Lavatory Stand, made in Walnut or Mahogany, with No. 36 Ivoryware Basin and Fittings, complete.

Size	18″ × 18″	22″ × 18″	27″ × 20″	30″ × 22″
Price	£7 4 9	£8 5 9	£9 6 0	£10 13 0

NICKEL-PLATING FITTINGS, **3/5** Extra.

No. 31. Lavatory Stand, 6″ Tiled Back and Shelf, made in Mahogany or Walnut, with No. 37 Ivoryware Spray Basin and Fittings, complete.

Size	27″ × 20″	30″ × 22″
Price	£11 16 3	£13 1 0
If with No. 35 Basin instead of No. 37...	£10 10 3	£11 15 0

NICKEL-PLATING FITTINGS, WITH No. 37 BASIN, **6/1** Extra.

" " " No. 35 BASIN, **3/5** "

CABINET LAVATORIES, WITH MARBLE SLABS.

No. 56.

No. 57.

No. 56. Lavatory Stand, High Mirror (Bevelled Edges) and Tile Back; made in Walnut, Mahogany, or Oak; 1¼" St. Ann's Marble Slab, Moulded Edges, Soap Sinkings; No. 64 D Tip-up Bowl, "easy to lift out"; Hot and Cold Cam Action Taps, Complete—

Size of Slab	30" × 24"	36" × 24"
Size of Bowl	17"	20"
Price	£17 0 6	£18 12 0
If fitted with No. 66 Lift-up Waste, 20" D Bowl and No. 61 Hot and Cold Taps	Bowl 20" £16 9 0	Bowl 20" £17 13 0

No. 57. Lavatory Stand, High Mirror (Bevelled Edges) and Tile Back; made in Mahogany, Walnut, or Oak, with 1¼" Marble Slab, Moulded Edges, Soap Sinkings, and No. 66 D Bowl and Quick Waste, Hot and Cold No. 61 Taps, Complete—

Size of Slab	30" × 24"	36" × 24"
Size of Bowl	18"	20"
Price	£16 15 0	£18 0 0

NICKEL-PLATING TAPS AND JOURNALS, 3/5 Extra.

NICKEL-PLATING TAPS AND WASTE, 3/5 Extra.

For Decorated Bowls, see Page 7.

DOULTON'S

IMPROVED TIP-UP LAVATORIES.

SPECIALLY DESIGNED TWO-PERSON LAVATORY.

No. 508.

PRICES.

				£	s.	d.
No. 508.—Two-person Lavatory, fitted with 15½ in. Gold-lined Tip-up Basins, Veined Marble Top and Plinth, Two Soap and Two Brush Trays, Cold Valves, Mahogany or Walnut Enclosures, Tiled Skirting, and Looking-glass Back,				£41	0	0
Do.,	do.,	do.,	but with 17½ in. Basins,	43	0	0
Do.,	do.,	do.,	but with St. Anne's Marble Top and 15½ in. Basin,	44	0	0
Do.,	do.,	do.,	but with 17½ in. Basins,	46	0	0
Do.,	do.,	do.,	but with Rouge Royal Top and 15½ in. Basin,	45	10	0
Do.,	do.,	do.,	but with 17½ in. Basin,	47	10	0

Special Fancy Basins extra, from 5/- to 20/-, according to design.

Hot Valves extra according to class.

Special Designs can be given for these Lavatories if desired, or they may be executed to Architect's own drawings.

DOUBLE CABINET LAVATORY.

No. 68.

No. 68. Lavatory for Two Persons, comprising Mahogany or Walnut Stand and High Mirror Back, with Hand-painted Tiles; $1\frac{1}{4}''$ White Veined Marble Top, Moulded Edges and Soap Sinkings, No. 66 D Bowls 20″, Hot and Cold No. 61 Taps and Quick Waste Arrangement.

Size of Slab	5′ 0″ × 2′ 0″
Price complete	£37

NICKEL-PLATING TAPS AND WASTE, 3/5 per Bowl Extra.

SHANKS' CABINET LAVATORIES.

Design No. 263.

The above Lavatory is fitted with Shanks' Patent No. 96 Lavatory and Marble Slab, as shewn. In addition to the Hot and Cold Taps with Waste, a Shampooing Fitting is fixed, suitable for use at either basin.

The Cabinet is of the best workmanship, and may be had in different woods, according to order.

SHANKS' DOUBLE LAVATORY CABINET.

Design No. 221.P

This splendid Lavatory is shewn fitted with Shanks' Patent Imperial **Lavatory Basins, Marble Slab** Top, and Hot, Cold, and Waste Fittings. The Back is fitted with high-class Tiles and Bevelled Plate-Glass Mirrors. It may be fitted with Shanks' Improved Oval or Round Tip-up Basins. The Cabinet-work is of the best material and workmanship, and may be made in different Woods, according to order.

RADCLIFFE BASIN

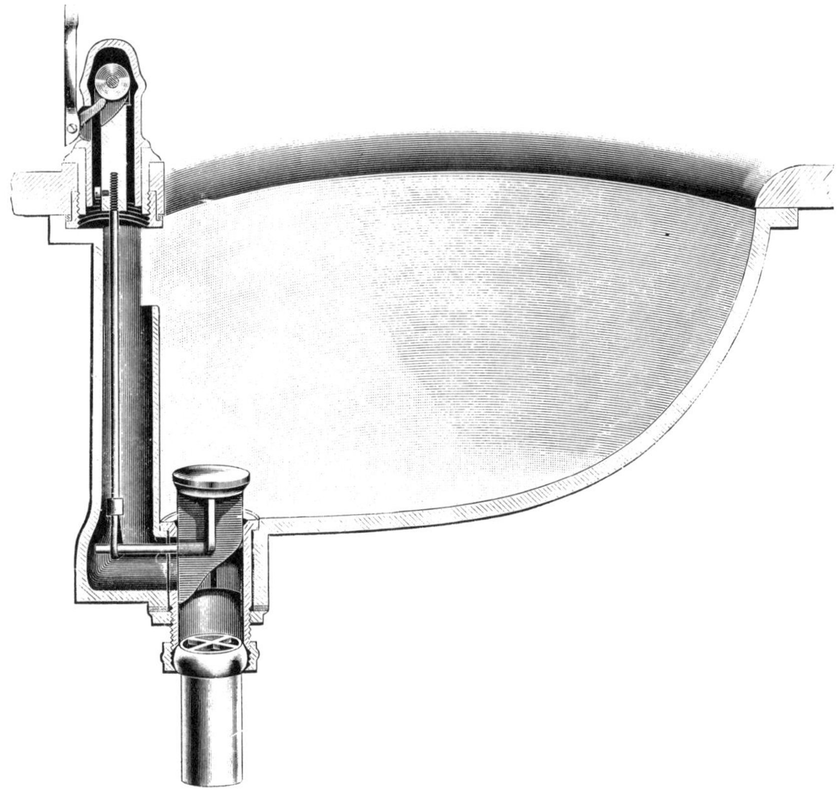

Plate 652-B.

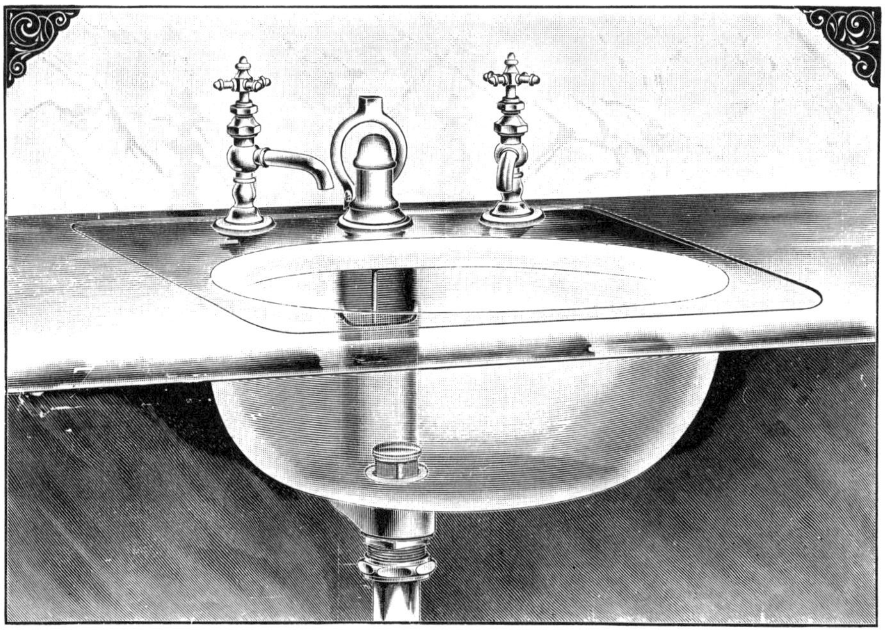

Plate 654-B.

SECTIONAL VIEWS OF RADCLIFFE BASIN WITH RING HANDLE LIFT AND PLUG

Price, 14 x 17 inch Radcliffe Vitreous Basin with nickel-plated ring handle lift, waste and plug..................................$11.50
Price, 15 x 19 inch Radcliffe Vitreous Basin with nickel-plated ring handle lift, waste and plug.................................. 12.50

Add if with embossed basin..$1.00

The plug which sets in a ground socket is lifted by throwing the ring handle back.

The Radcliffe basins with lifts and plugs as shown in Plates 648-B to 654-B readily recommend themselves as fixtures simple and sanitary in construction and convenient in operation.

RADCLIFFE LAVATORY

Plate 656-B.

"RADCLIFFE" VITREOUS BASIN, 15 x 19 inch, with nickel-plated lever handle lift and plug; Elliptic design 1¼ inch countersunk slab and back of selected Italian marble; size of slab 33 x 22 inches; height of back, 12 inches; "Belmont" pattern nickel-plated basin cocks with china scalps marked "Hot" and "Cold" on handles; nickel-plated brass supply pipes to floor; "Richmond" 1½ inch nickel-plated basin trap with vent; Plate 898-B 20 x 20 inch nickel-plated brass brackets.

Price as described with cream tint or marbleized basin.......................................$55.00

Light or Dark Tennessee marble may be substituted at same price.
Ring handle lift may be substituted at same price.
Supply pipes or trap to wall may be substituted at same price.

Add if with embossed basin.......................................$1.00
Add if with embossed basin decorated in gold inside and outside....................... 9.00
Add if with air chambers on supply pipes....................... 3.00
Add if with wheel handle stops on supply pipes....................... 2.50
If with 14 x 17 inch basin, deduct....................... 1.00

* * *

Add for 33 x 22 inch countersunk Italian or Tennessee marble floor slab.......................$7.50

Price on this lavatory in any Foreign or Domestic Marble, Onyx or Jasper will be furnished upon application.

"EMPRESS" PORCELAIN-WARE LAVATORY

Plate 608-B.

"EMPRESS" PORCELAIN-WARE ROLLED RIM LAVATORY with slab and basin combined in one piece with porcelain back and porcelain legs; basin fitted with nickel-plated "Yale" basin waste and "Belmont" pattern nickel-plated basin cocks; china scalps on waste and cocks marked "Hot" and "Cold" and "Waste."

Size of basin, 16 x 13 x 6½ inches.

Price as Described	CLASS A.	CLASS B.	CLASS C.
No. 1—Slab 30 x 24 inches, back 16 inches high	$48.00	$42.00	37.00
No. 2—Slab 33 x 24 inches, back 16 inches high	53.50	47.00	40.00
Deduct if without back, No. 1	4.50	3.50	2.50
Deduct if without back, No. 2	5.00	4.00	3.00

When used without back the slab is usually set into the tile wall, the tiles forming the back.

Deduct if without basin cocks	$4.00
Add if with nickel-plated brass instead of porcelain legs	5.00
Add if with nickel-plated Richmond basin trap	5.00
Add if with nickel-plated brass supply pipes	2.50

ENAMELED IRON LAVATORIES

Plate 616-B.

ENAMELED IRON LAVATORY with back; oval basin with nickel-plated overflow grate; waste plug with rubber stopper; nickel-plated brass soap dish; exterior bronzed, and bronzed iron brackets.

Price, 16 x 20 inch slab, 11 x 14 inch basin, 12 inch back........................$10.00

Price, 18 x 24 inch slab, 12 x 15 inch basin, 12 inch back........................ 12.00

(Cocks are not included in above prices.)

Add if enameled all over and with enameled iron brackets..$3.00

Plate 618-B.

ENAMELED IRON LAVATORY with back and end; oval basin with nickel-plated overflow grate; waste plug with rubber stopper; nickel-plated brass soap dish; exterior bronzed, and bronzed iron brackets.

Price, 16 x 20 inch slab, 11 x 14 inch basin, 12 inch back and end...........$13.00

Price, 18 x 24 inch slab, 12 x 15 inch basin, 12 inch back and end........... 15.00

(Cocks are not included in above prices.)

Add if enameled all over and with enameled iron brackets..$3.00

May be furnished with either right or left end as desired.

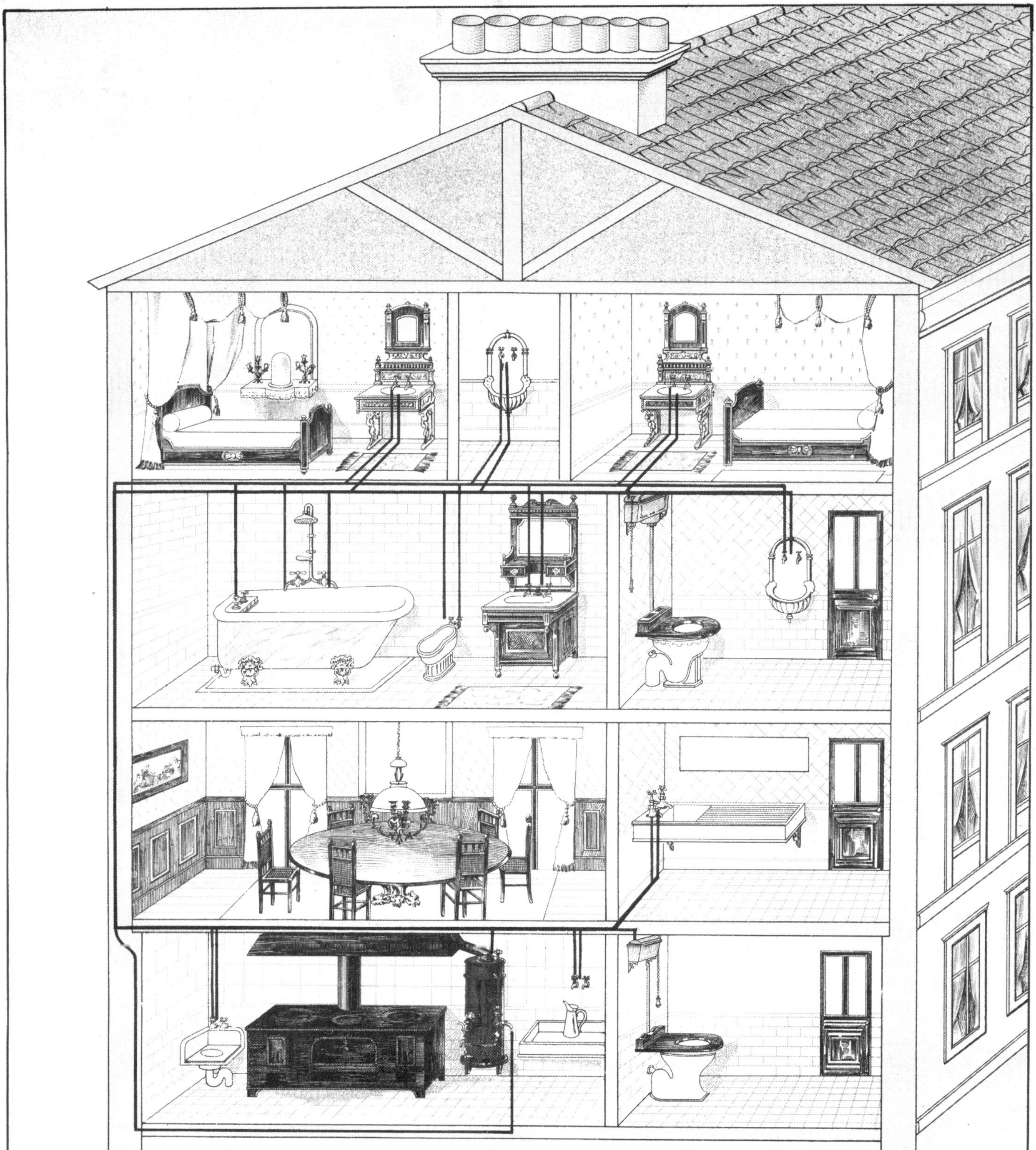

Type d'installation d'une Maison

Alimentée d'eau chaude par notre Chauffe-Bains à **PRESSION "L'IDÉAL"**
distribuant l'eau chaude en pression à tous les étages

La canalisation d'eau chaude est représentée par un trait rouge ——
et celle d'eau froide par un trait bistre ——

ÉTABLISSEMENTS PORCHER
52, Rue d'Hauteville, PARIS

IMP. EUGÈNE VERNEAU, 108, R. FOLIE MERICOURT. – PARIS

CHAPTER FOUR

GEYSERS, PIPES & PLUMBING

Pre-Victorian water supply systems could not cope with the large volume of water required in towns and cities, as they relied on pipes made of lead or timber, which leaked if water was forced through under high pressure. As early as the 1840s, however, the mass production of cast-iron pipes brought pressurised water to most industrialised parts of England and in 1846 Doulton introduced glazed earthenware sewer pipes. Following these improvements, the water companies shifted their attention to the problem of water being wasted in the home through leaking pipes and joints, and through the careless extravagance of domestic customers.

The manufacturers patented many devices to reduce waste. Self-closing taps suitable for use in schools and public bathrooms were available by 1885. Shanks' 'Patent Combined Hot, Cold and Waste Interlocking Bath Fitting' prevented waste by making it impossible to open the taps while the waste outlet was open. Doulton's patent 'Metallo-Keramic' joint was advertised as 'an absolutely perfect joint between the outlet and ventilation connections of a Pottery Closet' ... Every joint is tested up to a pressure of 45 feet head of water before being sent out.'

Each water company enforced its own regulations, and building by-laws could vary from town to town (and of course from country to country). British manufacturers noted the water companies' endorsements of their products, Shanks for example adding 'Approved by the Bristol Water Company' to several of their product descriptions. Their Waste Preventing Cistern was advertised as having been 'approved by the New River Water Co., London, and other leading companies'. The Webb Manufacturing Co. helpfully provided an appendix to their catalogue consisting of an update of the local plumbing and gas fitting regulations for Boston, 'Revised and Corrected to August 1, 1900. Compiled From Official Sources.'

Equal attention was given to ensuring a good supply of hot water within the house. Gas- or oil-fired boilers, or 'geysers', were widely used to heat the water just before it entered the bath. Doulton sold a patent 'Instantaneous' water heater, which despite its name could take as long as 20 minutes to provide a hot bath. Établissements Porcher showed how their 'Idéal' and 'Éclair' geysers might supply hot water throughout the house, using a cross-section of a four-storey townhouse with the hot water pipes printed in red and the cold in silver. Their estimate of the number of lavabos one household – albeit a bourgeois Parisian family on the threshold of the new century – might require, is predictably generous.

Just five years after Établissements Porcher published a set of full-page colour plates of their impressive range of geysers, Hermann Muthesius predicted the extinction of these metal monsters: 'With the disappearance of the geyser we have seen the last of a piece of bathroom furniture that was difficult to use, sometimes dangerous and always unwelcome and the bathroom will become more hygienic, spacious and pleasanter in general appearance.' Despite Muthesius' confidence, the geyser was remain a feature of the bedsit bathroom until the 1960s.

SHANKS' LAVATORY TAPS AND FITTINGS.

No. 26A.

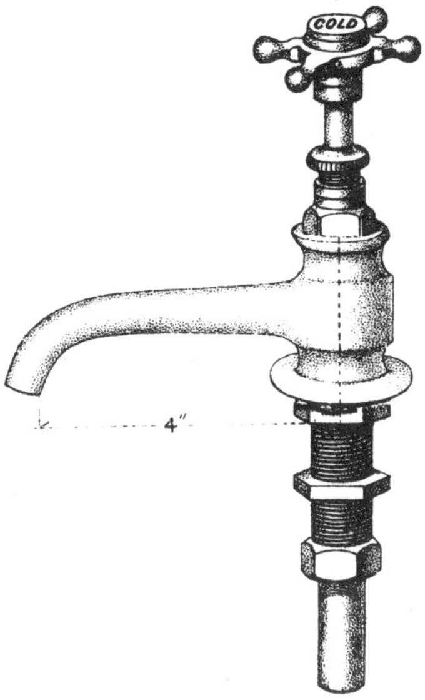

No. 26.

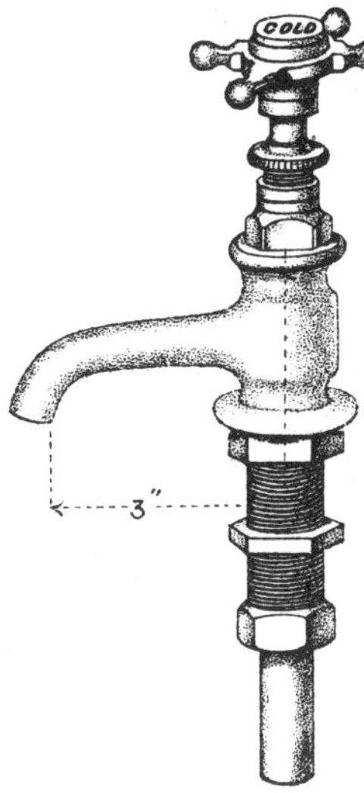

No. 26B.

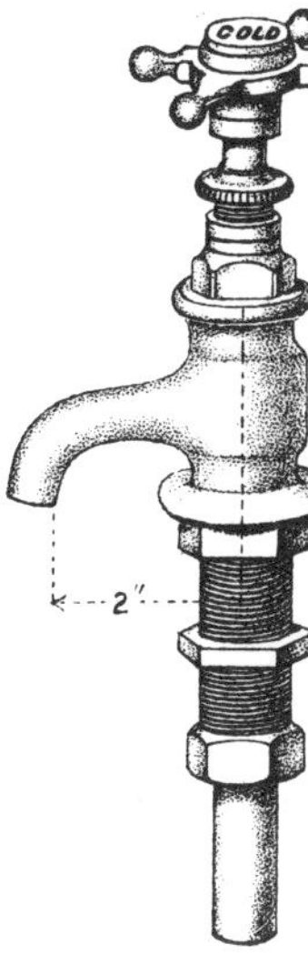

No. 34

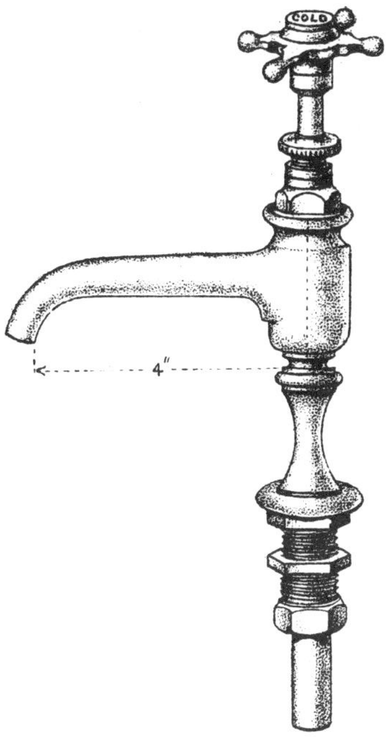

Sizes of above are for ½ inch Taps.

No. 28. Lavatory Fittings

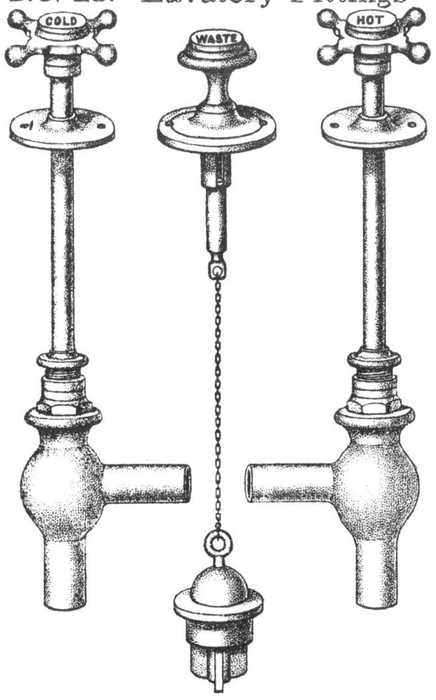

Pillar Cock.
No. 27.

Waste-Pulls and Valves.

No. 31.

No. 40.

Index Plates.

No. 32. For Marble.

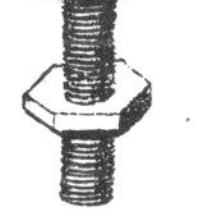

No. 33. For Wood.

No. 38.

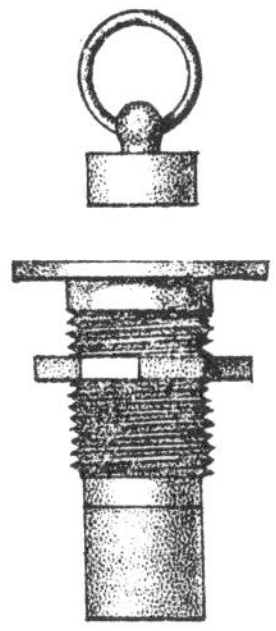

No. 39.

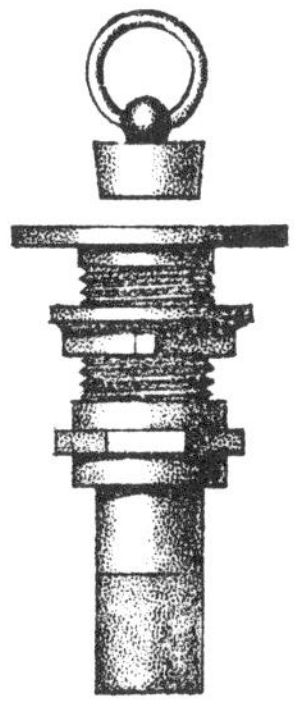

The above Taps are in best material and workmanship, and are suitable either for Hot or Cold Water.

SHANKS' PATENT "EUREKA" BATH FITTINGS.

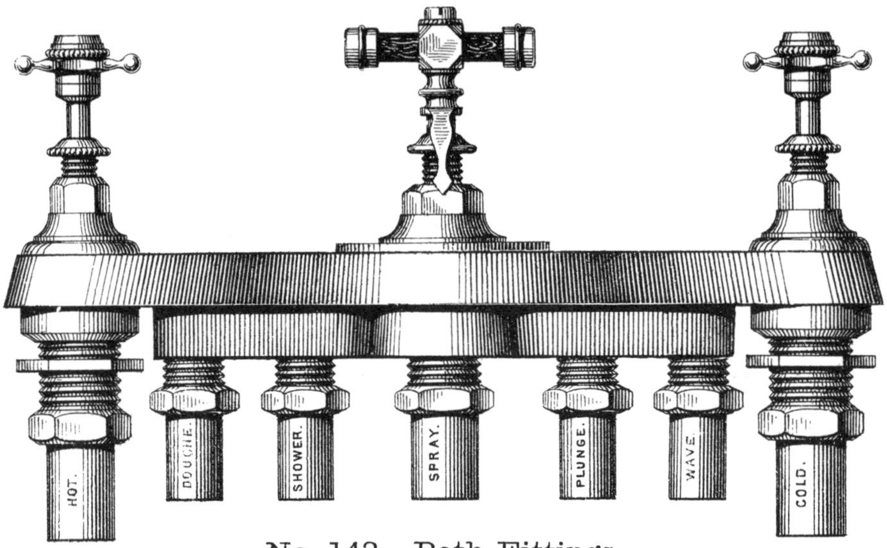

No. 143. Bath Fittings.

Five ways—for, say, Plunge, Spray, Shower, Douche, and Wave.

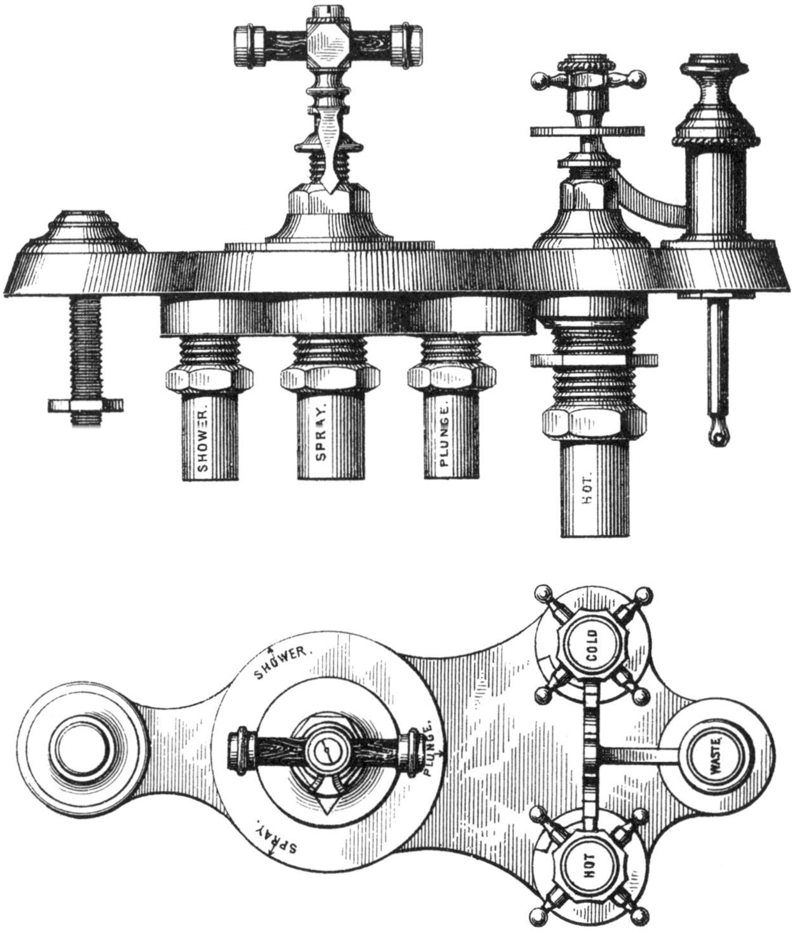

No. 144. Bath Fittings.

With Interlocking arrangement to suit Bristol Water Coy.'s requirements.

N.B.—The waste cannot be lifted until the water is turned off, thus preventing waste of water.

SHANKS' PATENT BATH FITTINGS.

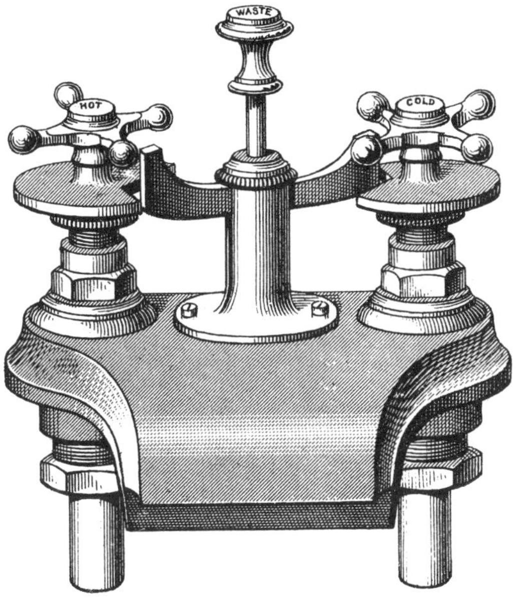

No. 236. Shanks' Patent Combined Hot, Cold, and Waste Interlocking Bath Fittings.

Arranged so that the Taps cannot be opened until the Waste is shut down, thus preventing waste of Water.

Approved by the Bristol Water Company.

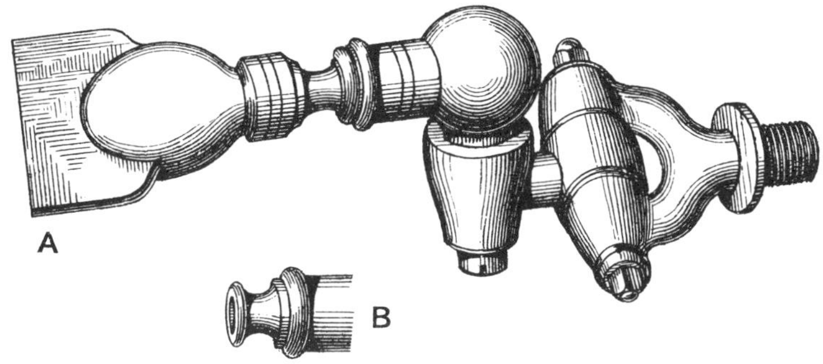

A Wave Outlet.

B Douche Nozzle, which can be made instead of the Wave.

No. 237. Wave Apparatus, with Universal Joint, for Fixing to Wall.

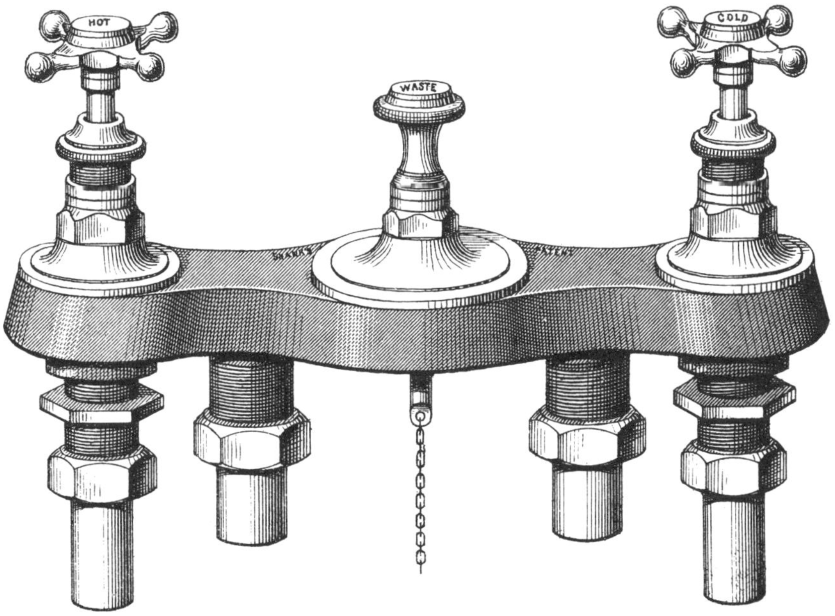

No. 138. Shanks' Plunge Bath Fittings.

These Fittings are suitable where it is desired to bring the water in at or near the bottom of Bath.

N° 208. Jeu de Robinetterie

Eau chaude et froide, avec robinet d'arrêt, cuivre nickelé. — Cette plaque de robinetterie s'emploie spécialement pour les baignoires alimentées par nos chauffe-bains « **Eclair** », « **Omnium** », « **Express** ».

PRIX : 100 fr.

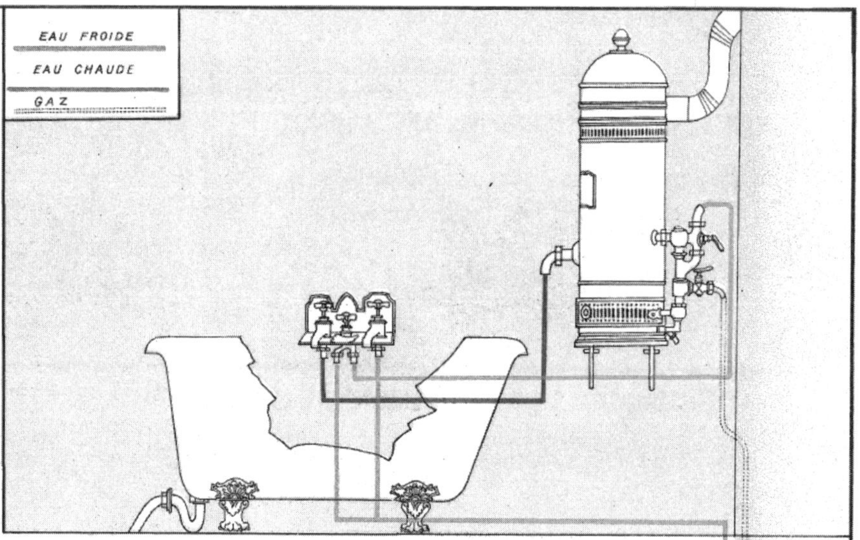

SCHEMA

Montrant le mode d'emploi du jeu de robinetterie N° 208, sur une baignoire alimentée par nos chauffe-bains « **Eclair** », « **Omnium** », « **Express** ».

N° 209. Robinetterie complète

Eau chaude et froide avec porte-bijoux, pour baignoire alimentée par nos chauffe-bains automatiques « **Auto-Éclair** » et « **Idéal** ».

PRIX : 80 fr.

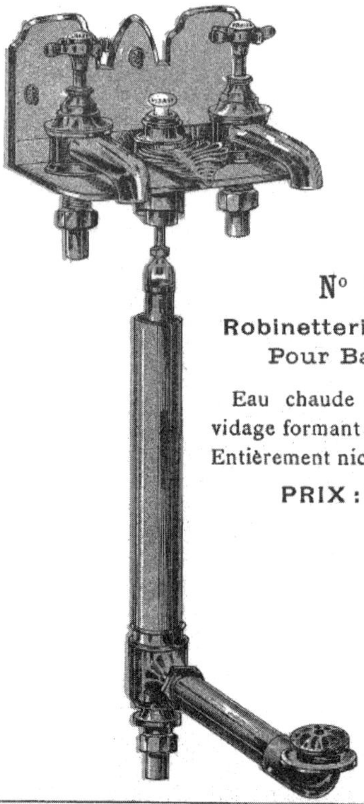

N° 210

Robinetterie compléte
Pour Baignoire

Eau chaude et froide avec vidage formant trop plein. — Entièrement nickelée.

PRIX : 140 fr.

N° 211. Robinetterie complète

Pour Baignoire

Eau chaude et froide avec vidage formant trop plein. Tuyaux d'alimentation descendant jusqu'au sol. — Le tout nickelé.

PRIX : 140 fr.

BATH TUB FITTINGS

Plate 1040-B.

"PRINCETON" NICKEL-PLATED COMBINED WASTE AND OVER RIM SUPPLY with yoke.

Price $29.00

Plate 1042-B.

"PRINCETON" NICKEL-PLATED COMBINED WASTE AND SPOUT SUPPLY with yoke.

Price $30.00

Add if with china scalps marked "Hot," "Cold" and "Waste" on handles.................................$2.00

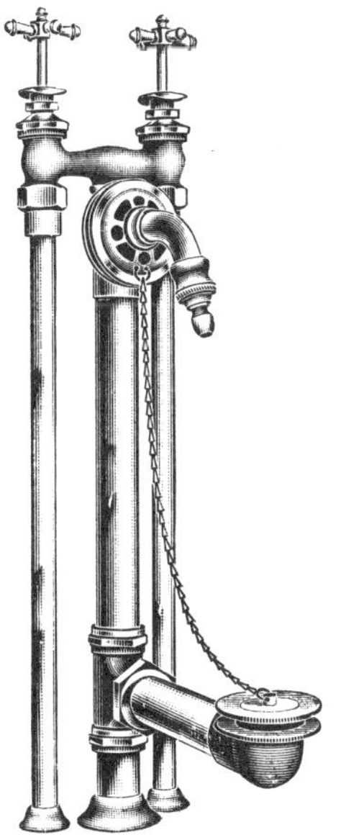

Plate 1046-B.

"CORNELL" NICKEL-PLATED COMBINED CONNECTED WASTE AND OVERFLOW AND SPOUT SUPPLY THROUGH STRAINER; compression valves with handles through rim and bevel flanges; nickel-plated brass supply pipes.

Price, each..$9.50

A simple and low priced combined fixture.

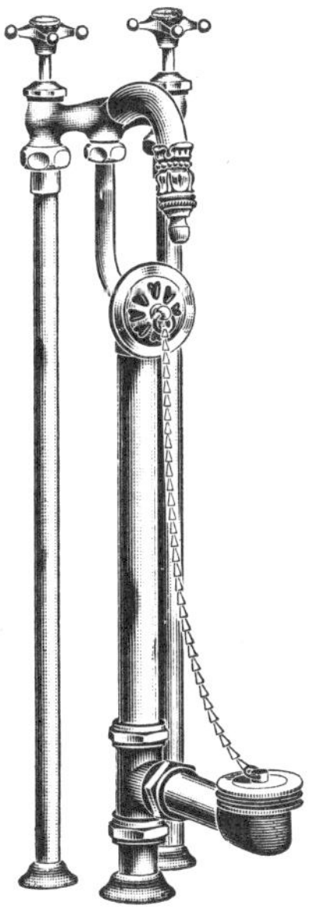

Plate 1047-B.

"BRANDON" NICKEL-PLATED COMBINED CONNECTED WASTE AND OVERFLOW AND OVER RIM SUPPLY; marked china scalps on handles.

Price, each..$12.50

SHOWER, DOUCHE AND SPRAY FITTINGS FOR BATHS.

No. 92.

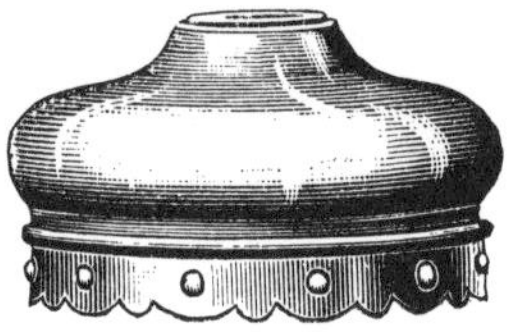
No. 201.

No. 160.

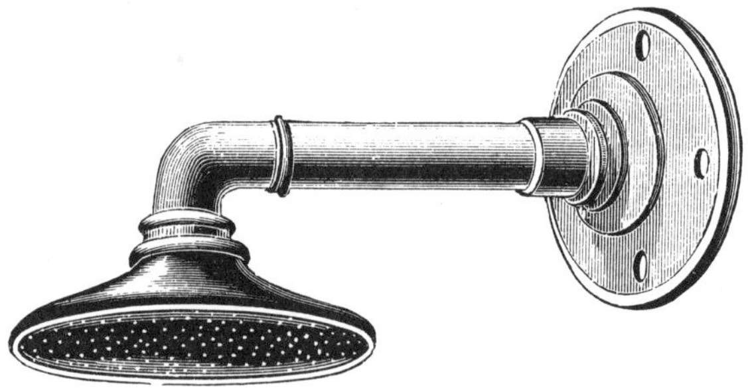
No. 159.
No. 159a.

No. 161.

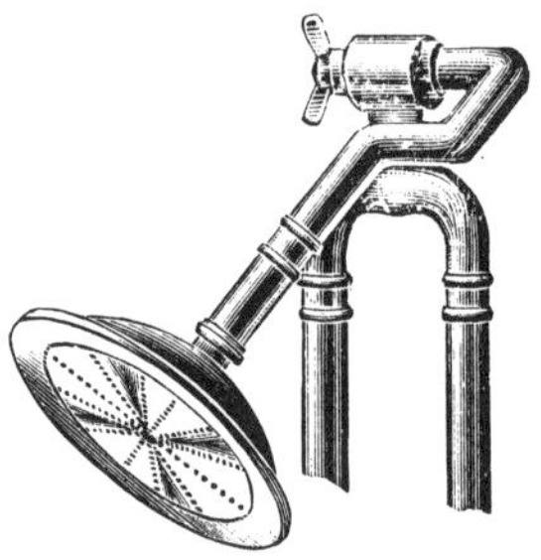
No. 202.

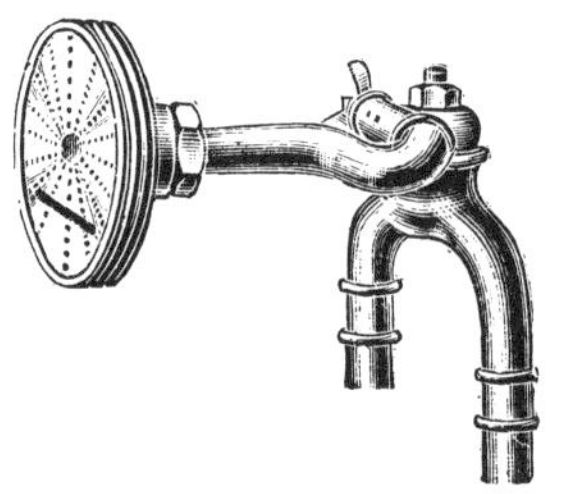
No. 203.

No.	Size	6″	7″	9″	Nickel-plated. 6″	Nickel-plated. 7″	Nickel-plated. 9″	
92	Shower Rose, Polished Gun Metal, Screwed for Iron ... ... 4½″ diameter, 10/- ; Nickel-plated, 13/- each.	—	—	—	—	—	—	
159	Bracket Shower, Iron Tube and Flange	18/-	—	21/-	21/-	—	24/-	each.
159A	Bracket Shower, Polished Copper Tube and Flange	—	28/4	31/4	—	37/4	40/4	„
160	Copper Shower Rose, Screwed for Iron	7/6	—	10/6	10/6	—	13/6	„
161	Bracket Shower, Self-closing Valve and Pull Handle	27/-	—	30/-	30/-	—	33/-	„
201	Fancy Shower Rose, Polished Copper, Screwed for Iron	—	8/6	12/-	—	11/6	15/-	„
202	Moveable Shower Bracket, Copper Rose, Gun Metal Breeches Piece and Mountings, Screwed for Iron	—	45/-	48/-	—	55/-	58/-	„
203	Universal Bracket, Breeches Piece, and Combined Spray, Wave and Douche Rose, each to act separately by a quarter-turn of the Rose, made of Gun Metal	—	73/-	—	—	83/-	—	„

OTHER COMBINATIONS OF SHOWERS TO ORDER.

SEE BATH SECTION FOR FULLER PARTICULARS.

IMPROVED BATH SHOWERS, DOUCHES & MIXING BOXES.

No. 84. No. 85.

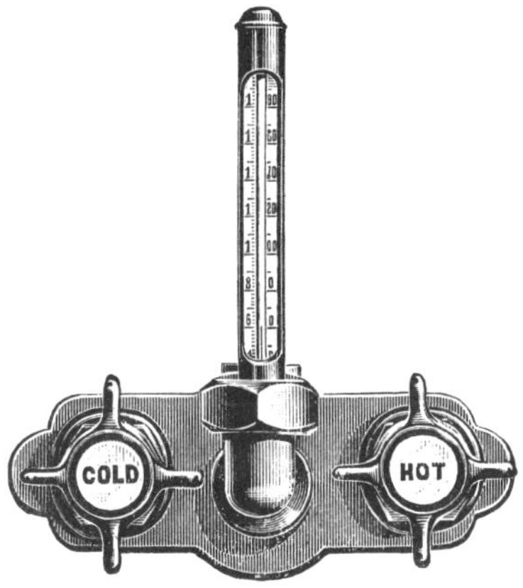

No. 208.
No. 209.

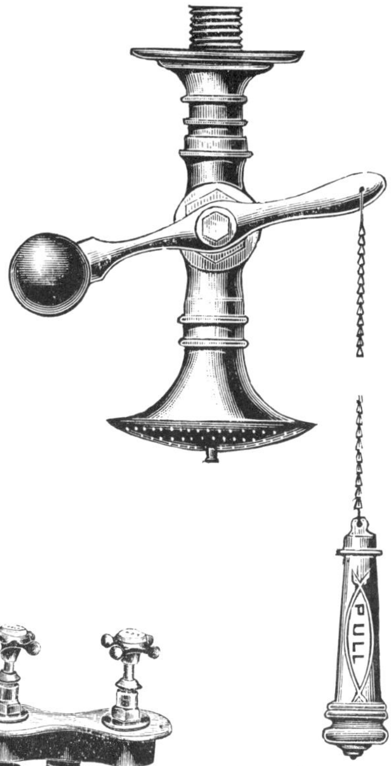

No. 86.
No. 87.

No. 83

No. 88. No. 89.

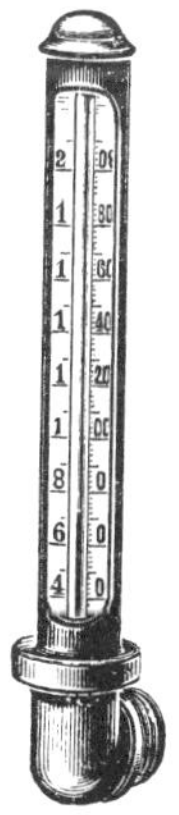
No. 206.
No. 207.

No. 82. No. 82a.

No.	Gun Metal			Nickel-Plated.			
Size...	½	¾	1	½	¾	1	inch.
82.—Combined Hot and Cold Shower or Douche Fittings for Baths	—	22/-	27/-	—	28/-	34/-	each.
82A.— Do. do. do. with Hose Connection on Front instead of Union at Back	—	24/-	29/-	—	30/-	36/-	„
83.—Combined Hot and Cold Shower or Douche Fittings for Lavatories ...	16/-	—	—	20/6	—	—	„
206.—Thermometer, with Bulb Elbow, Screwed for Iron	—	22/-	—	—	30/-	—	„
207.— Do. Straight, no Elbow, Screwed for Iron	—	20/-	—	—	25/-	—	„
208.—Combined Hot and Cold Shower or Douche Fittings, with Thermometer ...	—	42/-	49/-	—	53/-	60/-	„
209.—Do. Do. do do. Inlets Screwed for Copper or Iron Pipe, Vertical position, no Inlet Unions	—	42/-	49/-	—	53/-	60/-	„

		Nickel-Plated.	
84.—Bracket Shower and Douche, Polished Gun Metal, Tap and Pull Handle	45/-	... 60/-	each.
85.—Bracket Shower only do. do.	40/6	... 55/6	„
86.—Ceiling Shower and Douche do. do.	30/-	... 40/6	„
87.—Ceiling Shower only do. do.	25/6	... 36/-	„
88.—Bent Swivel Shower and Douche, Polished Gun Metal	49/6	... 64/6	„
89.—Bent Swivel Shower only, Polished Gun Metal	45/-	... 60/-	„

SHANKS' NEW PATENT "RELIABLE IMPROVED" VALVELESS WASTE-PREVENTING W. C. SUPPLY CISTERN,

ON THE SYPHON PRINCIPLE.

MANY THOUSANDS IN USE.

No. 16 Cast-Iron Cistern,

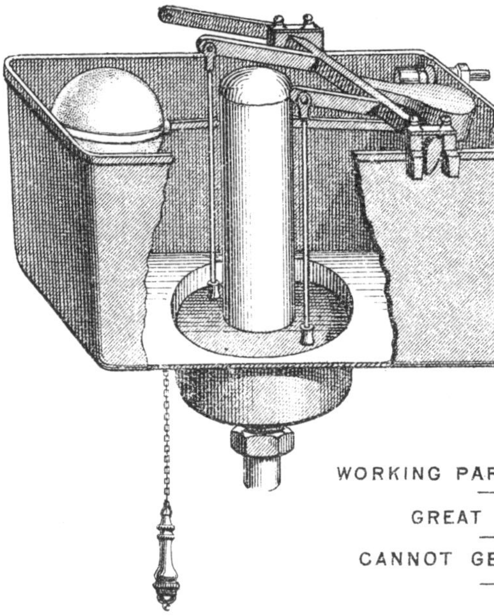

No. 16
Shewn with Cover.

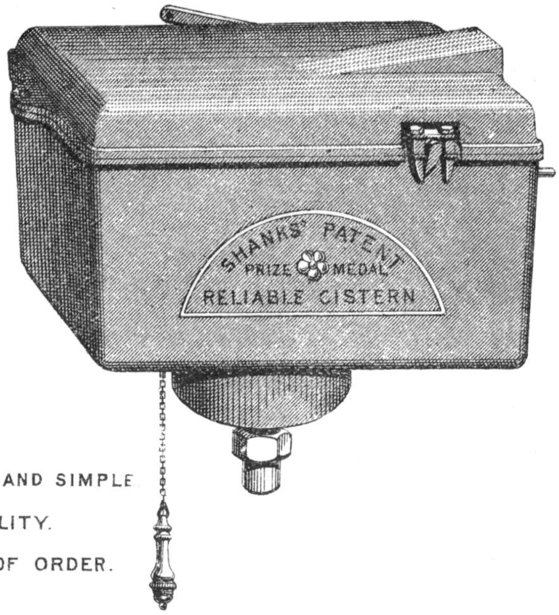

WORKING PARTS FEW AND SIMPLE

GREAT DURABILITY.

CANNOT GET OUT OF ORDER.

No. 16 Cast-Iron Cistern,
With Ornamental Front.

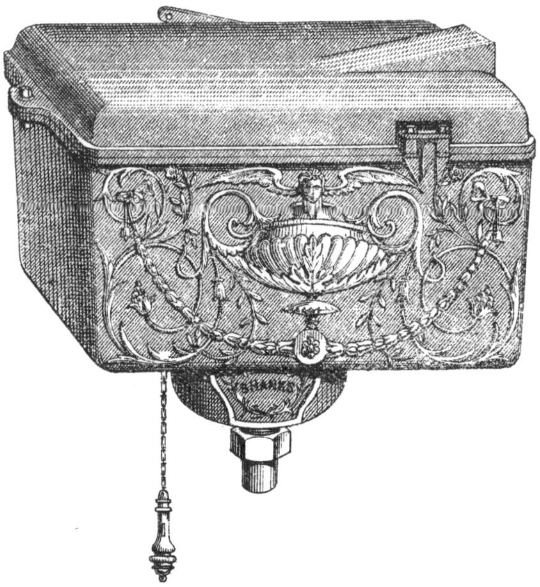

No. 16 Cistern,
Mahogany or Walnut Case, lined with Tinned Copper.

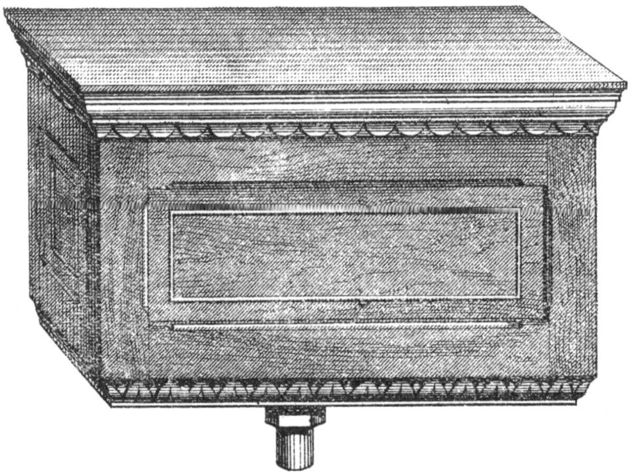

This Cistern is made entirely without Valves, on the Syphon principle. It is made with a Well or Dip in which an Annular Disc works, and through the centre of this Disc stands the Syphon Pipe. This Disc is depressed by the Lever and immediately starts the Syphon, emptying the Cistern with great force and rapidity. The advantages are:— that it acts noiselessly, and with the greatest possible certainty, with only $2\frac{1}{2}$ in. or 3 in. of a pull. We can confidently recommend it. It has been approved by the New River Water Co., London, and other leading companies.

IMPROVED SYPHON WASTE-PREVENTING, CAST-IRON CISTERNS.

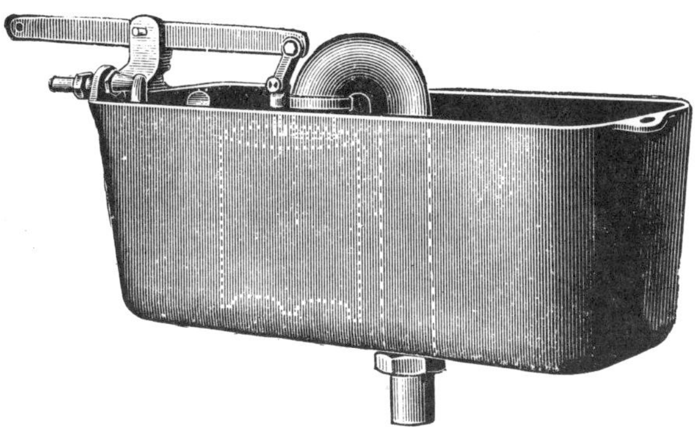

No. 202.—Disc Syphon Cistern.

No. 203.—Valve, Syphon Cistern, Cast Syphon.
„ **204.**—Valve, Syphon Cistern, Brass Syphon.

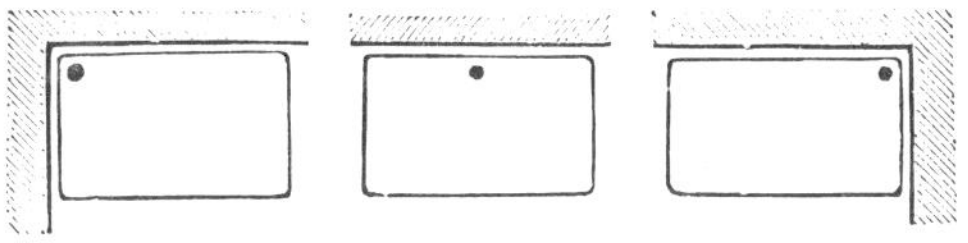

LEFT. CENTRE. RIGHT.

Plan shewing the 3 positions outlet in Cisterns Nos. 203 and 204 is made.

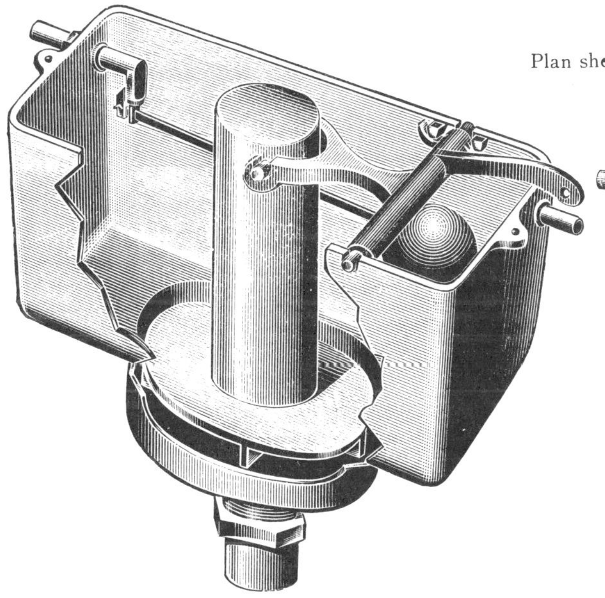

No. 150.—" Pull and let go " Syphon Cistern.
„ **150a.**— Do. do. with Dome as No. **206**.

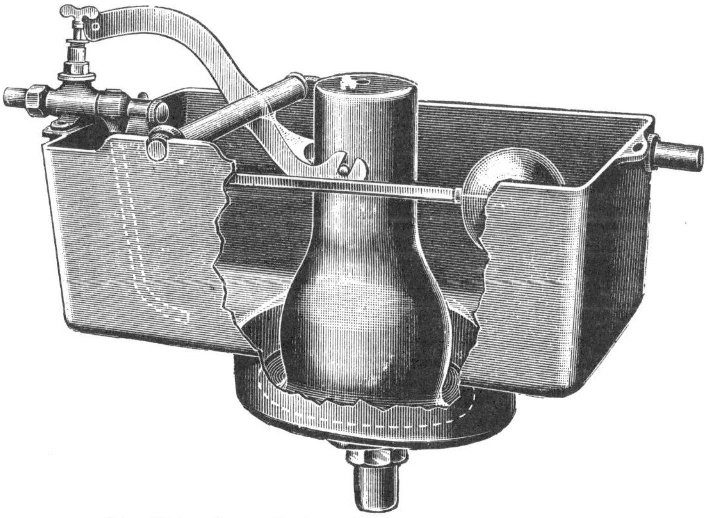

No. 206.—Spate Syphon Cistern, Journals Brass Bushed.

	No. 150 Cistern.			No. 150A Cistern.			No. 206 Cistern.		
For	2	3	4	2	3	4	3	4	galls. flush.
Painted	14/-	15/4	18/6	14/-	15/4	18/6	20/-	23/-	each.
Galvanized ...	18/8	20/3	25/-	18/8	20/3	25/-	26/3	29/6	„
Porcelain Enamelled	21/4	23/4	27/6	21/4	23/4	27/6	28/-	32/-	„
Painted Cover ...	1/1	1/4	1/6	1/1	1/4	1/6	1/4	1/6	„
Galvanized do. ...	2/-	2/7	3/-	2/-	2/7	3/-	2/7	3/-	„

If with Lead Inner Syphon Pipe, 1/- extra. Cast Spelter Dome, 2/8 extra.

	No. 202 Cistern.		No. 203 Cistern.					No. 204 Brass Syphon Cistern.					
For	3	4	2	2½	3	4	6	2*	2½	3	4	6	galls. flush.
Painted	20/-	23/-	14/-	14/8	16/8	19/4	21/6	15/4	16/7	18/-	21/9	24/6	each.
Galvanized	25/3	29/6	18/6	20/6	23/-	26/8	29/-	19/10	22/7	24/4	29/1	32/-	„
Porcelain Enamelled	28/-	32/-	19/6	20/8	22/8	26/4	31/-	20/8	22/7	24/-	28/9	34/-	„
Painted Cover ...	1/4	1/6	1/1	1/3	1/4	1/6	2/-	1/1	1/3	1/4	1/6	2/-	„
Galvanized do. ...	2/7	3/-	2/1	2/4	2/7	3/-	3/9	2/1	2/4	2/7	3/-	3/9	„

NOTE.—Cisterns Nos. 203 and 204 are made with outgo in either corner or in centre of Cistern at back, thus avoiding any swan-neck to flushing pipe.

Centre outgo always sent unless ordered right or left.

* The 2-gallon No. 204 Cistern has 1¼" Syphon, the others have 1½".

SHANKS' PATENT INSTANTANEOUS WATER HEATER,

FOR BATHS, LAVATORIES, &c.

Gives the Best Results, and is the Cheapest Heater in the Market.

Hot Water Instantly. A Hot Bath, at 105° Fahr., in 8 to 10 Minutes, for Three-Farthings. Boiling Water in a Minute.

THE TUBAL.

ADVANTAGES.

Constructed entirely of Strong Copper.

So arranged that all the internal parts may be removed for repairs or cleaning; an ADVANTAGE over others, which often get worn out, and cannot be repaired except at great cost.

The Heater being always full of water, there is no danger of explosion.

Made reversible, to suit any position.

Burns pure gas, and has no visible condensation.

ADVANTAGES.

Is very durable.

The internal surface is Tinned, to keep water pure.

The water does not come in contact with the gas, rendering it fit for culinary and drinking purposes.

The water may be heated to various temperatures, according to the rate at which it is passed through the Heater.

See results at foot.

Made in two sizes only, large and medium, thus obviating confusion in ordering.

The Low Price, Quality, Durability, and the Speed with which a Bath can be had, recommends it to all.

A Stream of Hot Water at any moment, Day or Night.

ESTIMATES FOR FITTING UP COMPLETE, WITH GUARANTEE OF ENTIRE SUCCESS.

PRICES.

No. 1. HEATER, Large.

Gives a continuous stream of Hot Water at the rate of—

1 Gallon per Minute, at	- - -	155 to 165 degs.
2 ,, ,,	- - -	120 ,, 130 ,,
3 ,, ,,	- - -	105 ,, 110 ,,
3½ to 4 ,, ,,	- - -	85 ,, 100 ,,

Size of Gas Pipe, ⅝″ or ¾″.

No. 2. HEATER, Medium.

Gives a continuous stream of Hot Water, at the rate of—

½ Gallon per Minute, at	- - -	160 to 170 degs.
1 ,, ,,	- - -	120 ,, 130 ,,
2 ,, ,,	- - -	100 ,, 110 ,,
2½ ,, ,,	- - -	95 ,, 100 ,,

Size of Gas Pipe, ½″.

In Stock, and to be seen in action at our various Warehouses and Show-Rooms.

DOULTON'S

PATENT "LAMBETH" INSTANTANEOUS WATER HEATER,

WITH AUTOMATIC CUT-OFF FOR GAS.

No. 296.

FOR BATHS, LAVATORIES, ETC.

CANNOT POSSIBLY GET BURNED.

A Hot Bath at 105° Fahrenheit in Ten Minutes for $\frac{3}{4}$D.

THE BEST RESULT OF ANY HEATER IN THE MARKET.

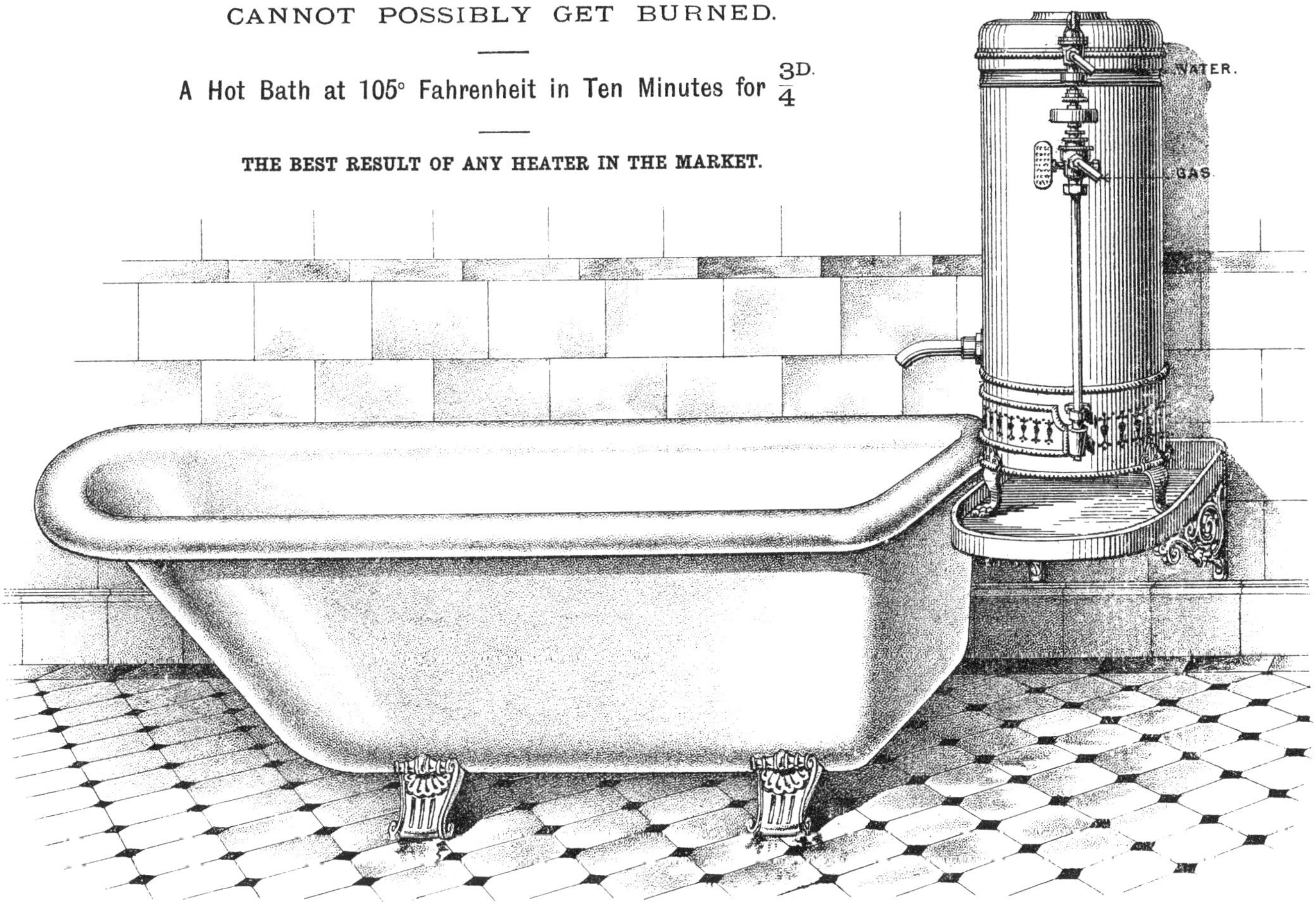

THIS Heater is constructed entirely of Copper, and the water passes through enclosed chambers, so that the Gas cannot (as is usually the case) come into contact with it. The automatic arrangement connected to the gas and water supply prevents the gas being lit until the water is turned on, and if by any chance the water supply fails the gas at once is lowered, so that it is harmless. This prevents any chance of the Heater being burned out—a feature very common in other forms. The gas is not completely extinguished, and rises again directly the water-pressure comes on.

Hot water may be obtained at once.

The Heater is strongly made, handsome in appearance, and may be had with the outer shell enamelled if desired.

The cold water is raised 55° in passing through the Heater, but water of higher temperature can be obtained if the quantity is reduced.

For Prices and Particulars see page 110.

INSTALLATION (Modèle G)

1 Chauffe-bains " AUTO-ÉCLAIR " N° 1 à douche (distributeur automatique d'eau chaude, breveté) en cuivre rouge poli . . . . 575 fr.
1 Socle chauffe-linge, grand modèle, en cuivre rouge poli . . . . 85 »
1 Baignoire modèle " ROMAINE ", émail porcelaine blanc à l'intérieur et sur la gorge, extérieur laqué et joli décor Iris peint à la main, montée avec robinetterie eau chaude et froide et vidage perfectionné formant trop-plein en cuivre nickelé avec siphon . . . . 525 »

PRIX de l'installation complète comme ci-dessus : **1185 »**

LA MÊME installation avec chauffe-bains N° 2 au lieu du N° 1, en moins. . . . 100 »
— — chauffe-bains et chauffe-linge, nickelés, en plus . . . . . 75 »

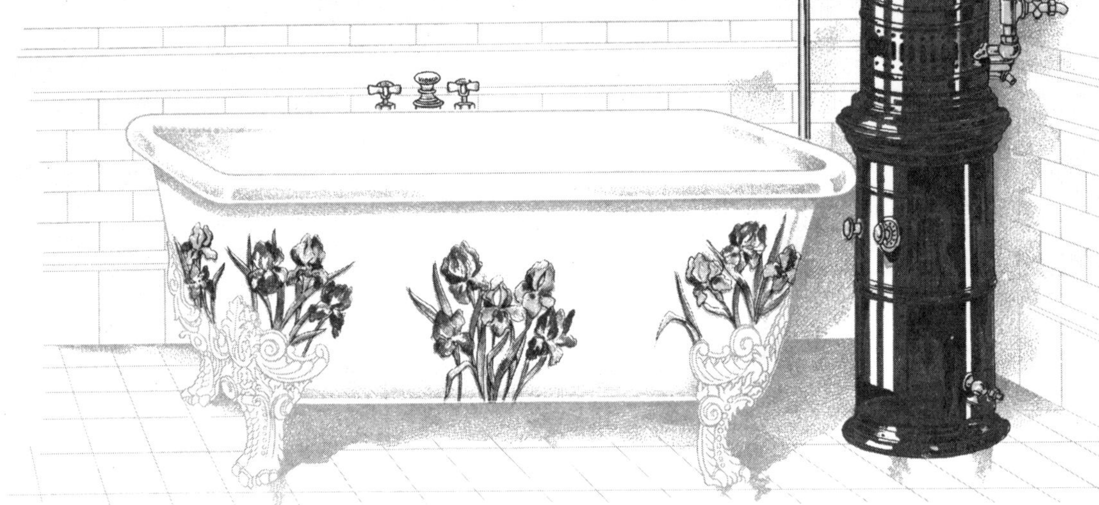

INSTALLATION (Modèle H)

1 Chauffe-bains " AUTO-ÉCLAIR " No 2 (distributeur automatique d'eau chaude, breveté), en cuivre rouge poli. . . . . 400 fr.
1 Socle chauffe-linge, grand modèle, en cuivre rouge poli . . . . 85 »
1 Baignoire modèle " ROMAINE ", émail porcelaine blanc à l'intérieur et sur la gorge, extérieur laqué crème et filets or, montée avec robinetterie eau chaude et froide et vidage perfectionné formant trop-plein en cuivre nickelé avec siphon . . . . 425 »

PRIX de l'installation complète comme ci-dessus : **910 »**

LA MÊME installation avec chauffe-bains et socle chauffe-linge nickelés, en plus. 75 »

ÉTABLISSEMENTS PORCHER

52, Rue d'Hauteville, PARIS

IMP. EUGÈNE VERNEAU, 108, R. FOLIE MERICOURT, PARIS

"L'OMNIUM", brévetó s. g. d. g.

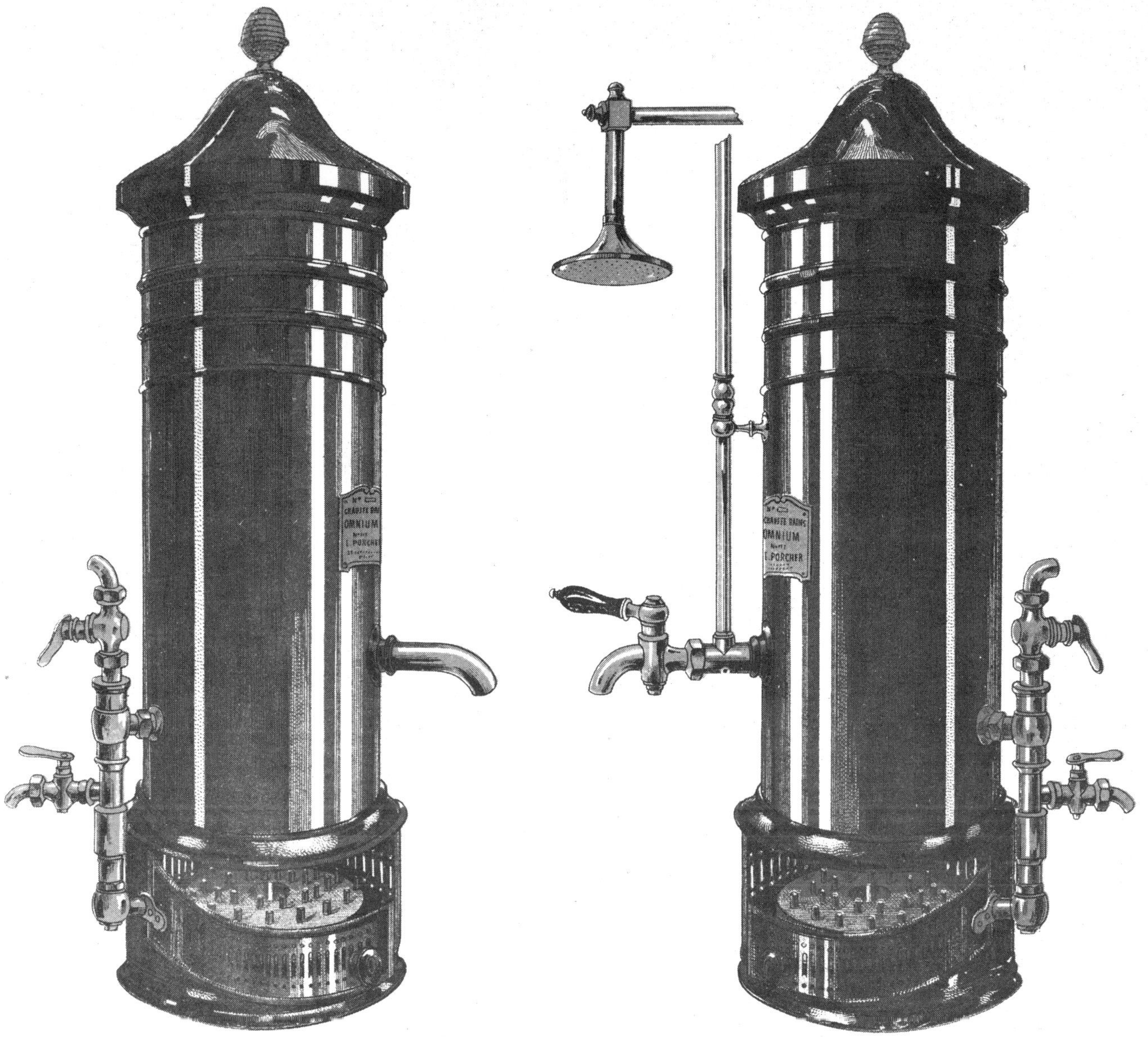

Par suite des demandes journalières qui nous sont faites pour des Chauffe-Bains meilleur marché que notre appareil " **L'ECLAIR** " quoique comportant la garantie de bonne fabrication, de durée et de bon fonctionnement que vaut notre nom attaché à ce genre d'appareil, nous nous sommes décidés à créer notre nouveau modèle " **L'OMNIUM** ".

Dans ce système, ainsi que dans " **L'ECLAIR** ", l'eau n'est pas en contact avec les flammes du gaz, et par conséquent jamais de noir de fumée dans le bain.

Tous nos Chauffe-Bains sont munis de notre valve automatique, rendant le gaz solidaire de l'arrivée de l'eau.

Dès que l'eau manque, le gaz retombe en veilleuse

Donc aucun danger d'explosion, ou de brûler ou de détériorer l'appareil.

Donne un bain en 14 minutes

PRIX A PARIS :	Avec Chauffe-Linge	**250** »
	Sans —	**235** »
	Avec Douche et Chauffe-Linge	**315** »
	Avec Douche sans Chauffe-Linge	**300** »
	Nickelage en plus	**50** »

RECOMMANDATION IMPORTANTE POUR LA POSE DE TOUS NOS CHAUFFE-BAINS. — Il est indispensable, une fois le Chauffe-Bains posé, de faire passer l'eau dans l'appareil afin de chasser l'air emmagasiné dans les cylindres avant d'en faire l'essai au gaz.

ÉTABLISSEMENTS PORCHER

52, Rue d'Hauteville, PARIS

IMP. EUGÈNE VERNEAU, 108, R. FOLIE-MERICOURT. — PARIS

F. W. WEBB MANUFACTURING CO. BOSTON. TRADE MARK

BATH ROOM FITTINGS

Plate 1484-B.

NICKEL-PLATED TOILET PAPER HOLDER.

Price each $1. 50

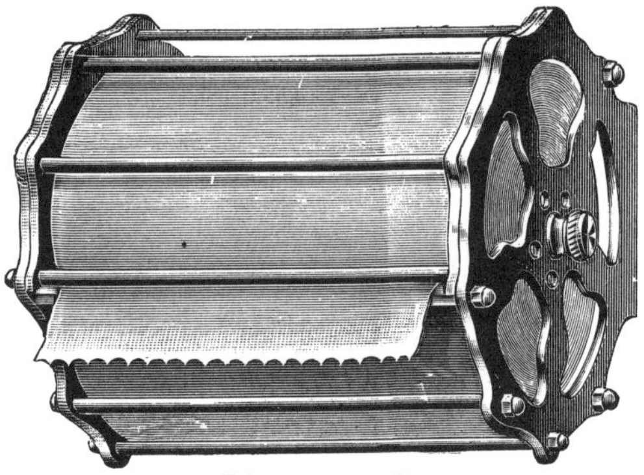

Plate 1486-B.

NICKEL-PLATED TOILET PAPER HOLDER.

Price each $2.75

Will hold rolls 5 inches wide.

Plate 1488-B.

NICKEL-PLATED TOILET PAPER HOLDER, heavy pattern.

Price each $6.00

Will hold rolls 5 inches wide.

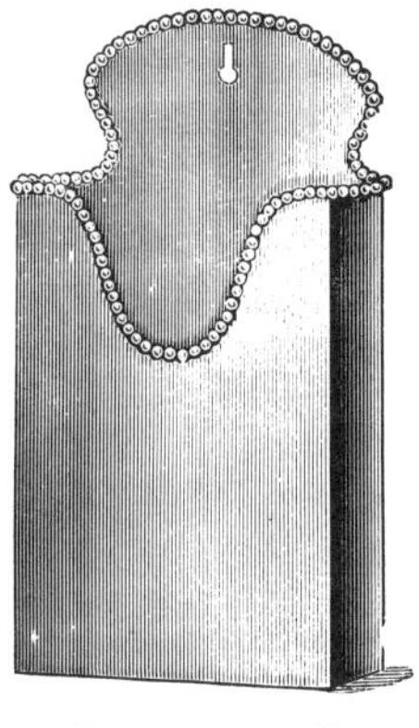

Plate 1490-B.

NICKEL-PLATED TOILET PAPER BOX.

Price each $2. 25

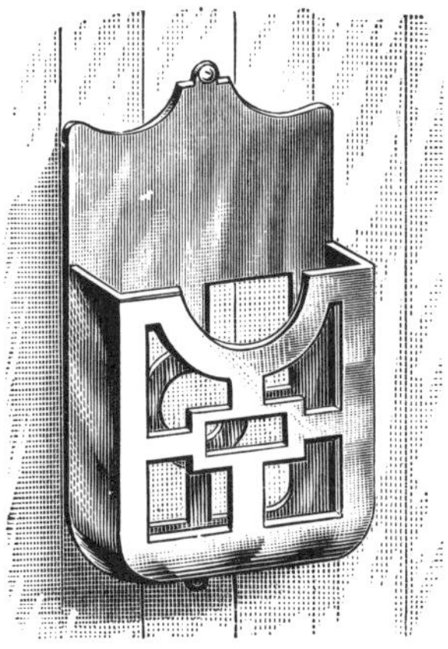

Plate 1492-B.

NICKEL-PLATED TOILET PAPER BOX, heavy pattern.

Price each $3. 50

Will hold sheet paper 5½ x 7½ inches.

CHAPTER FIVE

BATHROOM ACCESSORIES

The chief accessory of the Victorian bathroom, and the one to which most attention was devoted, was the closet seat. The material, style and finish of the seat was an unmistakable indication of the householder's status. When Thomas Crapper's toilets and urinals were installed at Sandringham, the Norfolk country retreat of the Prince of Wales, they were provided with seats made of cedar: sweet-smelling, warmer than mahogany and even more expensive. The majority of the population would have been familiar with scrubbed pine, at less than half the cost of mahogany or polished walnut. The Webb Manufacturing Co. included one enamelled steel seat in their range in 1900, 'in keeping with the idea of discarding the use of woodwork in bathrooms'.

The chain and pull could be a simple galvanised iron chain with a D-ring pull, or an elaborate brass rod passing through a shaped backplate and terminating in a turned and polished metal pendant. Coloured cord pulls with padded and tasselled handles added a touch of luxury, and china handles were approved of as being more hygienic.

Throughout the nineteenth century, paper was supplied in sheets, which were kept in special china or mahogany boxes that fitted on the shelf at the back of the closet seat or clipped onto the downpipe. Or one might improvise a container, as one visitor to an English country house between the Wars remembered: 'there was marvellous lavatory paper that came in little sheets that the housemaids would arrange in a swirl on a lovely china saucer. They always left a lavender bag on top.' Rolls of perforated paper were first produced in 1880, necessitating the invention of the modern roll holder. This appears not to have caught on as fast in Britain as in France and the United States.

The American bathroom benefited from an extensive array of other fittings designed to maximise comfort and convenience. Towel rails, hooks for dressing gowns and metal baskets for used towels were complemented by jewel cups into which ladies might drop their rings and bracelets for safekeeping while they washed their hands and, for the gentlemen, match holders and a cigar rest.

DOULTON'S IMPROVED SEATS

For PEDESTAL "SIMPLICITAS" CLOSETS,

No. 150.

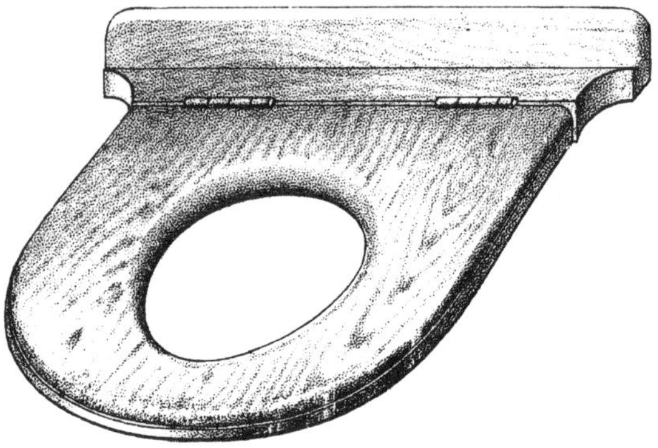

No. 150A.

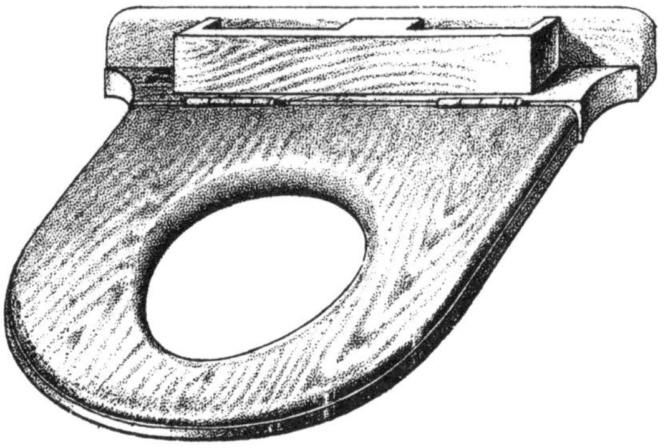

No. 150B.

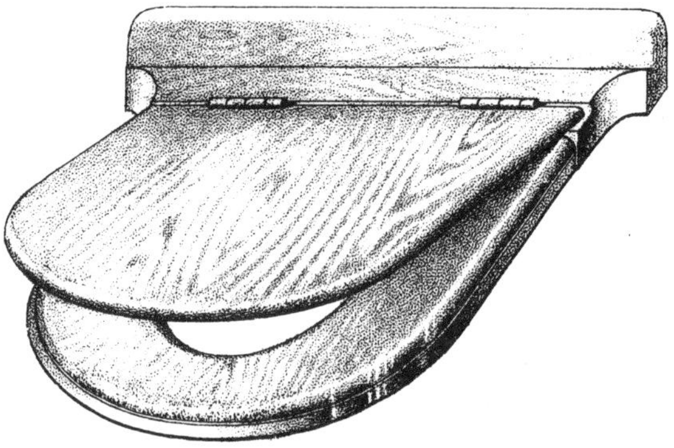

No. 150C.

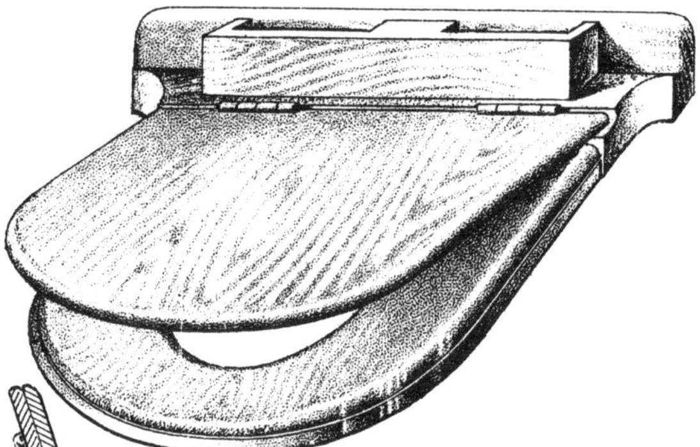

No. 150E.

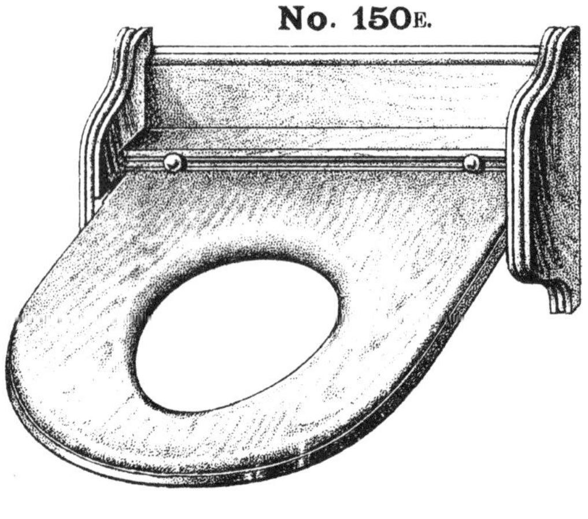

SECTION. No. 150E.

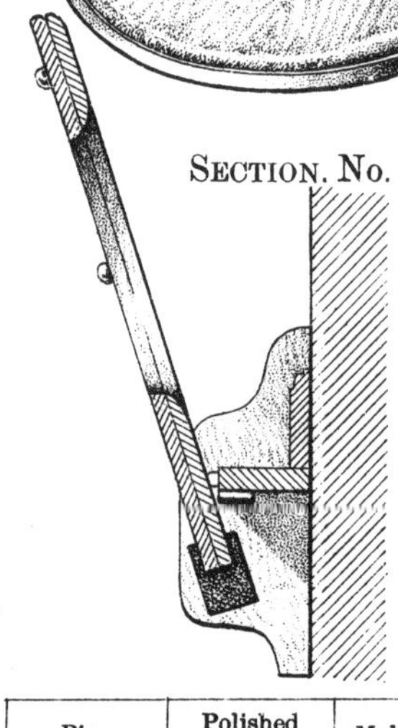

PRICES.	Pine.	Polished Pine.	Mahogany.	Walnut.	Teak.
	£ s. d.	£ s. d.	£ s. d.	£ s. d.	£ s. d.
No. 150. —Pedestal "Simplicitas" Closet Seat, - each,	0 13 6	0 17 0	1 1 0	1 1 0	1 1 0
No. 150A.—Do., do., with Paper Box, - ,,	0 15 0	0 18 6	1 4 0	1 4 0	1 4 0
No. 150B.—Do., do., ,, Hinged Flap, - ,,	1 1 0	1 7 6	1 15 0	1 15 0	1 15 0
No. 150C.—Do., do., with Hinged Flap and Paper Box, ,,	1 4 0	1 10 0	1 17 6	1 17 6	1 17 6
No. 150E.—Do., do., with Self-lifting arrangement, - ,,	1 5 0	1 11 0	1 15 0	1 15 0	1 15 0

No. 150D.—Cheap Mahogany Seat, as No. 150, in single thickness, with Back Rail same width as seat, 15/-.

All Seats with the exception of No. 150D. are made in double thickness.

DOULTON'S IMPROVED SEATS

For PEDESTAL "COMBINATION" CLOSETS.

No. 148.

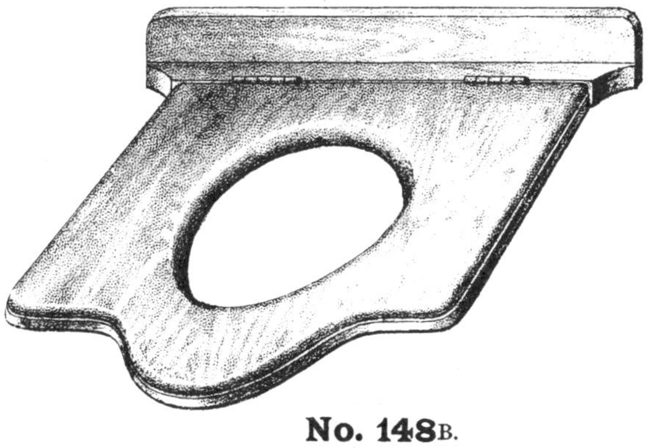

No. 148A.

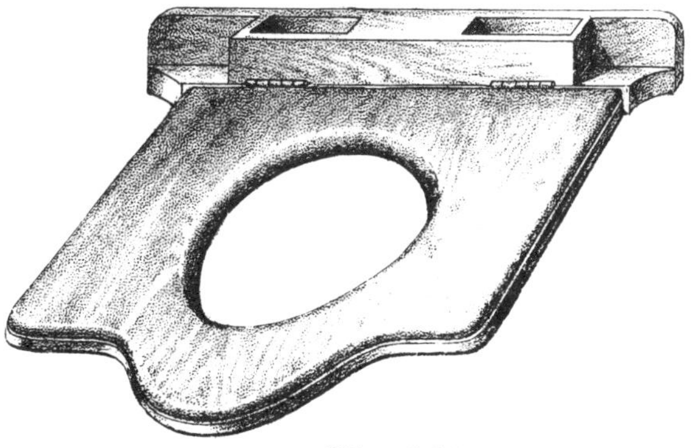

No. 148B.

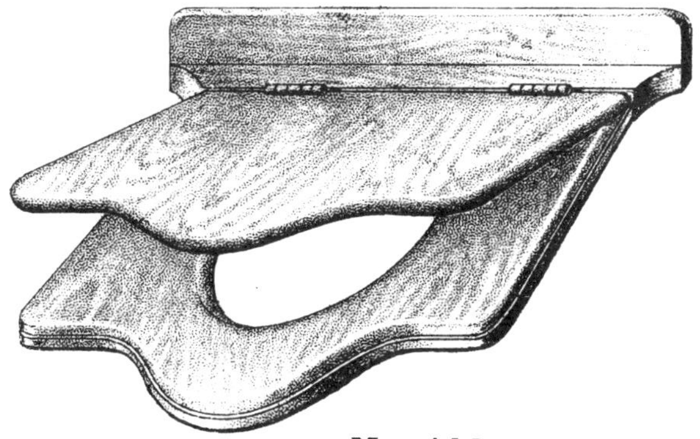

No. 148C.

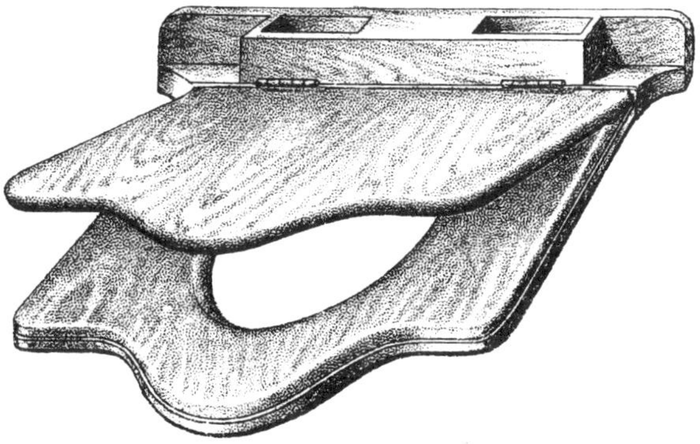

No. 148E.

SELF-LIFTING.

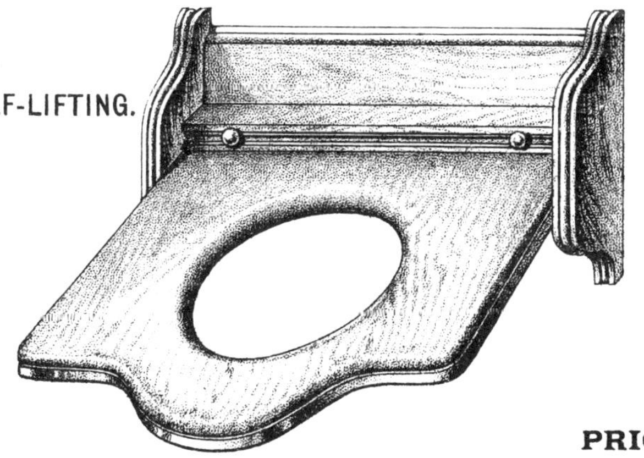

No. 149.

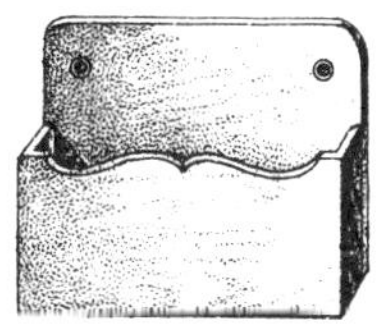

PRICES.	Pine.	Polished Pine.	Mahogany.	Walnut.	Teak.
No. 148. —Pedestal "Combination" Closet Seat, - each,	0 13 6	0 17 0	1 1 0	1 1 0	1 1 0
No. 148A.—Do., do., with Paper Box, - ,,	0 15 0	0 18 6	1 4 0	1 4 0	1 4 0
No. 148B.—Do., do., ,, Hinged Flap, - ,,	1 1 0	1 7 6	1 15 0	1 15 0	1 15 0
No. 148C.—Do., do., with Hinged Flap and Paper Box, ,,	1 4 0	1 10 0	1 17 6	1 17 6	1 17 6
No. 148E.—Do., do., with Self-lifting arrangement, - ,,	1 5 0	1 11 0	1 15 0	1 15 0	1 15 0
No. 149. —Paper Box, - - - - - - -	0 4 0	0 4 6	0 5 6	0 5 6	0 5 6

No. 151. —Cheap Mahogany Seat, as No. 148, in single thickness, with Back Rail same width as seat, 15/-.

All Seats with the exception of No. 151, are made in double thickness.

SHANKS' WATER-CLOSET SEATS.

These Seats are made in S. & Co.'s own Cabinet Factory by special machinery, so that a first-class job is ensured. They are made with Solid Brass Hinges, and of Mahogany, Walnut, or other Woods.

No. 1 Closet Seat.

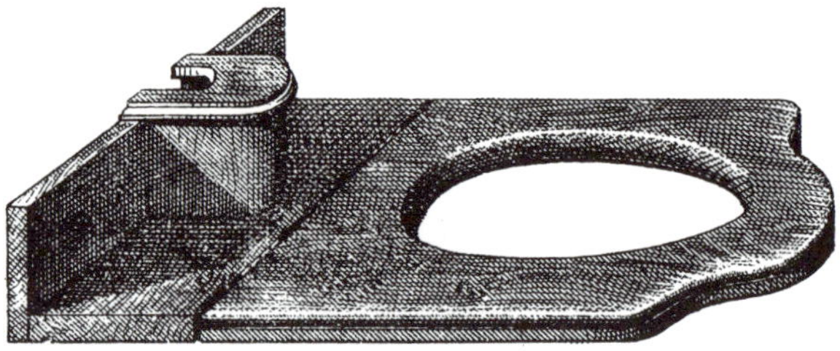

No. 2 Closet Seat,
With Paper Boxes.

No. 3 Closet Seat,
With Hinged Lid.

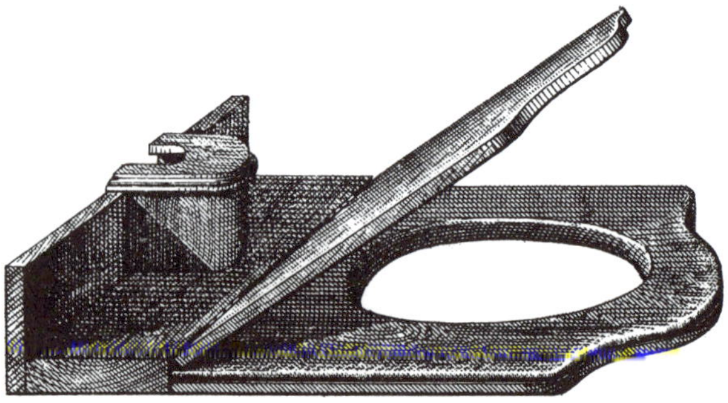

No. 4 Closet Seat,
With Improved Shape of Front, having in view considerations of comfort and cleanliness.

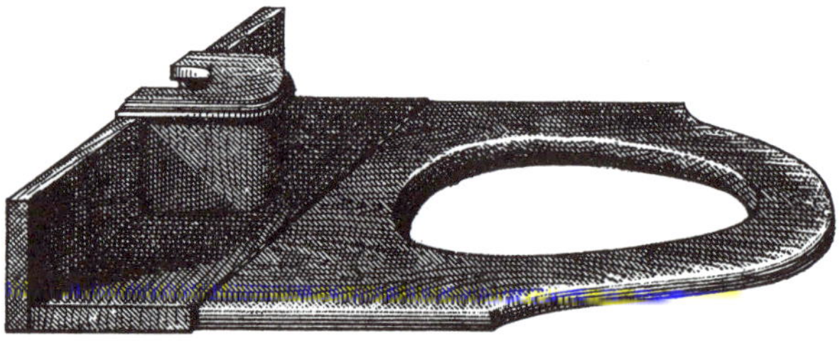

Shanks' Improved I.-R. Cone,
For connecting Down-Pipe to Tubal Closets.

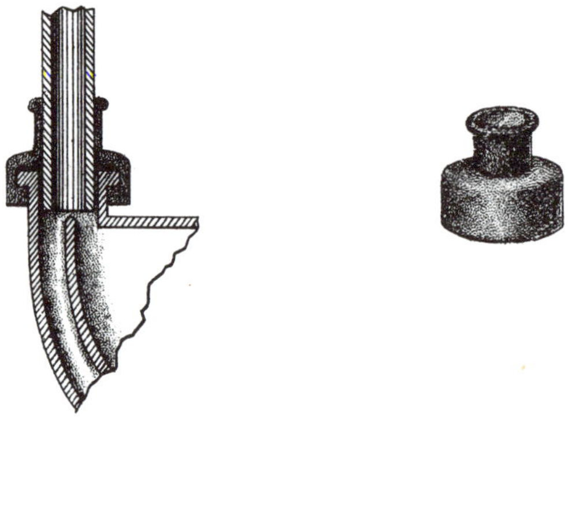

IMPROVED CLOSET SEATS.

No. 181.—Framed Closet Seat, Best Quality, with Improved Side, Stop-hinges.

	Plain Whitewood.	Pitch Pine.	Walnut or Mahogany.
As drawn	8/2	10/-	15/-
Do. with Straight Plinth	8/11	11/2	16/7
Do. with Shaped Plinth	9/10	12/-	17/6

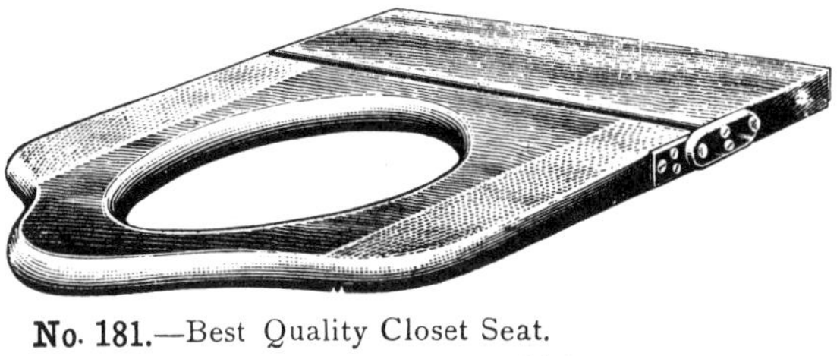

No. 181.—Best Quality Closet Seat.
,, 181A.— Do. do. 2-thickness crossways.
,, 182.—Second Quality do.
,, 182A.— Do. do. 2-thickness crossways.

No. 181A.—Best Quality Closet Seat, two-thickness, crossways, screwed together.

	Pitch Pine.	Walnut or Mahogany.
As drawn	11/-	18/8
Do. with Straight Plinth	12/3	20/3
Do. with Shaped Plinth...	13/-	21/2

No. 182.—Framed Closet Seat, Second Quality; Mahogany or Walnut.

As drawn	11/-
Do. with Straight Plinth	12/2
Do. with Shaped Plinth	13/-

No. 182A.—Second Quality Closet Seat, two-thickness, crossways, screwed; Mahogany or Walnut.

As drawn	13/4
Do. with Straight Plinth	14/6
Do. with Shaped Plinth	15/4

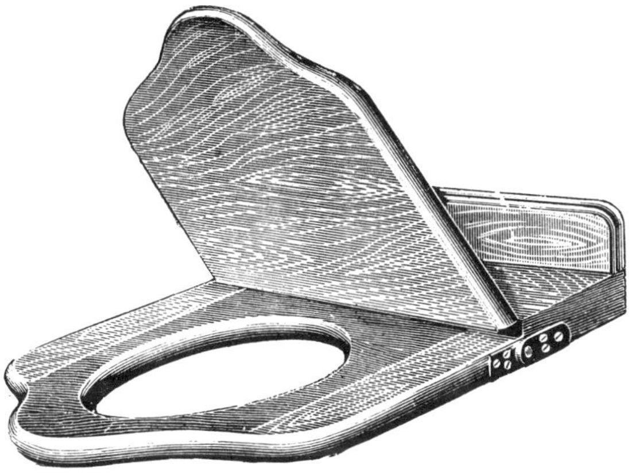

No. 183.—Best Quality Closet Seat.
,, 183A.— Do. do. 2-thickness.
,, 184.—Second Quality do.
,, 184A — Do. do. 2-thickness.

No. 183.—Framed Closet Seat, with Hinged Cover, Best Quality.

	Pitch Pine.	Walnut or Mahogany.
As drawn, with Straight Plinth	16/9	29/10
Do. with Shaped Plinth	17/7	30/9
Do. without Plinth	15/7	28/3

No. 183A.—Best Quality Closet Seat, two-thickness, with Hinged Cover.

	Pitch Pine.	Walnut or Mahogany.
As drawn, with Straight Plinth	17/10	33/6
Do. with Shaped Plinth	18/7	34/6
Do. without Plinth	16/7	32/-

No. 184.—Framed Closet Seat, Second Quality, with Hinged Cover; Walnut or Mahogany.

As drawn, with Straight Plinth	22/6
Do. with Shaped Plinth	23/3
Do. without Plinth	21/3

No. 184A.—Second Quality Closet Seat, two-thickness, with Hinged Cover; Walnut or Mahogany.

As drawn, with Straight Plinth	24/9
Do. with Shaped Plinth	25/7
Do. without Plinth	23/7

No. 148.—Self-Tipping Closet Seat, Best Quality, Walnut or Mahogany, with Plain Painted Brackets ... ... Complete, 26/4

No. 148A.— Do. do. without Painted Brackets... ,, 21/4

Seats fitted with Polished Copper Buffer Plate, 2/4 extra. This simple contrivance prevents urine trickling down front of Closet.

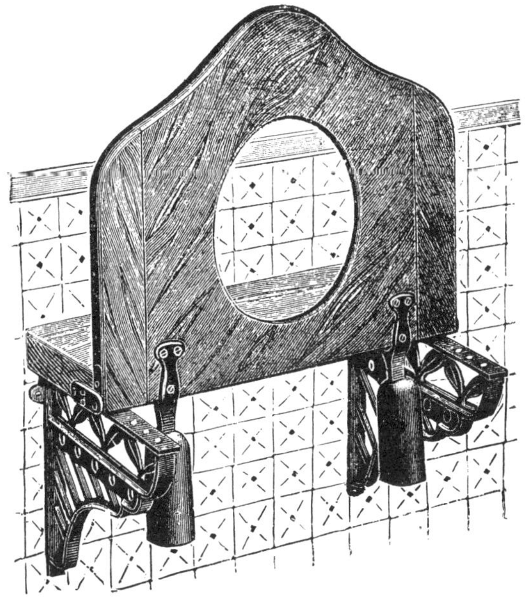

No. 148.—Self-Tipping Closet Seat and Brackets.
,, 148A.— Do. do. no Brackets.

DOULTON'S IMPROVED CLOSET FITTINGS.

No. 53. No. 54. No. 153. No. 153A. No. 153C No. 153D. No. 111. No. 111D.

PRICES.

		s.	d.
No. 53. —Galvanized Iron Chain and Pull, -	each	1	0
No. 54. —Brass Chain Pull and Handle, -	„	1	9
No. 153 —Do., do., Pottery Handle. -	„	1	3
No. 153A.—Do., do., Wood „ -	„	2	0
No. 153B.—Do., do., Doulton Ware Handle,	„	4	0
No. 153c.—Coloured Cord Pull, with Padded Handle, - - - - -	„	3	0
No. 153D.—Do., do., do., -	„	3	6

		s.	d.
No. 111. —Brass Pull Plate with Ebonized Handle, - - - - - -	each	6	6
No. 111A.—Brass Pull, Plate with Ebonized Handle, Plated, - - - -	„	10	0
No. 111B.—Do., do., Brass, with Doulton Ware Handle, - - - -	„	8	6
No. 111C.—Do., do., Plated, - - -	„	12	0
No. 111D.—Do., do., Specially Designed, Brass,	„	10	0
No. 111E.—Do., do., do., Plated, - -	„	15	6

IMPROVED ASYLUM PULL FOR BUILDING INTO WALL.

No. 323.

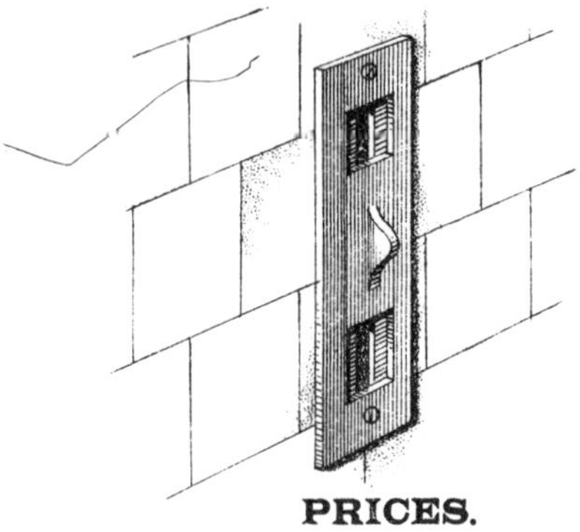

PRICES.

No. 323. —Brass, - - - 3/- each.
No. 323A.—Do. Plated, - 4/- „

CAST-IRON BRACKETS.

No. 57.

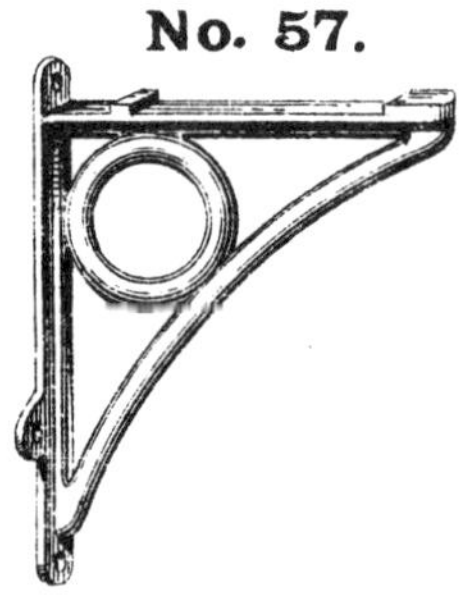

No. 58.

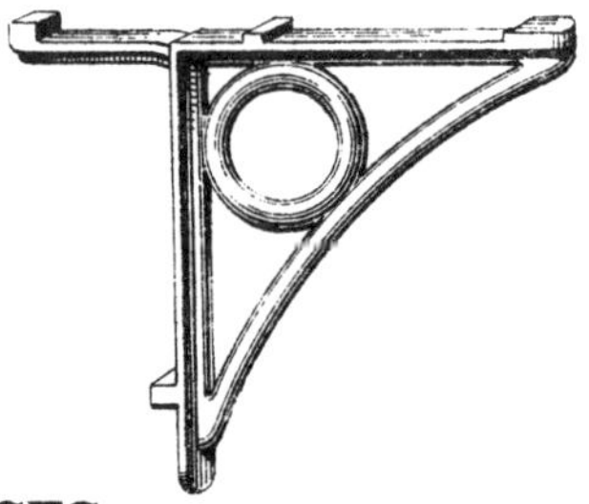

PRICES.

		Per Pair.
No. 57.—Cast-iron Brackets, Painted, -		1 6
„ „ Galvanized, -		2 6
No. 58.— „ „ Painted, -		1 6
„ „ Galvanized, -		2 6

CRANKS.

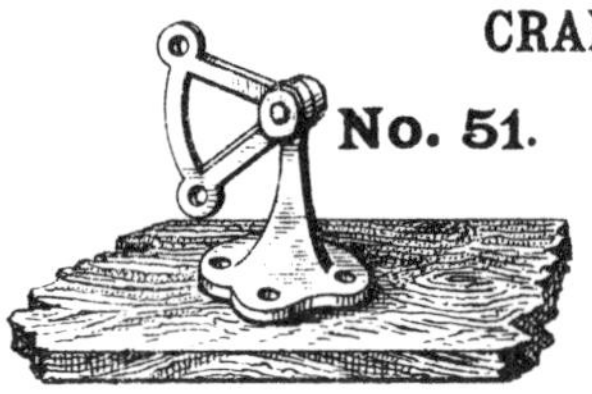

No. 51.

No. 52.

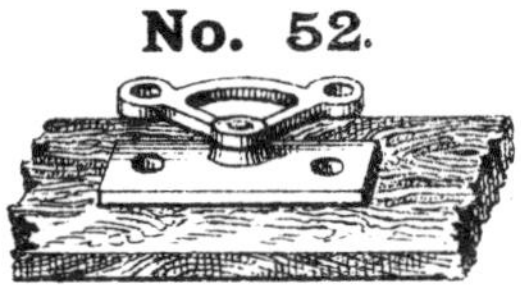

PRICES.

		s.	d.
No. 51.—Upright Cranks, - -	each,	0	6
No. 52.—Side „ - -	„	0	6

INDIA RUBBER CONES.

No. 154.

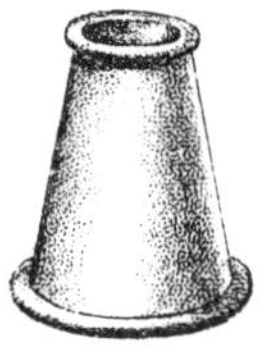

PRICE.—1/6 each.

CLOSET PULL AND LIFT-UP HANDLES.

No. 3.—Pull Handle.

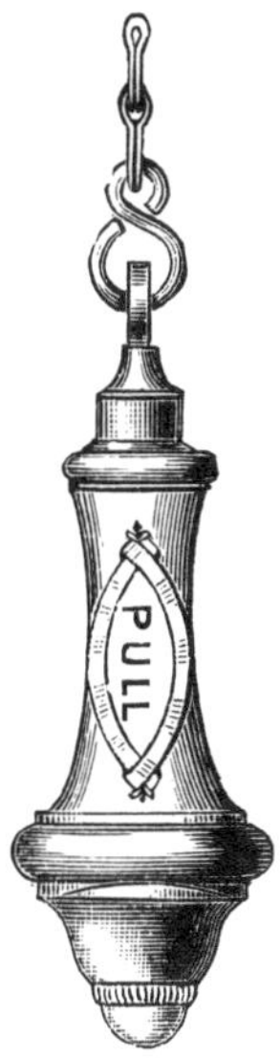

No. 4.—Pull Handle.

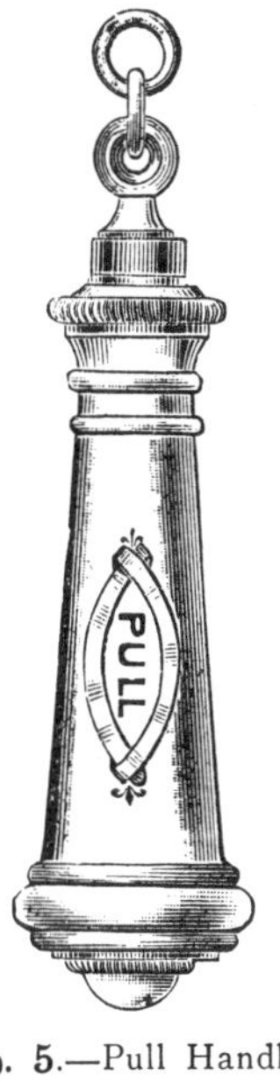

No. 5.—Pull Handle.

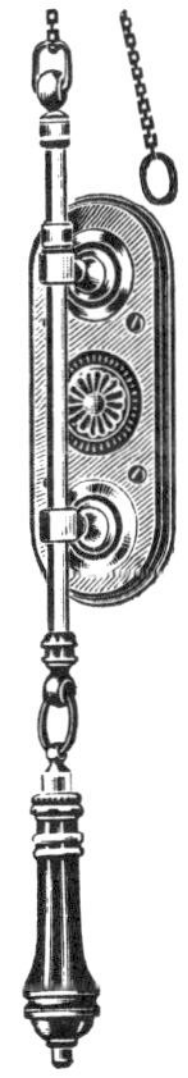

No. 147.—Bracket Pull.

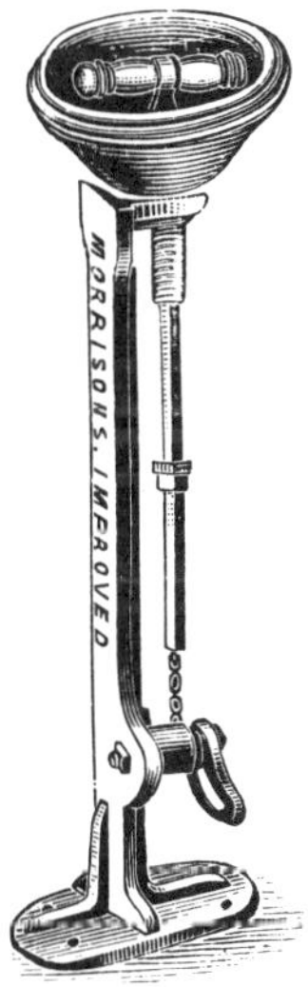

No. 1.—Cup & Support.

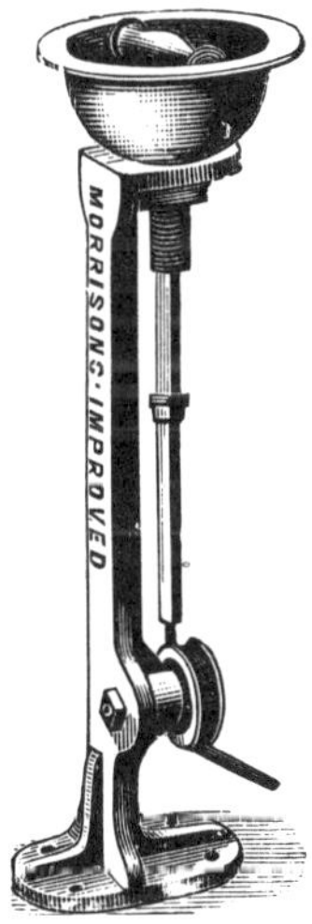

No. 2.—Cup & Support.

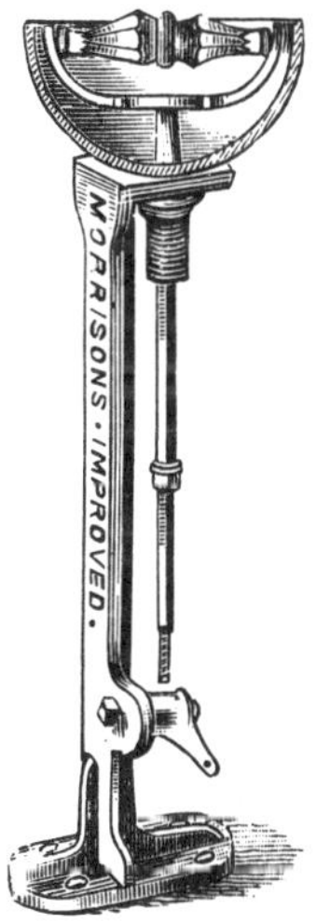

No. 6.—Cup without Flange, and Support.

		Nickel-Plating extra.
No. 1.—Encased China Cup, Ebony Handle, and Painted Cast-iron Regulating Support	8/9	1/- each.
,, 2.—Brass Cup, Ebony Handle, and Painted Cast-iron Regulating Support	7/6	1/6 ,,
,, 6.— ,, ,, Cut Glass, Amber Colored Grip	7/6	1/6 ,,
,, 3.—China Pull, Indiarubber Ring, and Chain and Split Ring	1/4	
,, 4.— ,, ,, ,, ,, ,, ...	1/-	
,, 5.— ,, ,, ,, ,, ,, ...	1/1	
,, 147.—Bracket Pull, Ebony Handle, Rod and Strong Chain ; with Walnut or Mahogany Fancy Back-plate ...	4/8	1/4 ,,

Pull Handles are supplied in real Ebony without extra charge. China Handles are usually made in White, Ivory or Celadon Colors. No extra charge for Printing Customer's Name on China Handles except initial cost of Copper Name Plate, for which we charge 3/6 nett.

FOR OTHER DESIGNS OF CLOSET PULL HANDLES PLEASE SEE DRAWINGS OF CLOSET SUITES.

Accessoires pour Closets

TUYAUX ET COLLIERS
cuivre nickelé
pour Réservoirs de chasse

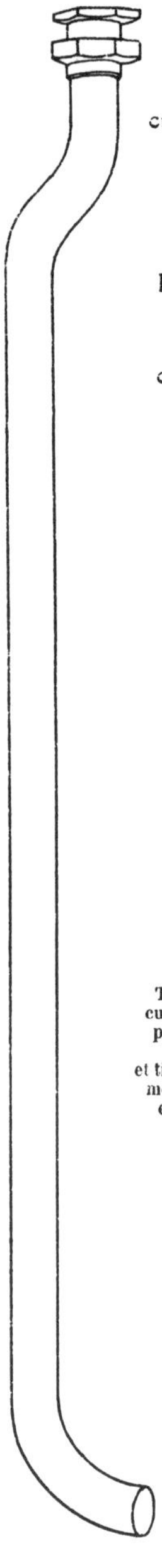

Prix complet
avec 2 colliers, **28** fr.

COLLIER
cuivre nickelé pour tuyau
de descente

Prix avec butoir, **1.50**

COLLIER
cuivre nickelé pour tuyau
de descente

Prix sans butoir, **1** fr.

VIS TÊTE NICKELÉE
pour fixer les Cuvettes au sol
N° **171** bis

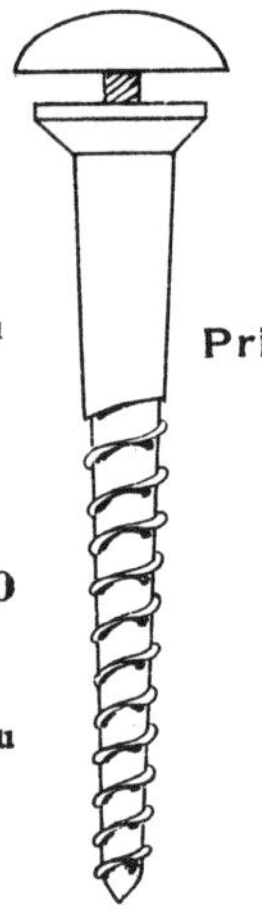

Prix : **0** fr.**25**

COUDE EN PLOMB
N° **199**

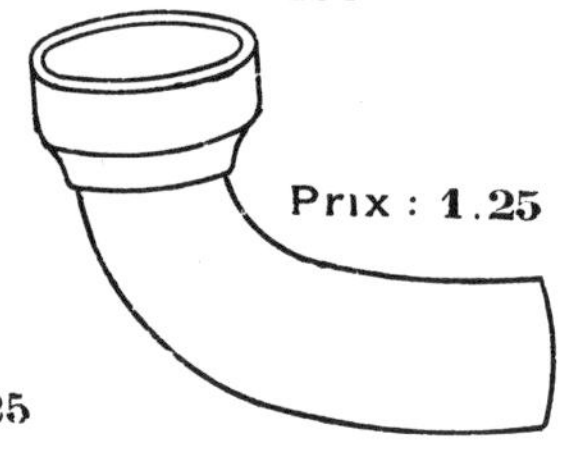

Prix : **1.25**

LIGATURE CAOUTCHOUC
servant à relier le coude ou le tuyau
à la cuvette
N° **281**

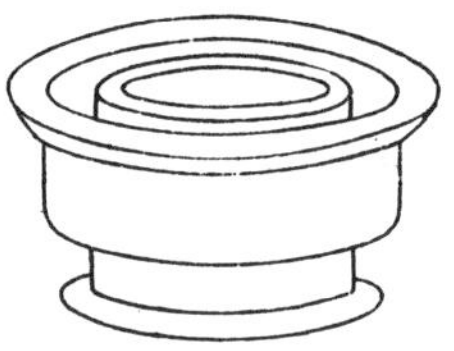

PRIX A PARIS :
1re grandeur . . . **1.50**
2me — . . . **1.25**

Nous montrons ci-dessous la façon la plus pratique de fixer la ligature

1re POSITION

Introduire le coude ou le tuyau dans l'intérieur de la ligature et rentrer ce tuyau ainsi recouvert dans la douille de la cuvette après avoir retourné la partie extérieure de la ligature.

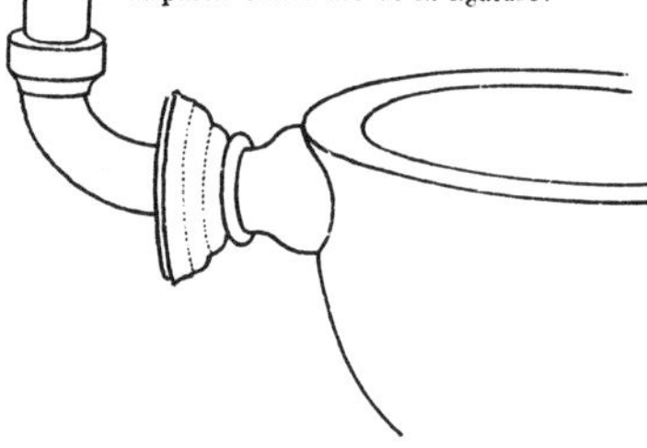

2me POSITION

Rabattre la partie extérieure de la ligature sur la douille de la cuvette et l'y fixer ainsi que sur le tuyau.

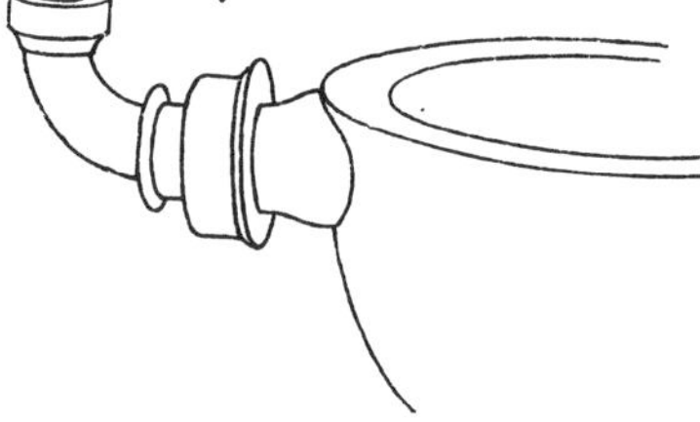

CHAINES DE TIRAGE

N° **196**

Tirage à glissière cuivre nickelé avec poignée porcelaine blanche et tige en cuivre massif monté sur applique en acajou massif

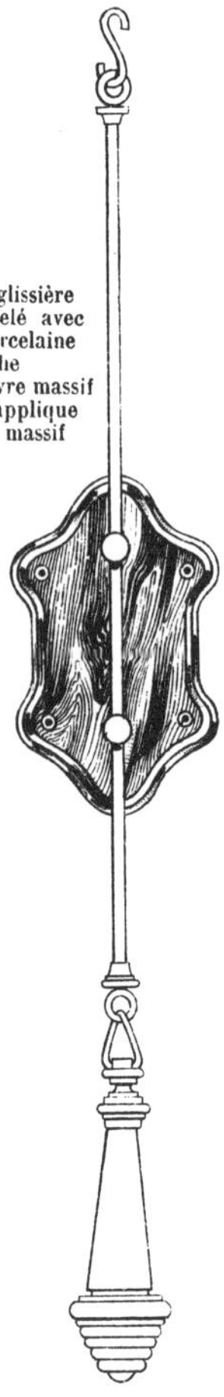

Prix : **12** fr.

N° **196** bis

Tirage à glissière cuivre nickelé avec poignée porcelaine blanche avec tige et chaîne, monté sur applique acajou massif.

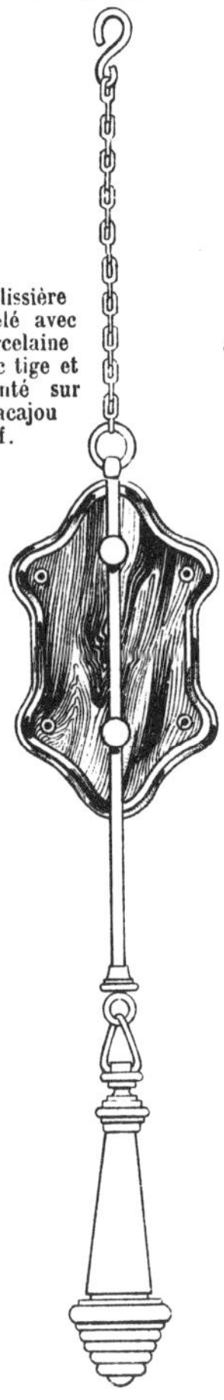

Prix : **8** fr.

N° **197**

Chaîne de tirage cuivre nickelé avec poignée porcelaine blanche.

Prix : **2** fr.

N° **197** bis

Chaîne de tirage cuivre nickelé avec poignée porcelaine décorée.

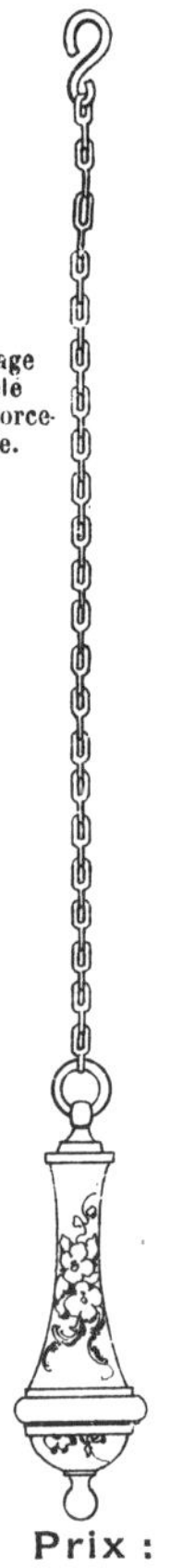

Prix :
Poignée décor d'une seule couleur. **2.50**
» » de plusieurs » **2.75**
» » filet or . . . . . **3.** »
» » impression or. . . **3.50**

N° **198**

Chaîne de tirage en fer étamé avec poignée bois

Prix : **0.75**

IMP. EUGÈNE VERNEAU, 108, R. FOLIE-MÉRICOURT, PARIS

CLOSET PULLS

HARDWOOD CLOSET PULL

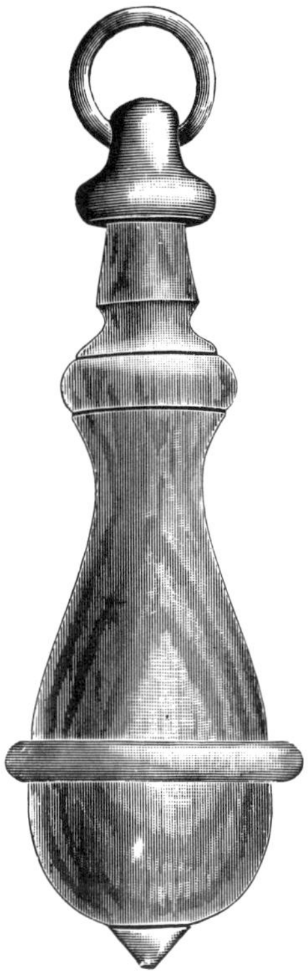

WITH RUBBER RING

Plate 575-B.

Price, each..................................$0.25

HARDWOOD CLOSET PULL

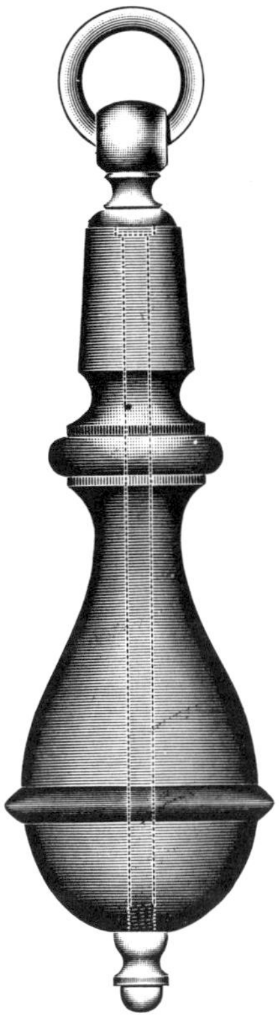

WITH ROD RUNNING THROUGH
AND RUBBER RING

Platc 577-B.

Price, each,..................................$0.35

WHITE CELLULOID
CLOSET PULL

Plate 580-B.

Price, each.................................. $0.60

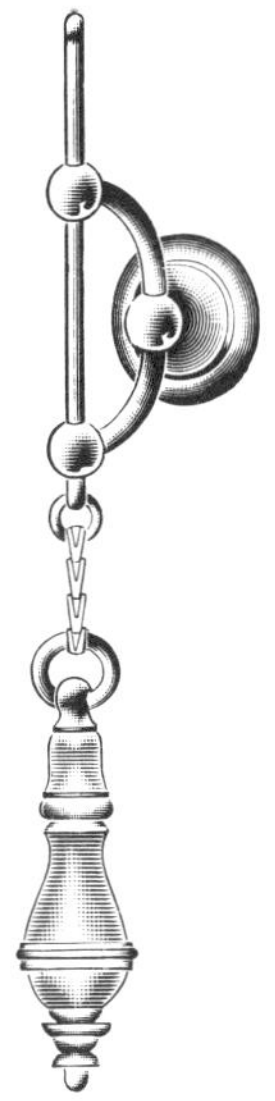

NICKEL-PLATED BRASS
GUIDE

Plate 585-B.

Price with White Celluloid pull
and link chain, each.................$1.75

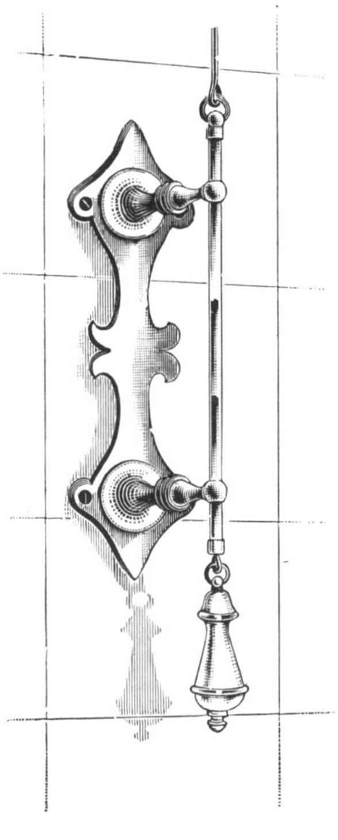

NICKEL-PLATED BRASS
GUIDE

Plate 587-B.

Price with White Celluloid pull
and link chain, each.................$1.75

PANELLED AND DECORATED ENCLOSURES FOR WATER WASTE PREVENTER.

No. 310.

No. 312.

No. 311.

No. 313.

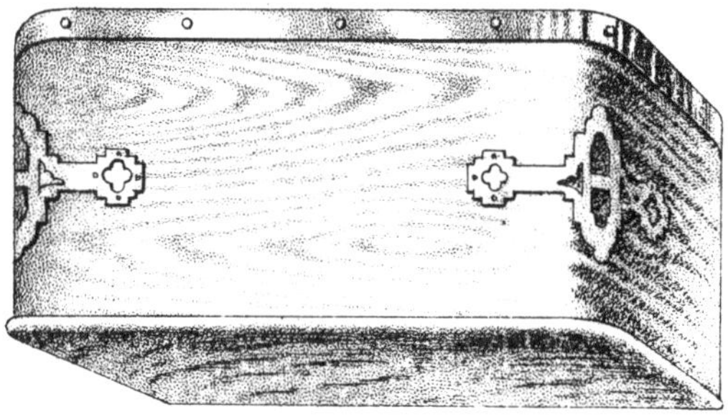

PRICES.

Polished Mahogany or Walnut Enclosure, with Tiled Panels in Front, and Carved Wood Panel below. Recessed at lower part. This Enclosure is Designed to cover both Cistern and Brackets.

No. 310. —To suit 2-gallon Cistern,	£7 15 0
No. 310A.— Do. 3-gallon do.,	7 17 0

Polished Mahogany or Walnut Panelled Enclosure, Designed to cover both Cistern and Brackets.

No. 311. —To suit 2-gallon Cistern,	£5 12 0
No. 311A.— Do. 3-gallon do.,	5 14 0

Polished Mahogany or Walnut Enclosure, with Tiled Panels, Designed to cover both Cistern and Brackets.

No. 312. —To suit 2-gallon Cistern,	£4 15 0
No. 312A.— Do. 3-gallon do.,	4 17 0

Polished Mahogany or Walnut Enclosure, with Rounded Corners and Polished Brass, or White Metal Decoration, etc. Band at top.

No. 313. —To suit 2-gallon Cistern with Brass Band,	£4 6 0
No. 313A.— Do. 3-gallon do., do.,	4 9 0
No. 313B.—To suit 2-gallon Cistern with White Metal Band,	4 10 0
No. 313C.— Do. 3-gallon do., do.,	4 13 0

All the above Enclosures may be made in other woods if preferred, or special designs can be had if required.

PANELLED AND DECORATED ENCLOSURES FOR WATER WASTE PREVENTER.

No. 314.

No. 319.

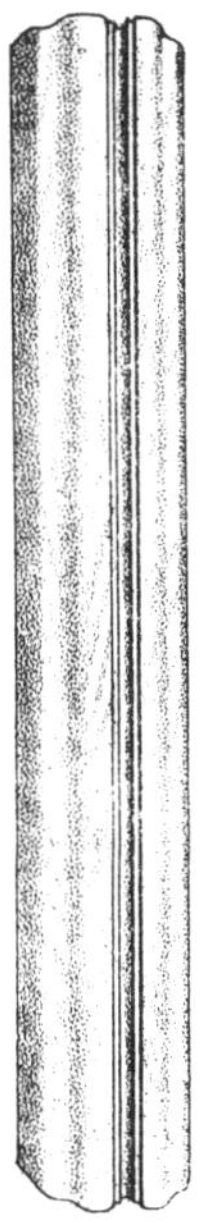

No. 320.

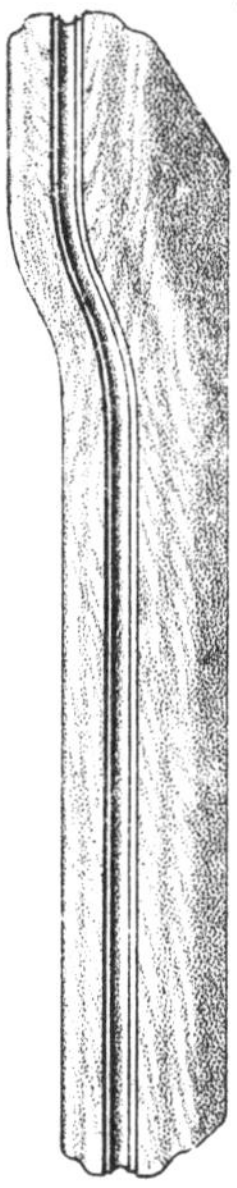

No. 315.

No. 316.

No. 317.

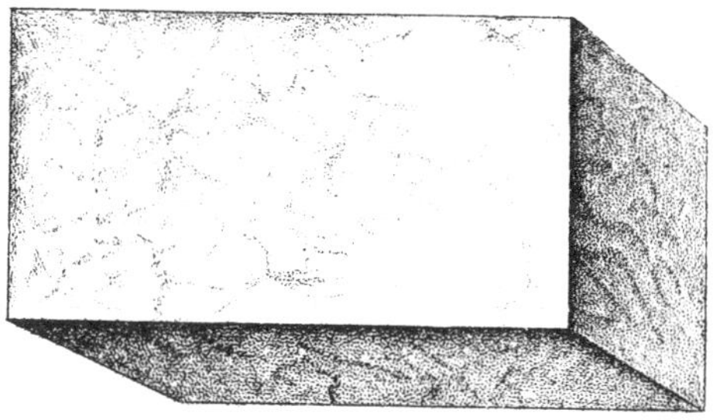

No. 318.

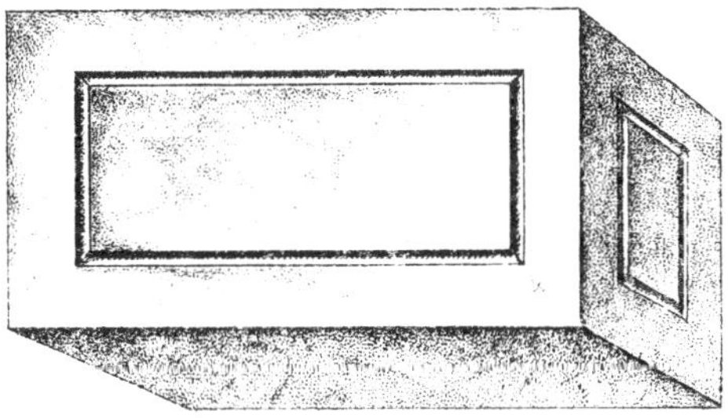

PRICES.

Polished Mahogany or Walnut Enclosure, with Tiled Panels.

No. 314. —To suit 2-gallon Cistern,	£4 0 0
No. 314A.— Do. 3-gallon do.,	4 2 0

Polished Mahogany or Walnut Enclosure as shown.

No. 315. —To suit 2-gallon Cistern,	£3 5 0
No. 315A.— Do. 3-gallon do.,	3 7 6

Polished Mahogany or Walnut Enclosure with Plain Panel.

No. 316. —To suit 2-gallon Cistern,	£2 10 0
No. 316A.— Do. 3-gallon do.,	2 12 0

MARBLE ENCLOSURES FOR WATER WASTE PREVENTER.

Polished Marble Enclosure.

	For 2-gallon Cistern.	For 3-gallon Cistern.
No. 317. —Veined Marble,	£2 0 0	£2 4 0
No. 317A.—St. Anne's,	2 9 0	2 15 0
No. 317B.—Rouge - Royal,	2 11 6	2 17 6

Panelled Marble Enclosure.

	For 2-gallon Cistern.	For 3-gallon Cistern.
No. 318. —Veined Marble,	£2 5 0	£2 10 0
No. 318A.—St. Anne's,	2 15 0	3 3 0
No. 318B.—Rouge Royal,	2 17 0	3 5 0

POLISHED HARDWOOD ENCLOSURES FOR DOWN-PIPES.

No. 319.—Polished Mahogany or Walnut Pipe Enclosure, to use with Nos. 310, 311 312,	£0 12 0
No. 320.—Polished Mahogany or Walnut Pipe Enclosure, to use with Nos. 313, 314, 315, 316, 317, 318,	0 15 6

All the above Enclosures may be made in other woods or marbles if preferred, or special designs can be had if required.

IMPROVED HOT WATER TOWEL RAILS.

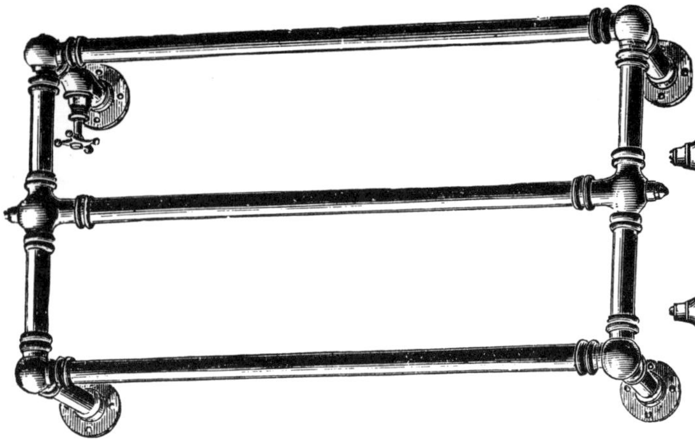

No. 34.

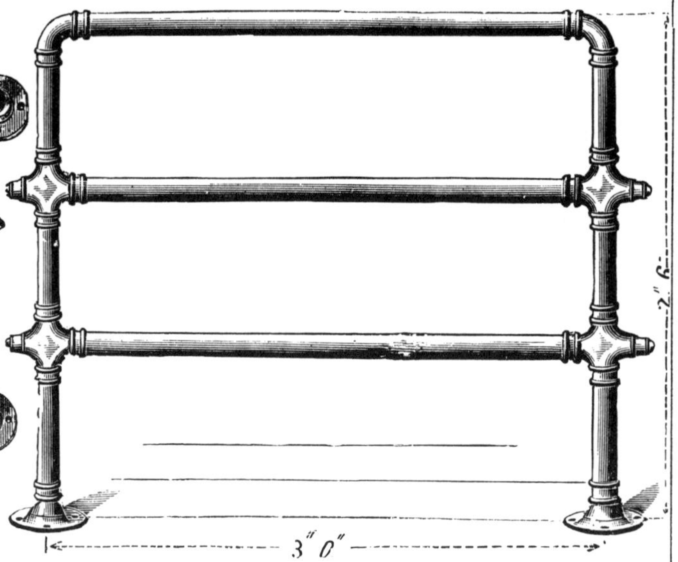

No. 22.

No. 98.

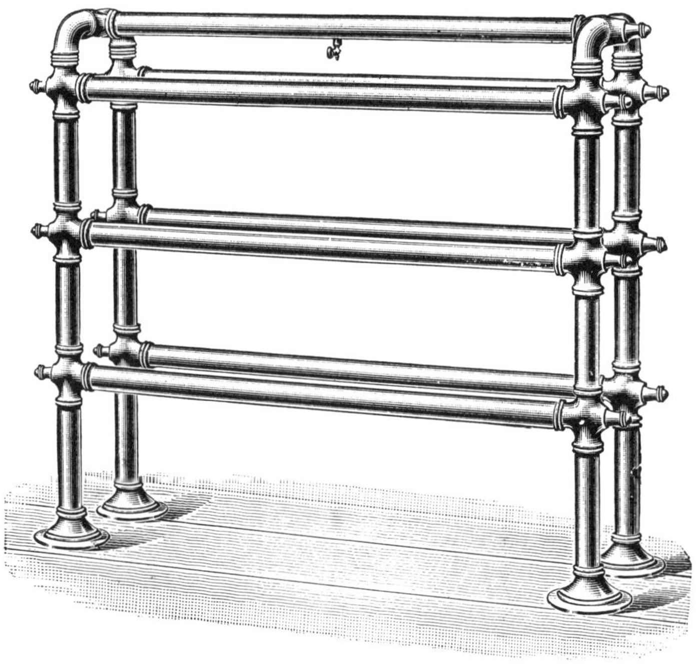

No. 99.

These Towel Rails are made of $1\frac{1}{2}''$ strong solid drawn Copper Tube, with Gun Metal Mountings, and are Finished Polished or Nickel-plated.

	No. 22.	No. 34.	No. 98.	No. 99.
Size	36″ × 30″	36″ × 30″	42″ × 36″	42″ × 36″
Price, Polished...	99/-	105/-	135/-	210/-
„ Nickel-plated	117/-	123/-	156/-	243/9

Our Towel Rails are greatly increasing in favor. They are a convenient acquisition to the bathroom and bedroom, and also afford when desirable a comfortable temperature in the apartment.

Towel Rails made specially to order. Fitting Taps to Nos. 22, 98 and 99, or altering from Stock sizes, charged extra.

THESE TOWEL RAILS ARE TESTED TO 300 LBS. TO THE SQUARE INCH BEFORE LEAVING THE WORKS.

DOULTON'S IMPROVED APPARATUS FOR HEATING AND DRYING BATH-ROOM TOWELS.

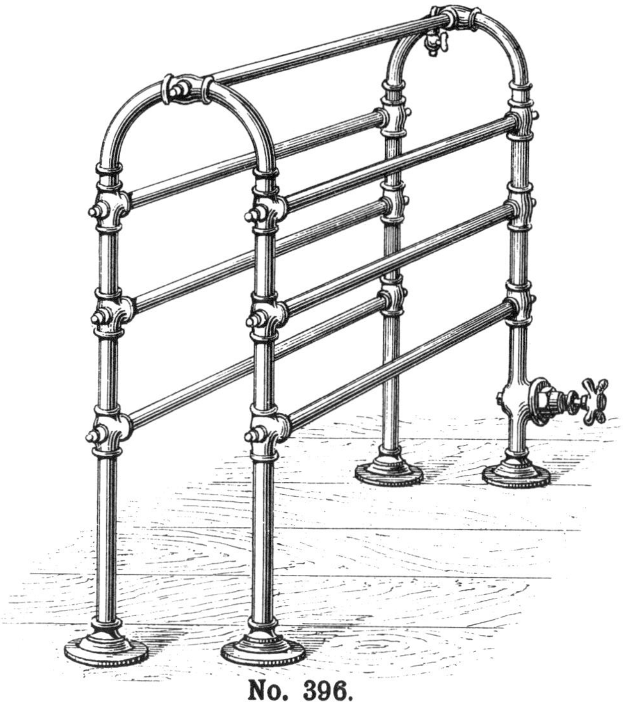

No. 396.

Standard Towel Rail.

No. 396. —Polished Brass,	- - complete,	£7	0	0
No. 396A.—Plated,	- - - - ,,	10	0	0

No. 397.

Standard Single Towel Rail.

No. 397. —Polished Brass, - - - - -	£3	7	6
No. 397A.—Plated, - - - - -	5	5	0

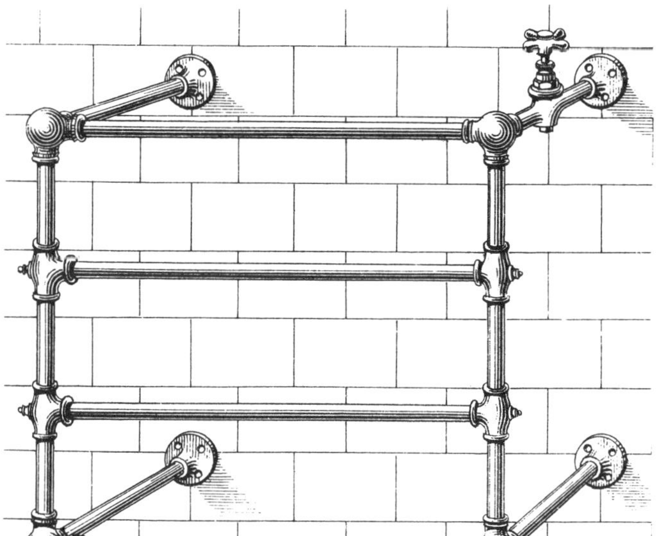

No. 398.

Towel Rail for Fixing Against Wall.

No. 398. —With Three Rails, Polished Brass,		£3	17	6
No. 398A.—Do.,	do., Plated,	5	17	6
No. 398B.—With Four Rails, Polished Brass,		4	10	0
No. 398C.—Do.,	do., Plated,	6	15	0

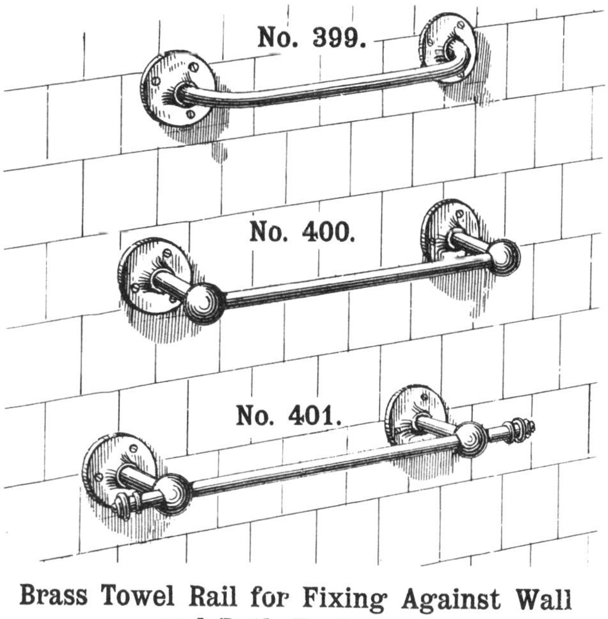

Brass Towel Rail for Fixing Against Wall and Bath Enclosures.

No. 399. —Towel Rail,	Polished Brass,	£0	9	0
No. 399A.— Do.,	- - - Plated,	0	14	0
No. 400. — Do.,	- Polished Brass,	0	11	0
No. 400A.— Do.,	- - - Plated,	0	17	0
No. 401. — Do.,	- Polished Brass,	0	11	0
No. 401A.— Do.,	- - Plated,	0	17	0

SEMI PLUG BASINS, BRACKET SOAPS, TOILET WARE, &c.

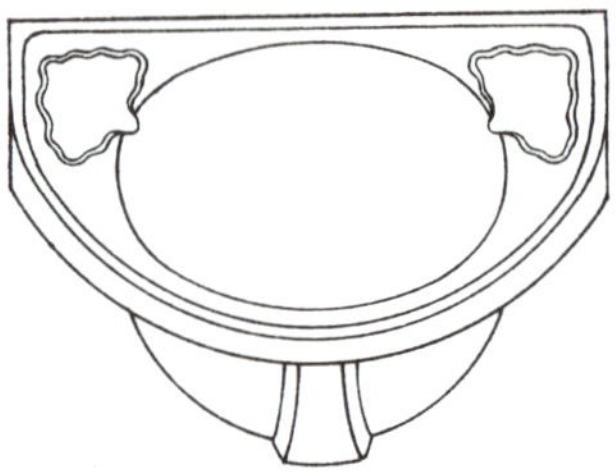

No. 206—SEMI PLUG BASIN.
With Patent Overflow.
$17 \times 10\frac{1}{2}$ in.; BASIN [oval], 11×9 in.

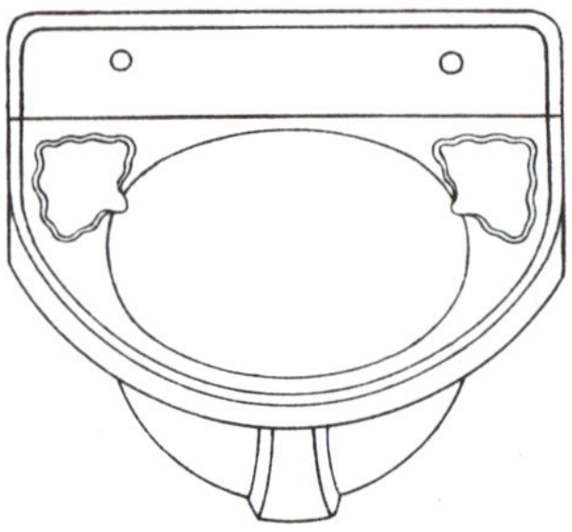

No. 207—SEMI PLUG BASIN.
With Back and Patent Overflow.
$17\frac{1}{2} \times 10\frac{1}{2}$ in.; BASIN [oval], 11×9 in.; Height of Back, 3 in.

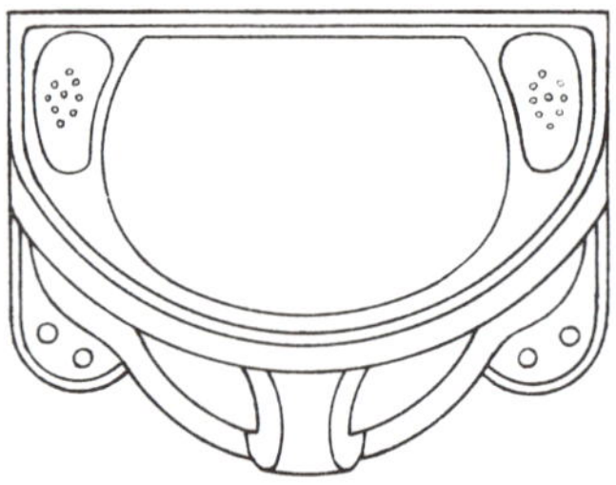

No. 213—SEMI PLUG BASIN, with Lugs.
With Patent Overflow and Drained Soaps.
$18\frac{1}{2} \times 12$ in.; BASIN [oval], $11\frac{1}{2} \times 10$ in.

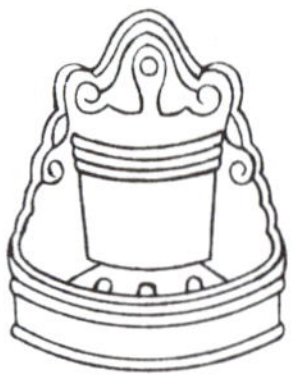

No. 215—FLAT WALL
Combined Bracket Soap and Brush Box.

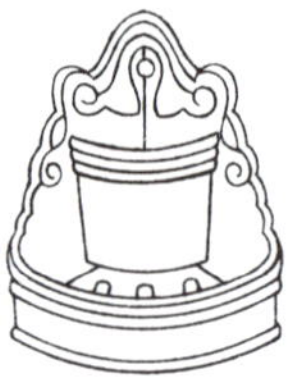

No. 216—ANGULAR
Combined Bracket Soap and Brush Box.

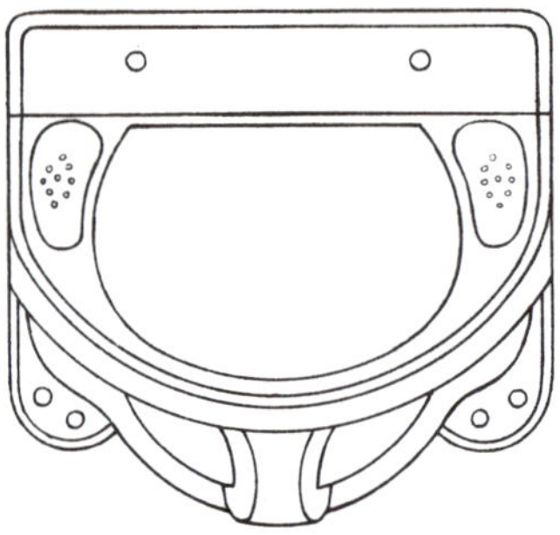

No. 214—SEMI PLUG BASIN, with Lugs.
With Back, Patent Overflow and Drained Soaps.
$18\frac{1}{2} \times 12$ in.; BASIN [oval], $11\frac{1}{2} \times 10$ in., Height of Back, 3 in.

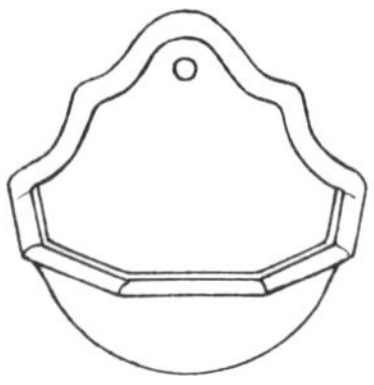

No. 217—FLAT WALL BRACKET SOAP.

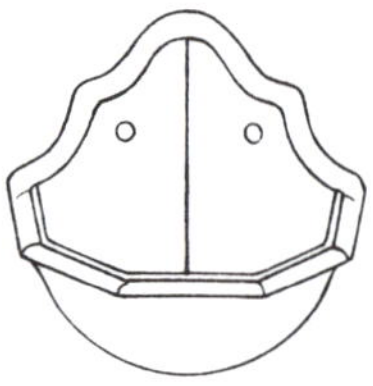

No. 218—ANGULAR BRACKET SOAP.

No. 219—BRUSH TRAY.

No. 220—BRACKET SOAP.

No. 221—EWER AND BASIN, Plain.

No. 221A as No. 221, but Basin with Plug Hole.

No. 222—CHAMBER.

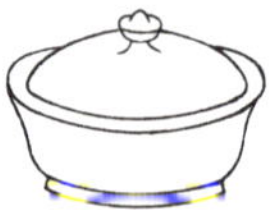

No. 223—SOAP TRAY.

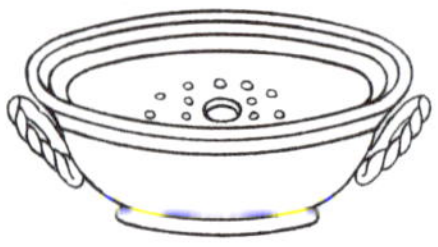

No. 224—SPONGE.

SPITTOONS FOR SWIMMING BATHS.

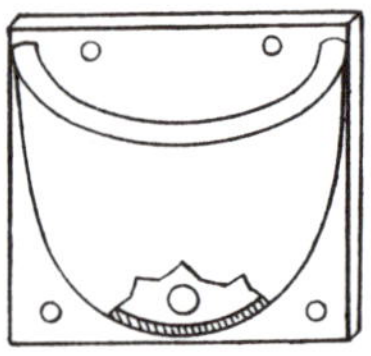

No. 208—SQUARE BACK.
Height, 8 in.; Diameter, 9×5 in.

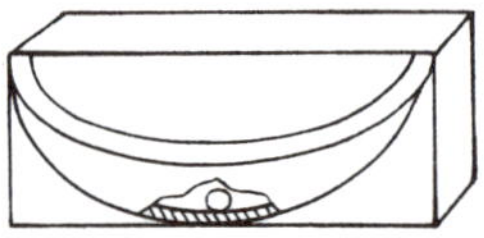

No. 209—BRICK SHAPE.
$10\frac{1}{2} \times 4\frac{3}{4}$ in.; Back to Front, $4\frac{3}{4}$ in.

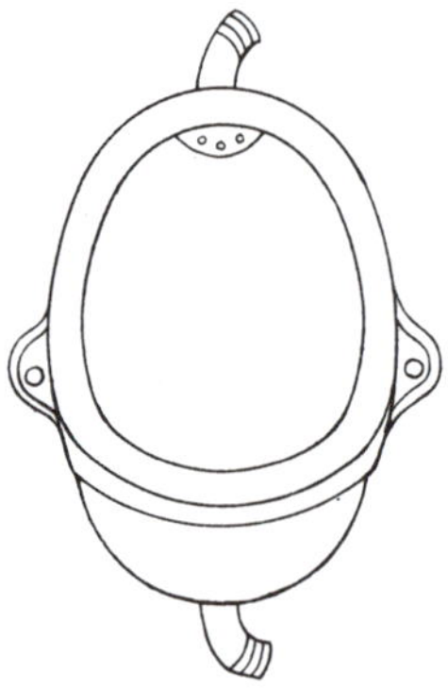

No. 210—FLAT WALL.
Height, 13 in.; Diameter, 10×6 in.

Accessoires de Toilette

	Nº 160	Nº 161	Nº 162	Nº 163	Nº 164
		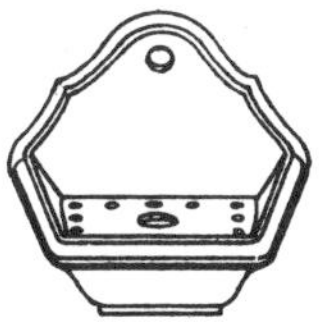	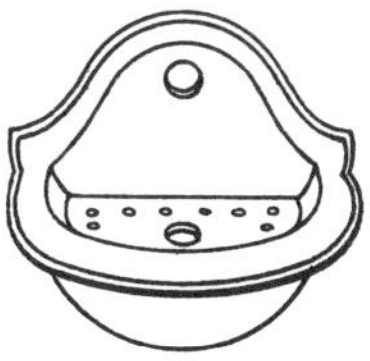	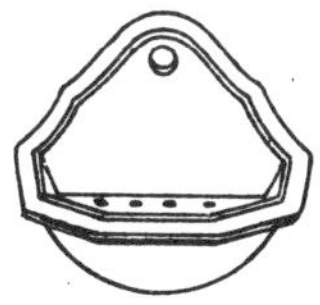	

PRIX A PARIS

	Nº 160	Nº 161	Nº 162	Nº 163	Nº 164
Blanc	2.50	3 75	3.75	3.75	1.50
Décors d'une seule couleur, nºs 1, 2 et 3	3.25	5. »	5. »	5. »	2. »
Décors riches de plusieurs couleurs, nºs 5 et 6	4.25	6. »	6. »	6. »	2.75

Nous possédons généralement en magasin ces Pièces en blanc dans les décors nºs 1, 2, 3, 5 et 6

BOITE A BROSSES
Nº 180

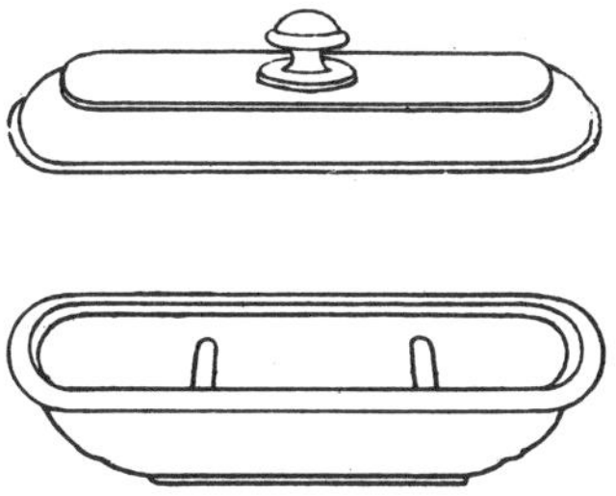

BOITE A SAVON
Nº 181

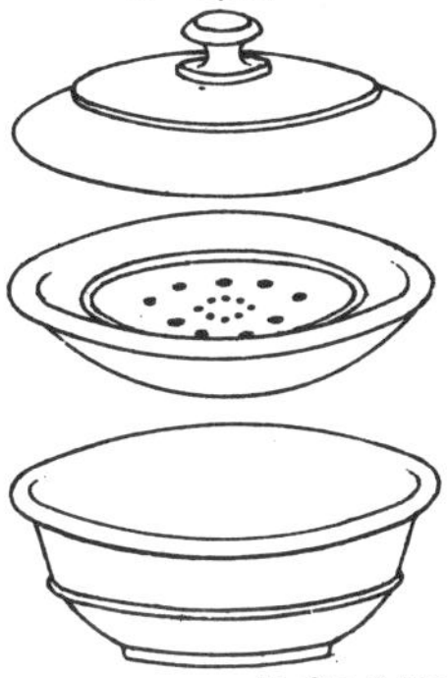

BOL A ÉPONGES
Nº 182

PRIX A PARIS :

	Boite à Brosses Nº 180	Boite à Savon Nº 181	Bol à Éponge Nº 182
Blanc	2.50	2.50	3 fr.
Décors d'une seule couleur	3.75	3.75	4.50
Décors riches de plusieurs couleurs	5. »	5. »	6.50
Décors avec filets or	6 »	6. »	7.50
Décor impression or extra riche	7. »	7. »	8.75

Nous possédons généralement en magasin ces Pièces dans les décors de nos Cuvettes basculantes, montrés aux pages 131, 132, 133

BOITE A PAPIER
Nº 171

VASE DE NUIT ROND
Nº 176

VASE DE NUIT OVALE
Nº 177

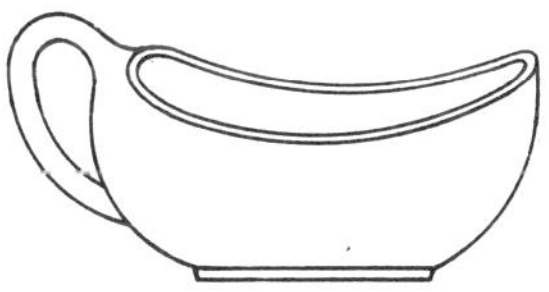

PRIX A PARIS :

	Nº 171	Nº 176	Nº 177
Blanc	6.50	3 fr.	6 fr.
Décors d'une seule couleur, nºs 1, 2, 3 et 4	8 50	4 »	7 »
Décors riches de plusieurs couleurs, nºs 5, 6 et 7	10 »	6 »	9 »

SEAU
Nº 173

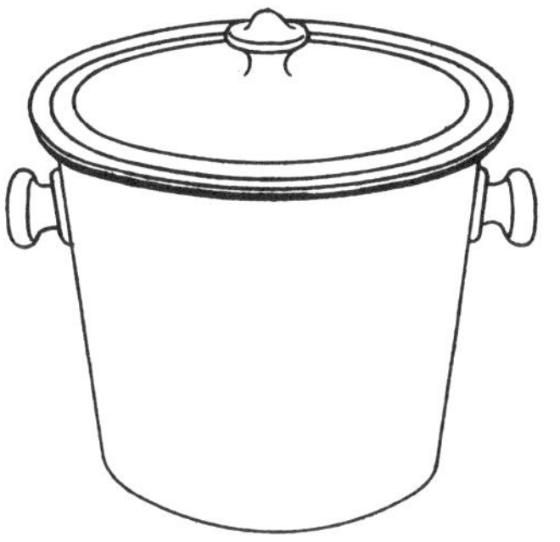

BROC A EAU
Nº 174

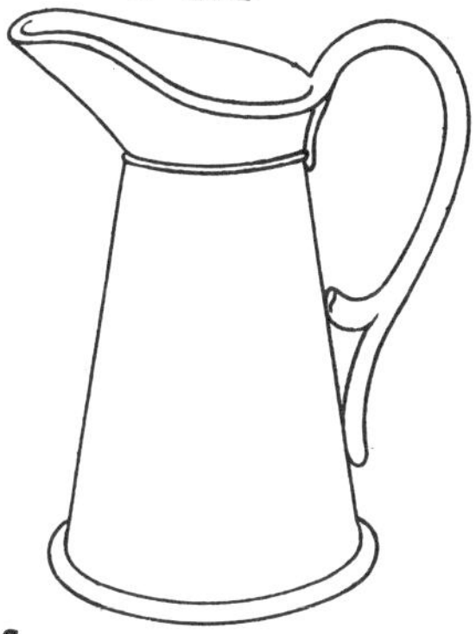

BAIN-DE-PIEDS
Nº 175

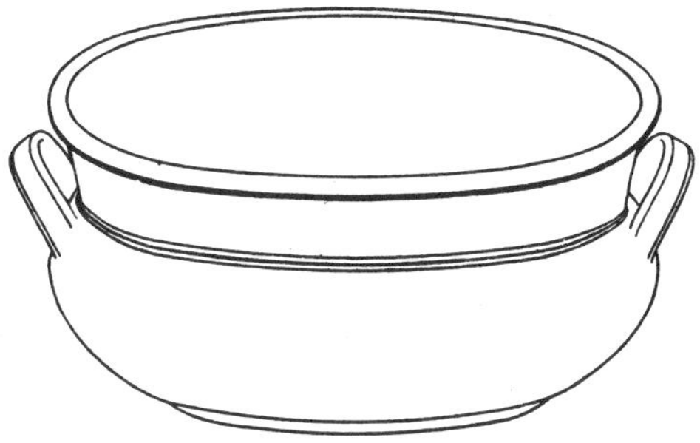

Dimensions : 30×50

PRIX A PARIS

	Seau, Nº 173	Broc, Nº 174	Bain-de-Pieds, Nº 175
Blanc	16.50	8.50	35 fr.
Décors d'une seuleur couleur, nºs 1, 2 et 3	20. »	9 50	40. »
Décors riches de plusieurs couleurs, nºs 5 et 6	28. »	13. »	47. »

Nous possédons généralement en magasin toutes ces Pièces en blanc et dans les décors nºs 2, 3, 5 et 6

Les Boîtes à papier se font dans tous les décors des Closets

Accessoires pour Closets

PORTE-ROULEAU EN FONTE BRONZÉE
L' " INDISPENSABLE "
N° **200**

Complet avec rouleau de papier et vis pour le fixer au mur.
Prix. . . . . **7** fr.

PORTE-ROULEAU EN FONTE BRONZÉE
Forme Fer à Cheval
N° **200** *bis*

Complet avec rouleau de papier et clous pour le fixer au mur.
Prix. . . . . **4** fr.

ROULEAUX PAPIER HYGIÉNIQUE
N° **201**

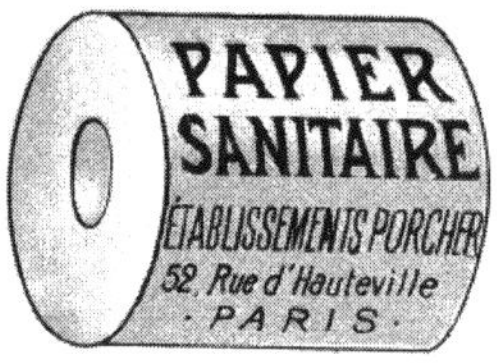

Nous possédons ces papiers en 4 qualités. La qualité **D** est un papier antiseptique et désinfectant. Les qualités **A**, **B** et **C** présentent des différences de force et de finesse de papier.

Qualités. . .	A	B	C	D
Le rouleau.	**0.75**	**1.** »	**1 25**	**2.50**
La douzaine	**8.40**	**10.80**	**13.40**	**24.** »
La grosse	**96.** »	**120.** »	**150.** »	**250.** »

CONSOLES EN FONTE
AVEC BANDE CAOUTCHOUC

Ces consoles sont destinées à supporter le siège, dans l'emploi des appareils en deux pièces (voir page 151).
Prix la paire. . . **5** fr.

VERROU INDICATEUR
N° **202**

Partie placée à l'intérieur du closet
Prix. . . . . . **10** fr.

Extérieur

PETITES CONSOLES EN FONTE

Ces petites consoles sont destinées à supporter les dormants des sièges fixés au mur, des modèles n°s 278, 279, 282, etc.
Prix la paire. . . . **2** fr.

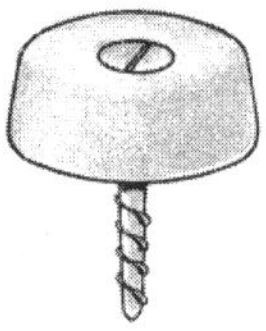

TAMPONS CAOUTCHOUC POUR SIÈGES
N° **280** *bis*

Nous recommandons particulièrement ce modèle ne détériorant pas le bois du siège et ne risquant jamais de se couper ou de s'écraser à l'usage.
Prix la pièce . . . **0** fr.**30**

IMP. EUGÈNE VERNEAU, 108, R. FOLIE-MÉRICOURT. — PARIS

BATH ROOM FITTINGS

Plate 1524-B.

NICKEL-PLATED CAST BRASS SPONGE HOLDER.

Size of dish, 5¾ x 7 inches.

Price, each..$2. 50

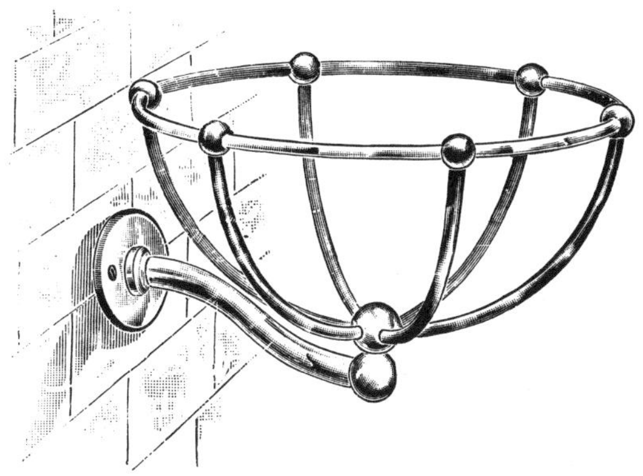

Plate 1526-B.

NICKEL-PLATED BRASS SPONGE HOLDER.

Size of dish, 7½ x 7½ inches.

Price, each..$1. 75

Plate 1528-B.

NICKEL-PLATED BRASS SOAP AND SPONGE HOLDER for roll-rim bath tub.

Size of sponge dish, 5¾ x 7 inches.
Size of soap dish, 3¼ x 5½ inches.

Price, each..$5. 00

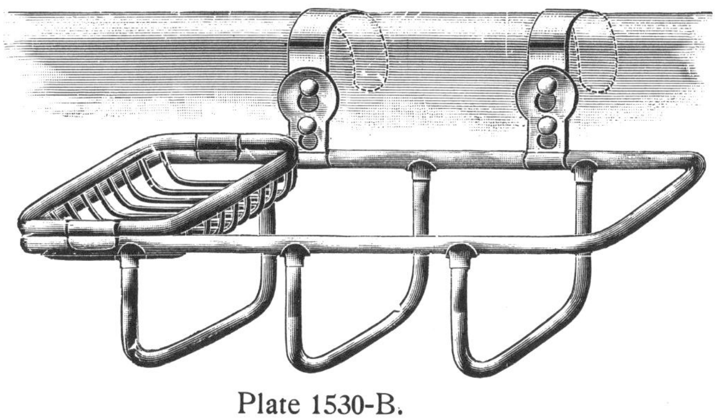

Plate 1530-B.

NICKEL-PLATED BRASS WIRE SOAP AND SPONGE HOLDER for roll-rim bath tub.

Price, each..$1. 50

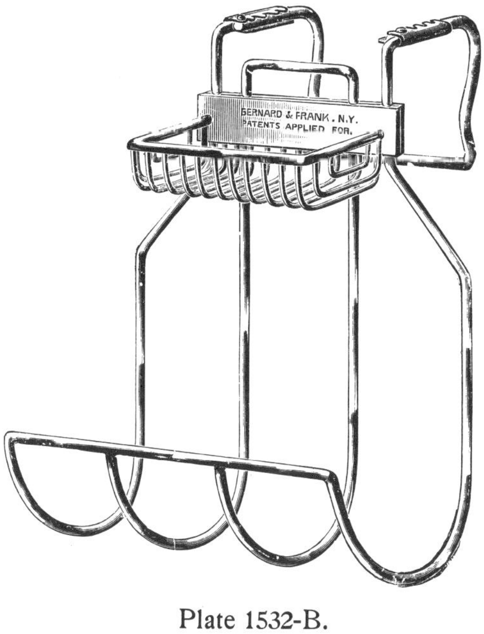

Plate 1532-B.

NICKEL-PLATED BRASS WIRE ADJUSTABLE SOAP AND SPONGE HOLDER for roll-rim bath tub.

Price, each..$2.25

F. W. WEBB MANUFACTURING CO. BOSTON. TRADE MARK

LAVATORY FITTINGS

Plate 846-B.

NICKEL-PLATED (No. 2) CHAIN STAY.

Price, per dozen.........$3.75

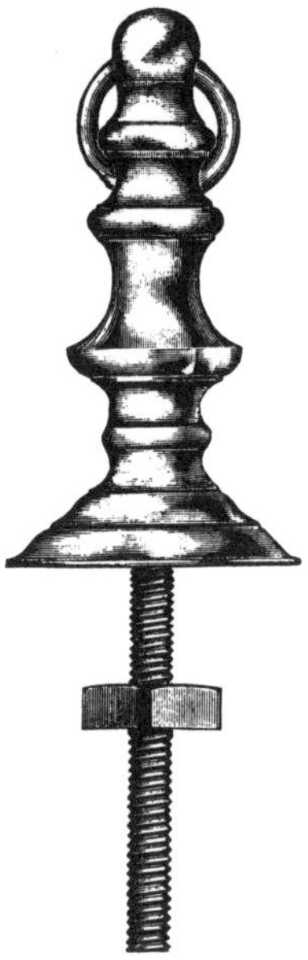

Plate 848-B.

NICKEL-PLATED (No. 4) CHAIN STAY.

Price, per dozen.........$6.50

Plate 850-B.

NICKEL-PLATED COCK HOLE CHAIN STAY.

Price, per dozen.........$4.50

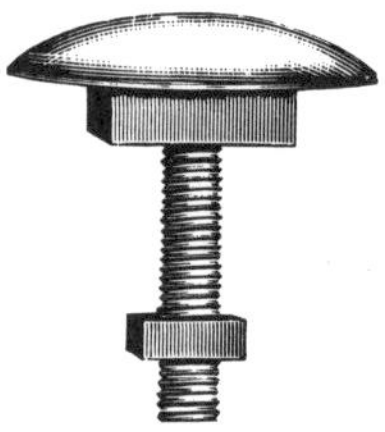

Plate 852-B.

NICKEL-PLATED COCK HOLE CAP.

Price, per dozen.........$4.25

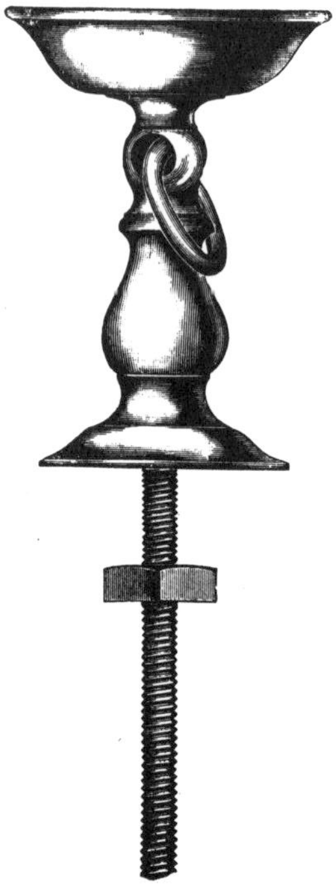

Plate 854-B.

NICKEL-PLATED (No. 6) RING CUP CHAIN STAY.

Price, per dozen.........$9.00

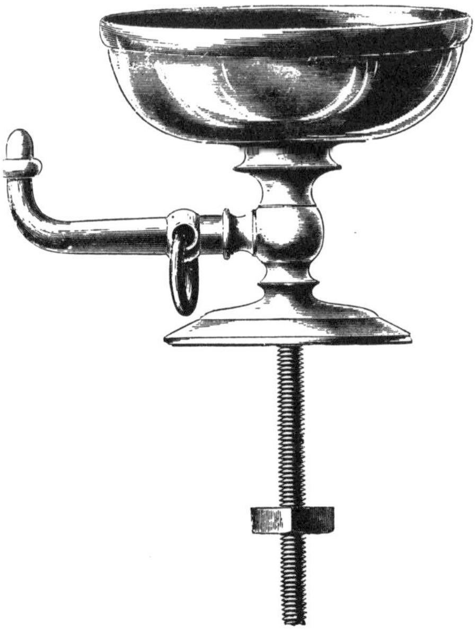

Plate 856-B.

NICKEL-PLATED JEWEL CUP AND RING HOLDER CHAIN STAY.

Price, each......................................$2.25

Plate 858-B.

NICKEL-PLATED "VENDOME" SOAP CUP CHAIN STAY with drip connection.

Price, each.......... ....$6.00

BATH ROOM FITTINGS

Plate 1550-B.

NICKEL-PLATED BRASS COMBINED TUMBLER, TOOTH BRUSH, TOOTH POWDER AND SOAP HOLDER.

Price, each.................................$4.50

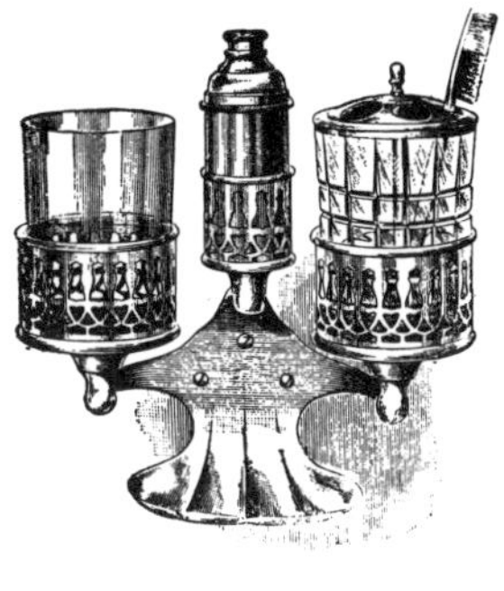

Plate 1552-B.

NICKEL-PLATED BRASS COMBINED TUMBLER, TOOTH BRUSH, TOOTH POWDER AND SOAP HOLDER.

Price, each.................................$5.00

Plate 1554-B.

NICKEL-PLATED BRASS COMBINED TUMBLER, TOOTH BRUSH AND SOAP HOLDER.

Price, each.................................$4.00

Plate 1556-B.

NICKEL-PLATED BRASS COMBINED TUMBLER AND TOOTH BRUSH HOLDER.

Price, each.................................$2.50

Plate 1558-B.

NICKEL-PLATED BRASS COMBINED TUMBLER, TOOTH BRUSH AND SOAP HOLDER

Price, each.................................$4.00

Plate 1560-B.

NICKEL-PLATED BRASS COMBINED TUMBLER AND SOAP HOLDER.

Price, each.................................$3.25

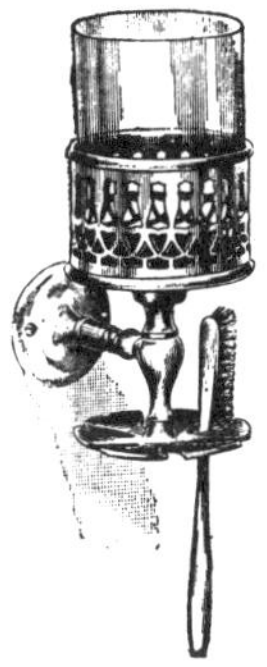

Plate 1562-B.

NICKEL-PLATED BRASS COMBINED TUMBLER AND TOOTH BRUSH HOLDER.

Price, each.................................$1.60

Plate 1564-B.

NICKEL-PLATED BRASS TOOTH BRUSH HOLDER.

Price, each.................................$1.50

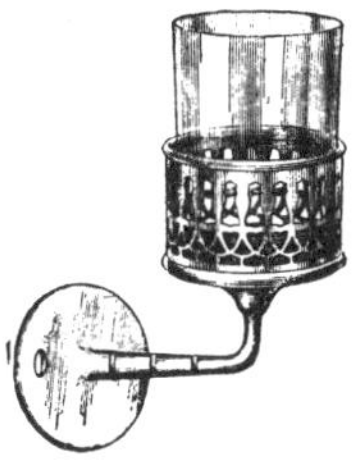

Plate 1566-B.

NICKEL-PLATED BRASS TUMBLER HOLDER.

Price, each.................................$1.00

Tumblers are included in above prices.

BATH ROOM FITTINGS

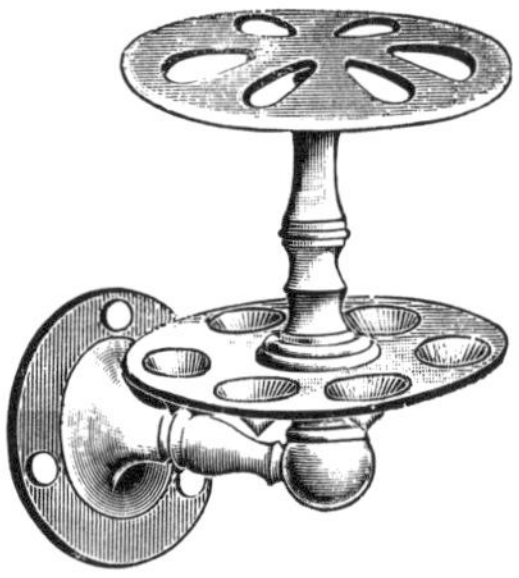

Plate 1568-B.

NICKEL-PLATED BRASS TOOTH BRUSH HOLDER.

Price, each...$2.00

Plate 1570-B.

NICKEL-PLATED BRASS TUMBLER HOLDER.

Price, each (without glass)..$1.00

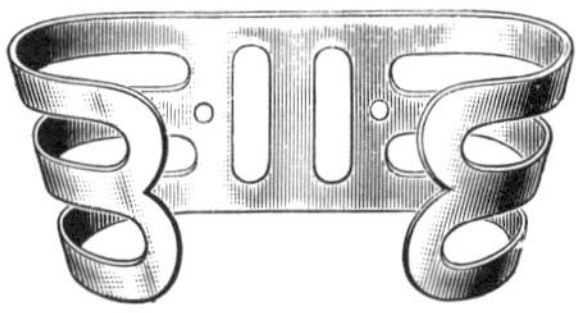

Plate 1572-B.

NICKEL-PLATED BRASS WHISK BROOM HOLDER.

Price, each......................$0.50

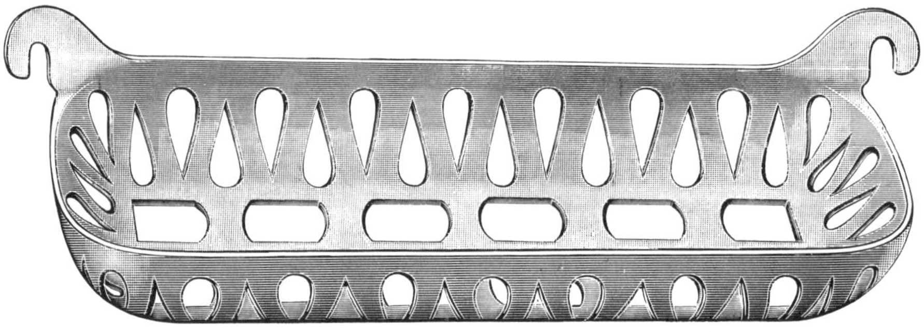

Plate 1574-B.

NICKEL-PLATED BRASS TOOTH AND NAIL BRUSH HOLDER.

Size, 8 x 3 inches.

Price, each...$2.00

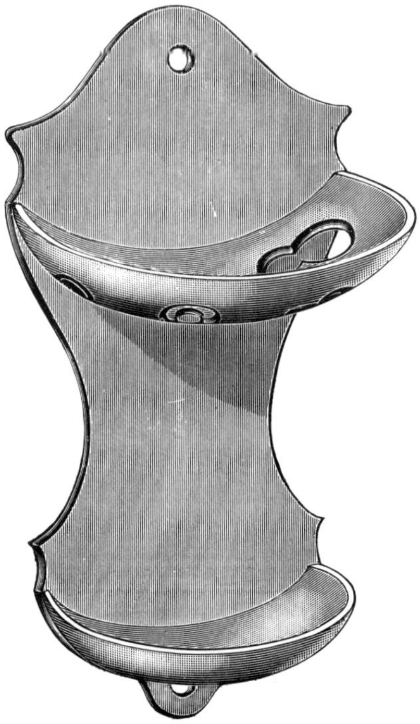

Plate 1576-B.

NICKEL-PLATED CAST BRASS TOOTH BRUSH HOLDER.

Price, each..........................$1.75

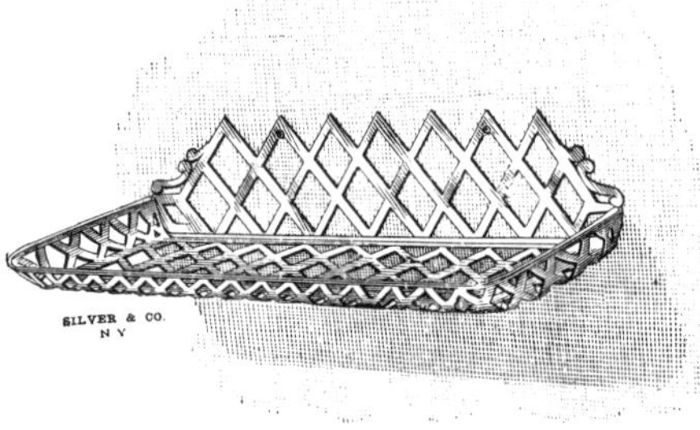

Plate 1578-B.

NICKEL-PLATED BRASS COMB AND BRUSH TRAY.

Size, 11 x 4 inches.

Price, each..$2.50

BATH ROOM FITTINGS

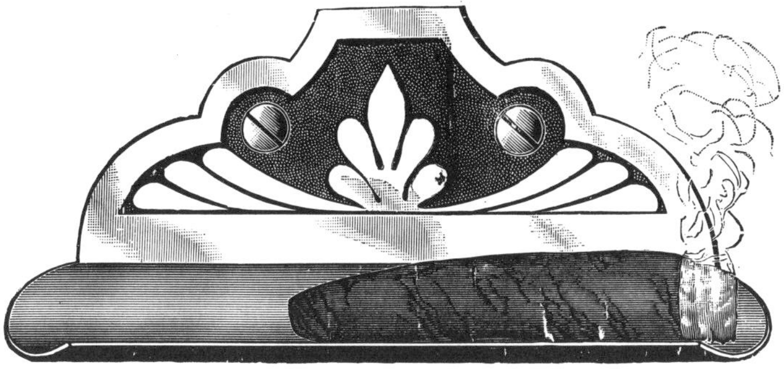

Plate 1580-B.

NICKEL-PLATED CAST BRASS CIGAR REST.

(Cut is full size.)

Prize, each...$0. 50

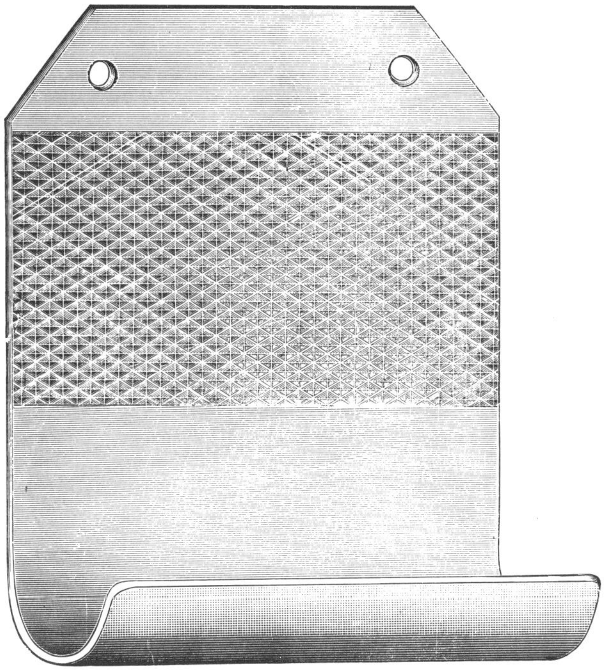

Plate 1582-B.

NICKEL-PLATED BRASS CIGAR REST AND MATCH SCRATCHER.

(Cut is full size.)

Price, each...$0. 50

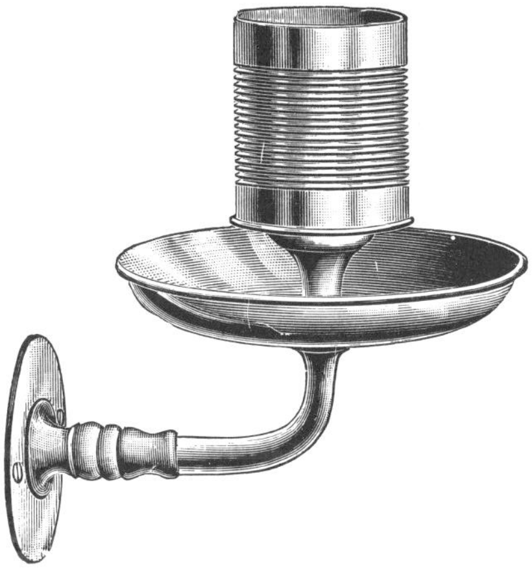

Plate 1584-B.

NICKEL-PLATED BRASS MATCH HOLDER.

Price, each...$1. 50

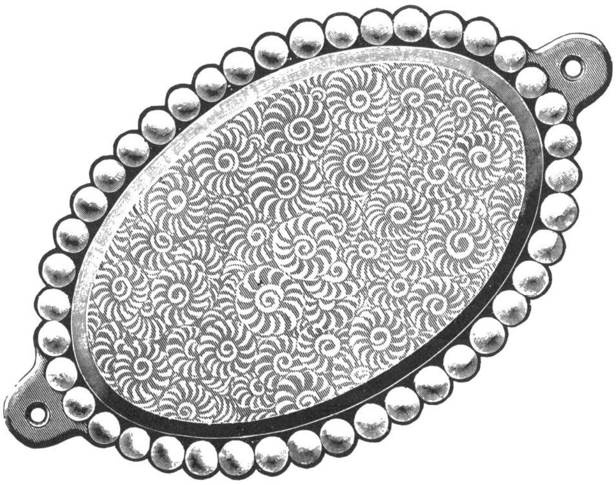

Plate 1586-B.

NICKEL-PLATED BRASS CORAL MATCH SCRATCHER.

(Cut is full size.)

Price, each...$0. 35

Plate 1588-B.

NICKEL-PLATED BRASS MATCH HOLDER.

Price, each...$1. 75

CLUB, HOTEL, OR RETIRING ROOM LAVATORIES.

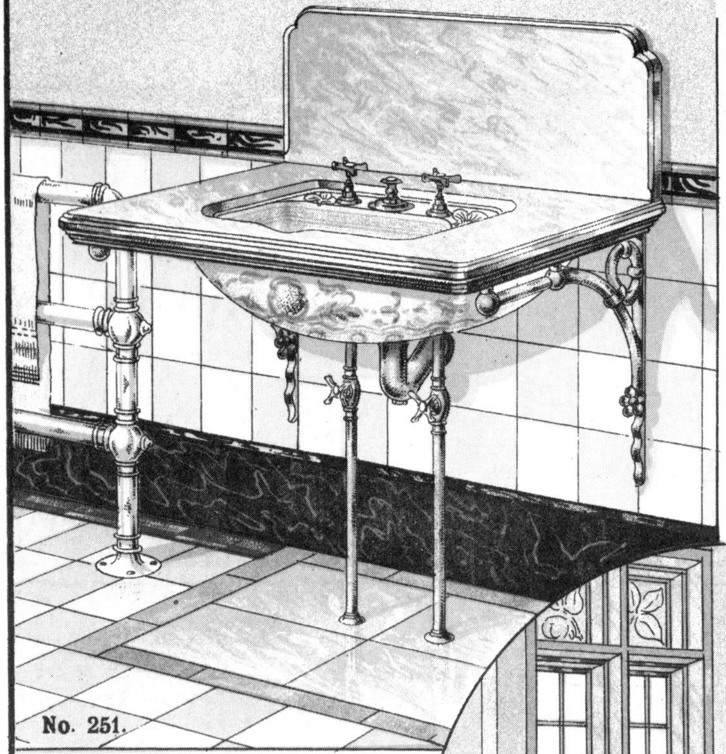

No. 251.

PATENTED AND REGISTERED LAVOZONIC.

No. **251.**—Lavatory, comprises No. 154 Patent Embossed Lavozonic, Decorated in Colors (no Gold) inside and outside; Hot and Cold Screw-down Taps, Quick Waste, 1½" Clearway P Trap, and Polished Copper Supply Pipes fitted with Stop Taps; White Veined Marble Top, 2' 10" × 2' 2" × 1¼", Moulded Edges, and ¾" × 12" Skirting, Chamfered Edges, supported upon Polished Brass Brackets and Moulded Beading.

Price complete **£16 13 9**

Nickel-plating Brass Work... ... **30/-** extra.

No. **252.**—Lavatory is made with 1¼" Marble Top, 3' 0" × 2' 2"; Moulded Marble Frieze, and the Skirting, which is ¾" thick, extends from floor to 12" above top. The Legs and Brackets are in Polished Brass, and the Bowl is No. 154a Patent Lavozonic, fitted with Polished Brass Trap and Supply Bends.

Price **£15 15 0**

Nickel-plating Fittings, Legs and Trap... ... ... **25/-** extra.

No. **253.** — Polished Marble, Framed, Bevelled Edge Mirror, Walnut or Mahogany Setting, and Polished Brass Mounts.

Size outside ... 3' 0" × 3' 0"

Price **£6 15 0**

Dished Veined Marble Soleplate, 3' 0" × 2' 3" ... **51/-** extra.

For prices of Towel Rails, see page 97.

No. 253.—Mirror.

No. 252.

CHAPTER SIX

PUBLIC BATHROOMS

The concept of public bathing was established in the ancient world. The Romans built bath complexes all over the empire, from the Baths of Titus (AD 80) and the Baths of Caracalla (AD 211), to the baths built around the hot springs at Bath in Somerset in the first century AD. By the sixteenth century there were bath houses in London, including one in Bagnio Court in Newgate, which was said to have had the first baths in England supplied with artificially heated water.

Spa towns such as Bath, Buxton and Cheltenham developed in the eighteenth century as fashionable resorts for the leisured classes, for whom 'taking the waters' (which meant sipping a glass of sulphurous spring water, rather than immersing oneself in it) was a social occasion. It was not until the mid-nineteenth century that the lack of washing facilities for the poor was taken seriously. In 1832, one Catherine Wilkinson of Liverpool 'began to lend her room and appliances to poor people for washing'; the City Council took over responsibility for providing this service in 1844. In the same year, public baths and wash-houses for the poor were established by a Mr. Bowie in the London Docks. Two years later Parliament passed an Act to encourage the establishment of public baths and wash-houses 'for the health, comfort and welfare of the inhabitants of populous towns and districts in England and Ireland'.

These early public baths were not swimming pools, but individual baths for people who had no facilities for washing at home. Because the essential problems of securing a supply of clean, hot water and adequate drainage were the same whether it was people or their clothes that were being washed, laundry and personal bathing facilities were frequently installed in the same building. Later, these could be found alongside swimming pools, making an explicit connection between personal hygiene and general physical fitness.

The Victorian period also saw the development of numerous new building types which all required public bathrooms. In institutions such as prisons, asylums and hospitals, security and economy were essential. Doulton's improved combined bath fittings 'For Asylums, Hospitals, Public Baths, etc.' were typical of the products designed to meet these needs: 'so constructed that the bather has no control over supplies or waste. Where large numbers of people have to be accommodated, it is essential that the Baths fill and empty very rapidly. Special attention has been paid to this important feature.'

The new, purpose-built pubs, large hotels, and railway stations of the Victorian age created a demand for luxurious, colourful and impressive bathrooms which gave the manufacturers ample scope for invention. Polished marble, brightly coloured tiles and gleaming pipework were lavished on luxurious washroom interiors. The design of urinals for public buildings also became a notable sub-discipline of the sanitary engineer's trade. While the inmates of prisons and workhouses lined up to use pressed metal troughs, their clubland counterparts enjoyed the privacy of gleaming stalls of 'St. Anne's marble' (a kind of ceramic) with footplate-operated flushes and engraved glass tanks mounted overhead to serve as cisterns.

LAVATORIES FOR SCHOOLS AND PUBLIC INSTITUTIONS.

No. **21**. — Lavatory, comprises Polished Slate Top and Skirting, No. 67 Bowl, 13″ inside, and Unremovable Plug, Hot and Cold No. 46 Taps, Cast-iron Brackets and Open Waste Trough.

Price complete, **48/6** per person, for 2 or more.

Without Hot Tap, **6/9** less each.

Also made with Standards instead of Brackets at same Price.

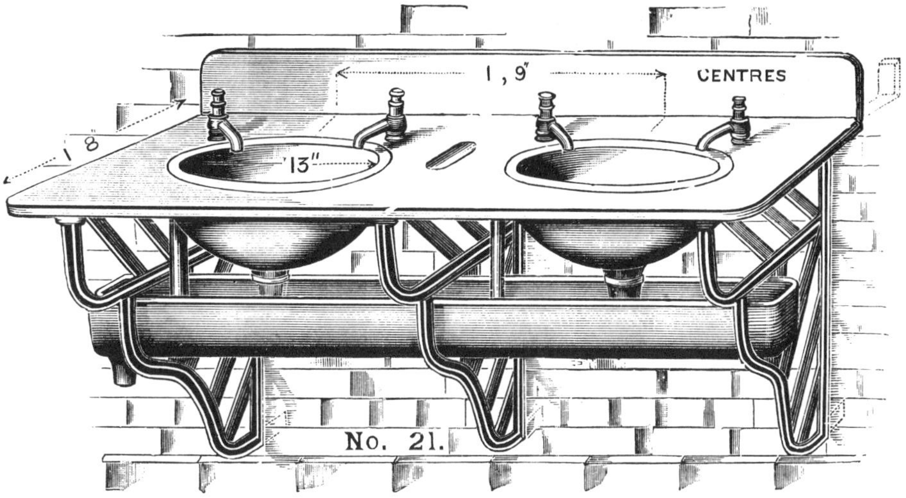

No. 21.

No. **20**.—Lavatory, Slate Top and Skirting, Earthenware Tip-up Bowl and Receiver, Self-closing Tap, side inlet, Cast-iron Standards, Waste Pipe, and Wrought-iron Framing.

Price, **66/-** per person, for 2 or more.

Hot Tap, **6/9** each extra.

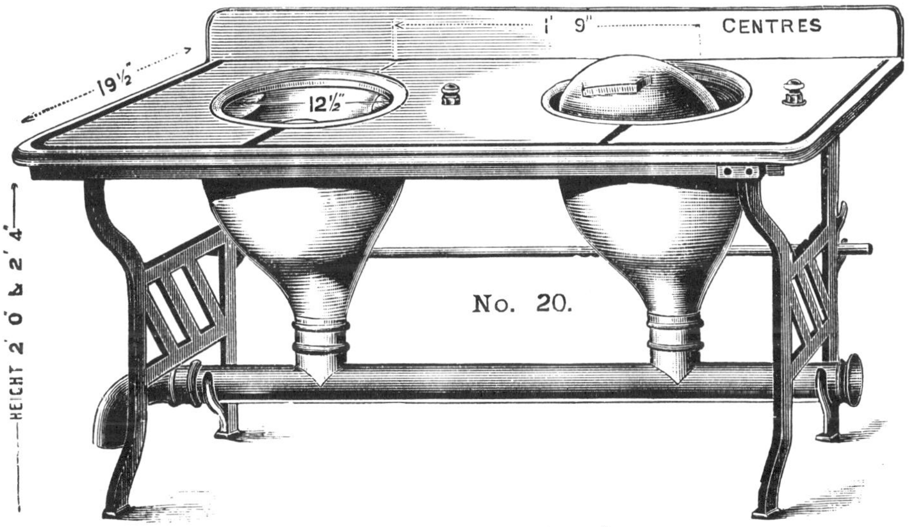

No. 20.

No. **24**.—Cast-iron Tip-up Lavatory Range, 14″ Bowl, having No. 179 Self-closing Cold Water Tap, Waste Pipe and Standards.

Price per person, for 2 or more—

Painted.	Top, Skirting, Receiver, and Bowl Porcelain Enamelled.
41/9	**79/3**

If with No. 42 Tap instead of No. 179, **2/4** each less.

Porcelain Enamelling Interior of Waste Pipe or Trough, **3/-** per person extra.

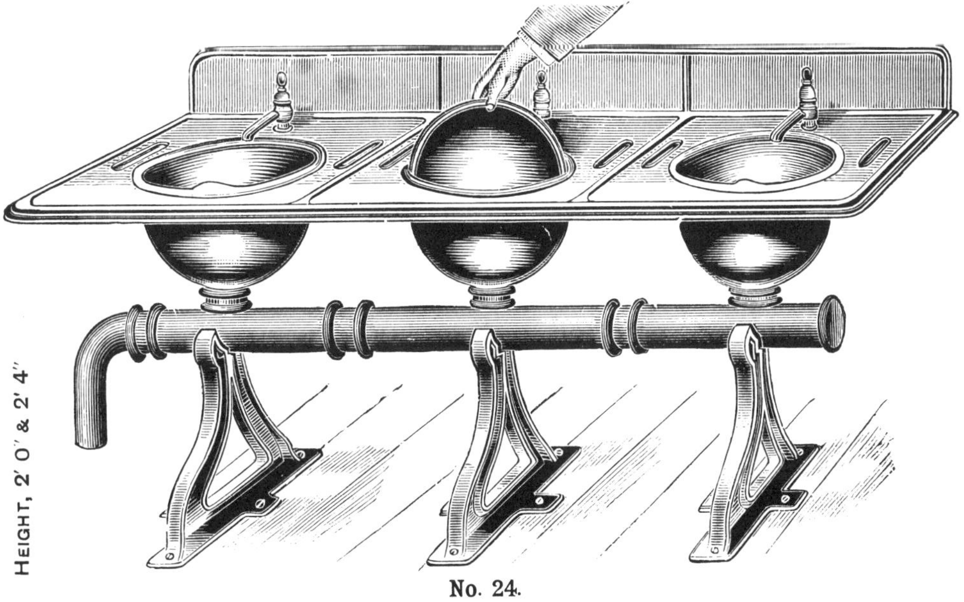

No. 24.

DOULTON'S SPECIAL BATH FITTINGS FOR ASYLUMS, HOSPITALS, PUBLIC BATHS, Etc.

No. 232.

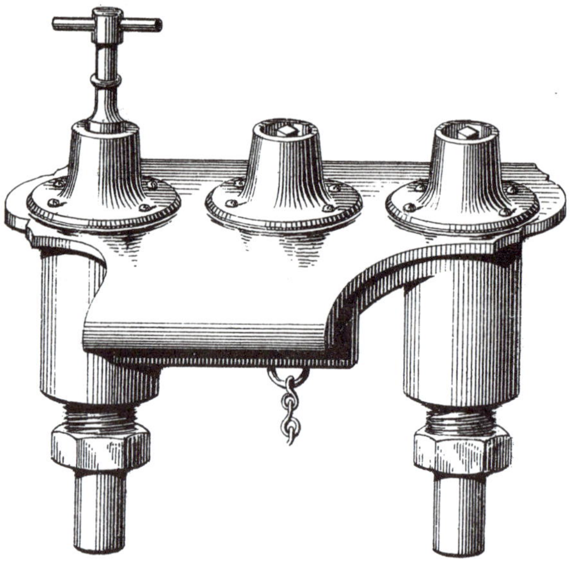

No. 232A.

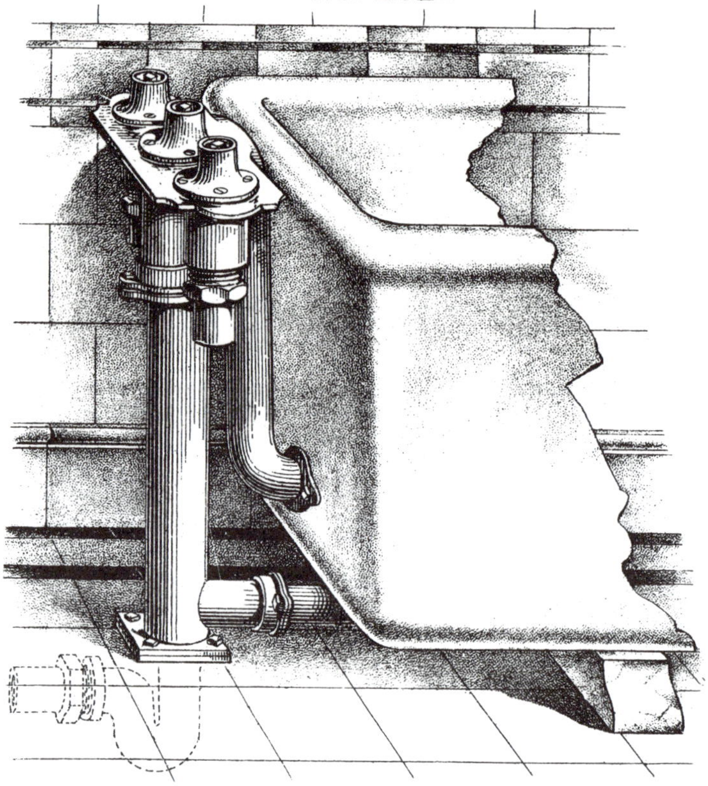

THESE Fittings have been designed to meet the requirements of Hospitals, Asylums, Workhouses, etc., and are so constructed that the bather has no control over supplies or waste. Where large numbers of people have to be accommodated, it is essential that the Baths fill and empty very rapidly. Special attention has been paid to this important feature.

PRICES.

No. 232. —Fittings complete as shown, with 1 in. Polished Brass Plate and Valves, and Cast-Iron Waste Pipe, - - - - - - - - - - - - - - - -	£4 8 0
No. 232A.—Fittings complete as shown, with Polished Brass Plate, and Inlet to Bath as drawing,	4 15 0

A Copper Waste and Brass Hollow Plug may be had with either of the above, £1 1s. extra,

If Waste is not required for the above, 15/- less.

PLUGS, WASHERS, AND CHAINS.

	Brass.	Plated.
No. 235.—2½ in. Plug, Washer, and Chains for Earthenware Baths, - - - -	£0 16 0	£0 19 0
Do., 3 in. Do., do., do., - - -	1 0 6	1 4 6
Do., 4 in. Do., do., do., - - -	1 8 0	1 13 0

For Designs of Tiling see pages 4, 6, 38, 57, 58, 59, 60, 61, 157, 158.

MORRISON, INGRAM & CO., MANCHESTER.

HOTEL, CLUB, OR BANK LAVATORIES.

No. 22.—Towel Rail. No. 126.—Lavatory.

No. 125.—Lavatory. No. 34.—Towel Rail.

No. 126.—Lavatory, 1½" Sicilian Marble Top, 5' 0" × 1' 11", Chamfered Edges, 6" × ⅜" Skirting, Fluted Soap Sinking; 17" Fire-clay D Bowls, Enamelled White Interior, and Waste Arrangement, ½" Hot and Cold No. 61 Taps; Cast-iron Brackets, Frieze and Shields, Enamel Painted and picked out in colors.

Price complete, for 2 persons, £14 10.

No. 125.—Lavatory with 1½" Sicilian Marble Top, 5' 0" × 1' 11", Chamfered Edges, ⅜" Skirting, 1' 4" high, and 4" × ⅜" Shelf and Brackets, Fluted Soap Sinking; 17" Fire-clay D Bowls, Enamelled White Interior, and Waste Arrangement, ½" No. 61 Hot and Cold Taps; Cast-iron Frieze and Standard with Shields, Enamel Painted and picked out in colors.

Price complete, for 2 persons, £15 16 6

White Hygeia Metal or Nickel-plating Fittings, 3/5 per Bowl extra.

If without Shields, 18/- per pair less.

If with 1½" Brass Trap, 4/6 each extra.

No. 22.—Polished Copper Towel Rail. Price, 99/-.

No. 34.—Polished Copper Towel Rail. Price, 105/-.

Nickel-plating either, 18/- extra.

LAVATORIES MADE SPECIALLY TO ORDER.

Complete Schemes prepared on receipt of indication of requirements.

JOHN HEYWOOD, CHROMO LITHO. MANCHESTER, LONDON, BRISTOL, LIVERPOOL.

SHANKS' URINALS.

SINGLE, AND IN RANGES OF EVERY DESCRIPTION.

No. 4 Angle Urinal,

With Lipped Basin, with Treadle-action Supply.

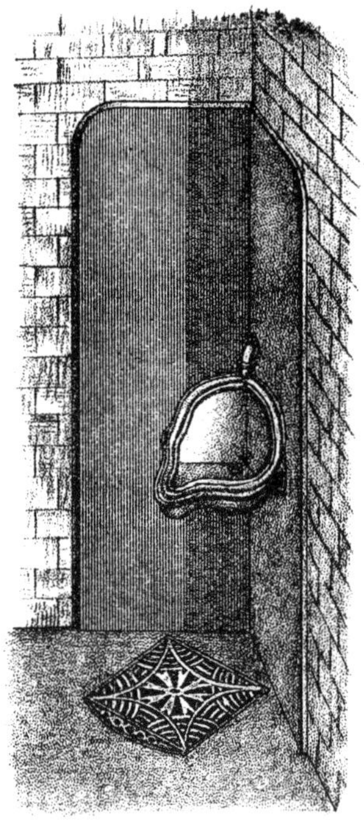

Other varieties of Angle Urinals on application.

No. 3 Urinal Range,

In Plain or Enamelled Slate, and White Porcelain Basins.

Supplied either continuously, by Self-closing Valves, or by Treadle-action Valves.

No. 3 Urinal, with or without Tiles.

The Divisions are raised from the ground and sustained by Iron Brackets. The floor may be made of Tiles, and Grating fixed to drain the surface water.

SELF-ACTING TREADLES,

FOR URINALS.

No. 5,

With Galvanized Iron Top or Polished Brass Top and Supply-Valve, complete.

No. 6,

In Galvanized Iron, with Ornamental Tile-top and Supply-Valve, as shewn.

SECTION.

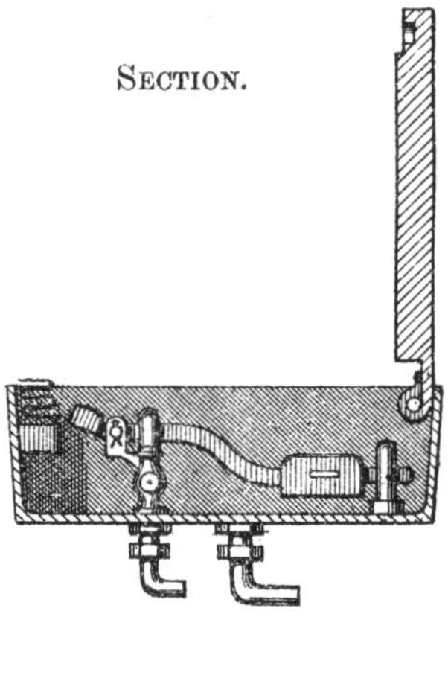

SHANKS' IMPROVED URINALS.

No. 13 Range,

In Plain Slate, Enamelled Slate, or Polished Marble, with Shanks' Improved No. 29 Urinal Basin, No. 9 Automatic Supply-Cistern, in White Earthenware; Nickel-Plated Down-Pipes, Strong Fireclay-Enamelled Gutter, and Nickel-Plated Brass Pillars for supporting Slabs, complete.

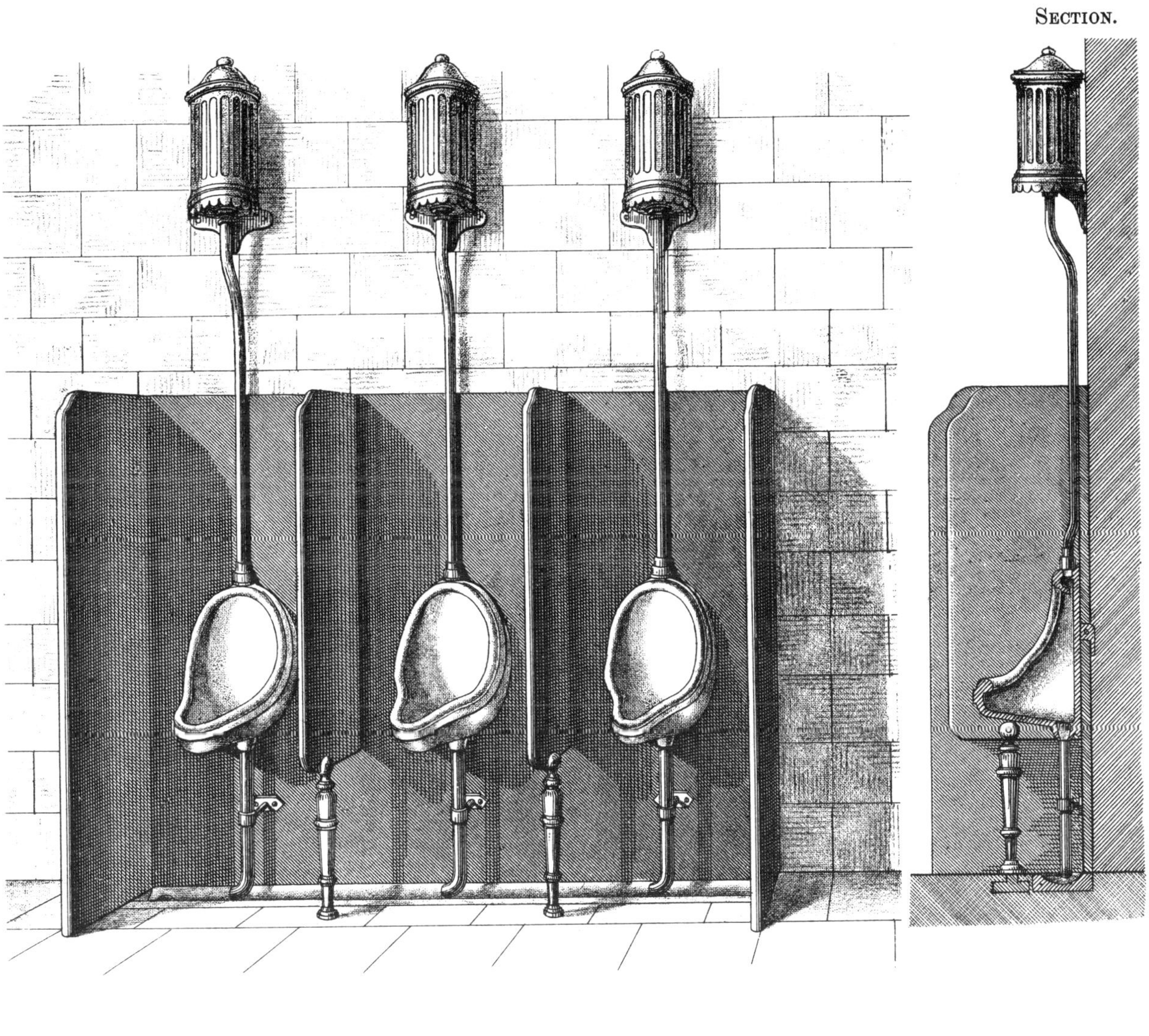

The above method of supporting Slabs is much superior to the ordinary method, as it is better for ventilation and for the cleanliness of the floor. The above Range, with St. Ann's Marble Backs, White Veined Divisions, and Nickel-Plated Pipes and Pillars, makes a really beautiful and Sanitary job.

SHANKS' URINALS FOR PUBLIC PLACES.

No. 7 Urinal,

For fixing against Wall.

The principle of this Urinal is as follows:—A centre Urinal Pan, common to all the divisions, is continuously full of water, which is as continuously refreshed and replenished by means of a Tap kept running into it, either a drop-by-drop or a larger supply as may be wished. This overflows down the Overflow-Valve Plunger arranged for the purpose.

A Grating, communicating with the Trap, is arranged on floor.

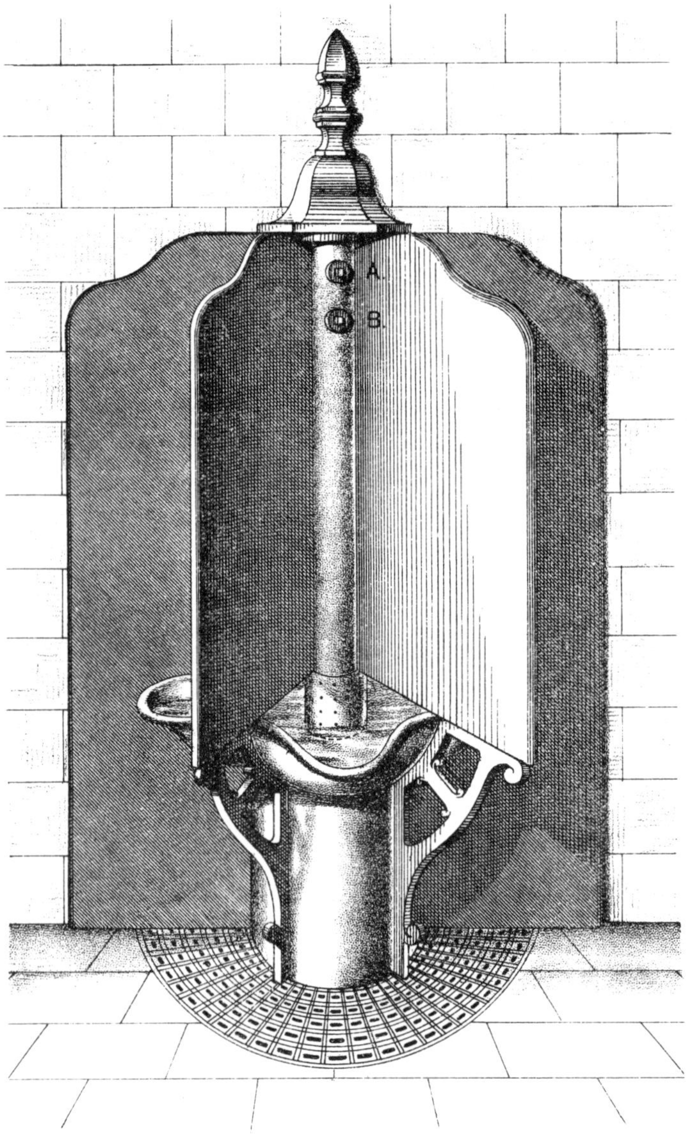

Centre Pillar and Urinal Pan is made of Porcelain-Enamelled Iron. Division and Back Slabs are usually Slate, Plain or Enamelled. **A** is a Brass Spindle, wrought by a key kept by attendant, for regulating Tap which supplies water to Urinal. **B** is a similar Spindle for lifting Overflow Plunger or Valve when it is desirable to empty the Urinal Pan.

PLAN.

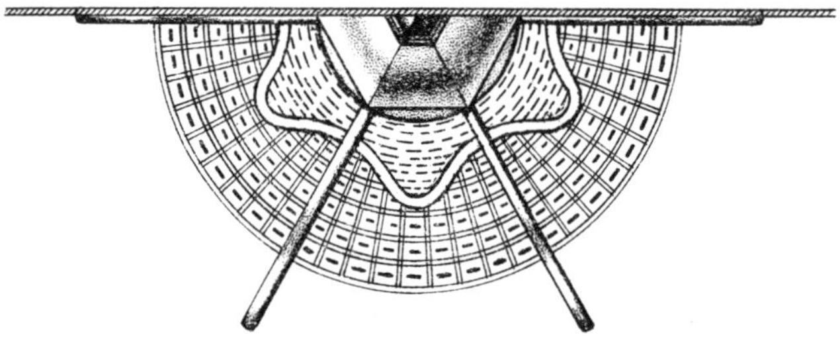

These Urinals have been largely used in Public Places, with very satisfactory results.

SHANKS' URINALS FOR PUBLIC PLACES.

No. 8 Urinal.

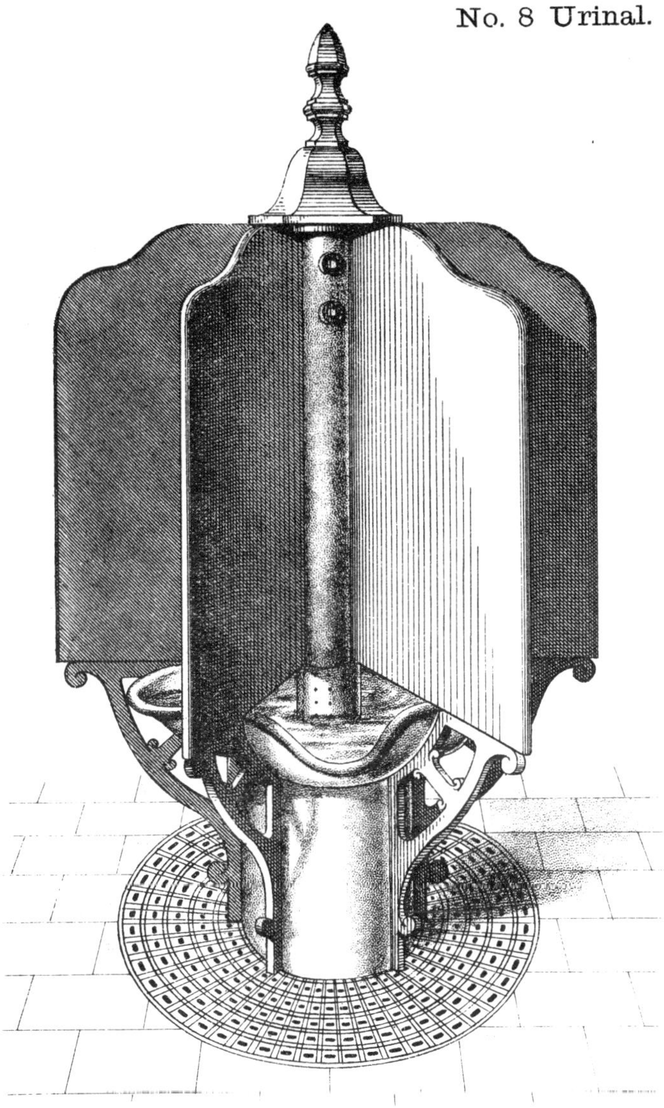

This Urinal is substantially the same as No. 7, only that it is arranged for Six persons, to stand in the middle of a floor.

The Iron-work may be entirely Galvanised or simply Painted.

The Centre Pillar and Pan may be White Porcelain-Enamelled, or enamelled with Shanks' Special Glass Enamel.

The Slate Slabs may be Plain Rubbed, or Metallic-Enamelled.

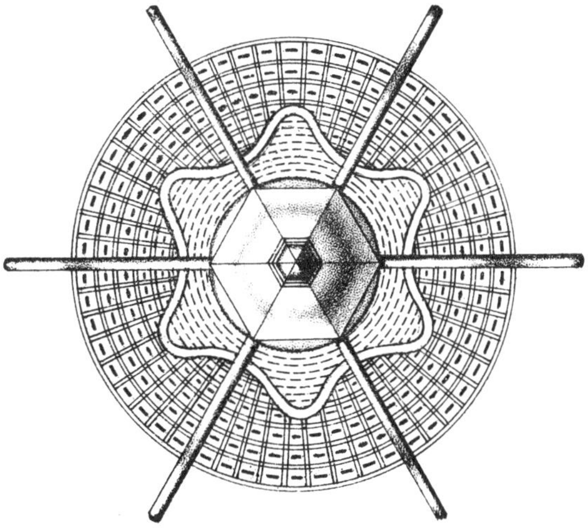

This Urinal may be supplied either with Slate Slabs right down to the floor, or with Cast-Iron Brackets, as shewn.

Price in each case will be the same.

DOULTON'S
IMPROVED CIRCULAR-BACKED URINALS.

No. 460.

THE drawing given below illustrates the method of erecting this Urinal in the centre of a room. In many cases the wall space is desired for closets and lavatories, and under such conditions independent Urinals are necessary. The outside diameter is only about 6 ft., so no great space is required.

The Urinal requires no extra support or centre column; it is compact, strong, and handsome in appearance.

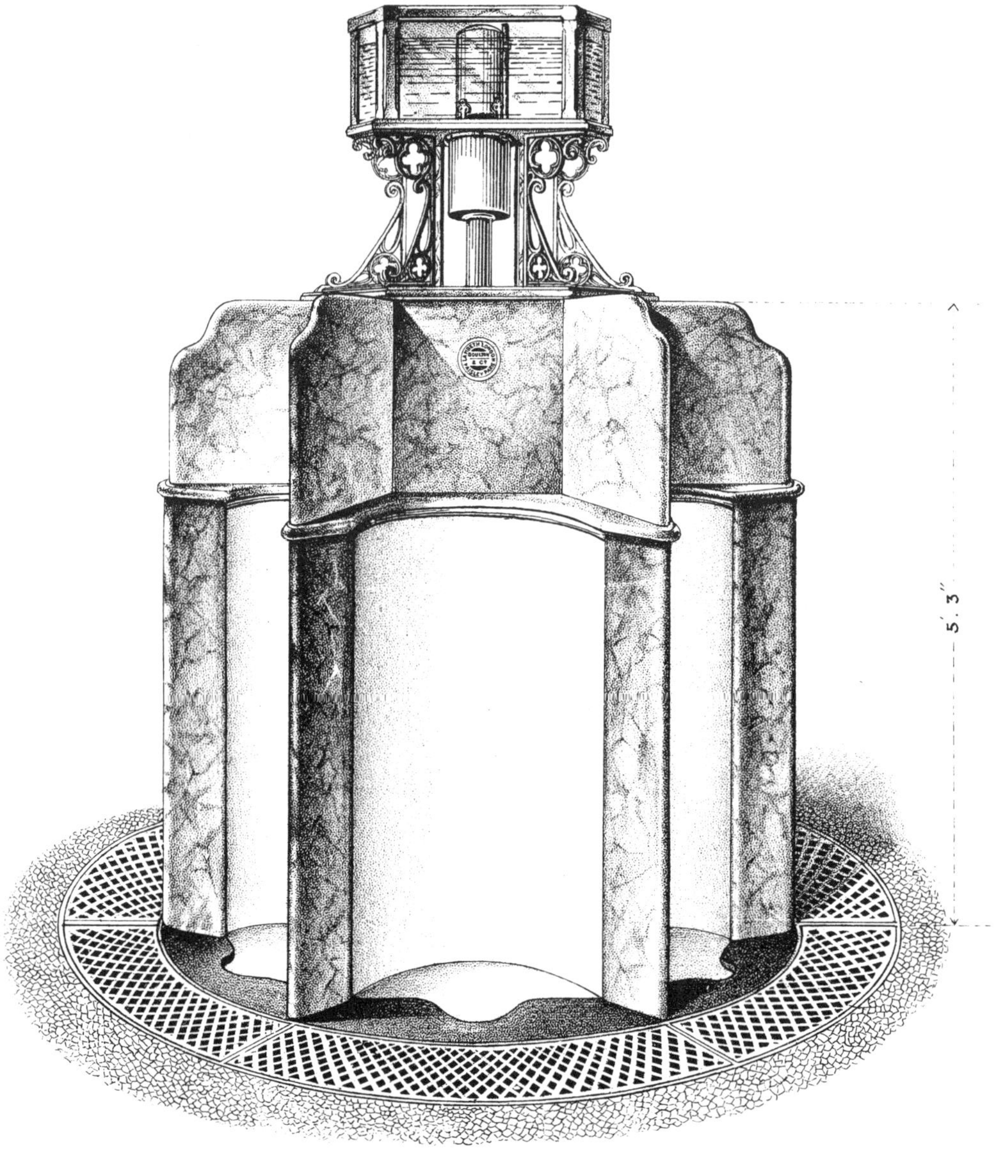

For Prices, see pages 178 and 179.

DOULTON'S IMPROVED PUBLIC URINAL.

No. 204.

THIS Design is very suitable for a Street Urinal where space is not limited. The interior portion is of Hexagonal form, and may be had either as No. 137, No. 460, or No. 198 in list. The Screen is composed of Slate Panels, supported by Cast-Iron Columns which are arranged so that a Panel can be removed without interference with the roof or grating. The roof is made of Wrought-Iron Framing, and covered with thick glass, with a grating in the centre for ventilation and gas lamp as shown.

These Enclosures are fitted up before being despatched, and each part marked so as to avoid any difficulty in fixing, and a template showing position of the holes for columns is sent with the work.

PLAN No. 204,
with No. 460 or No. 137 Urinal.

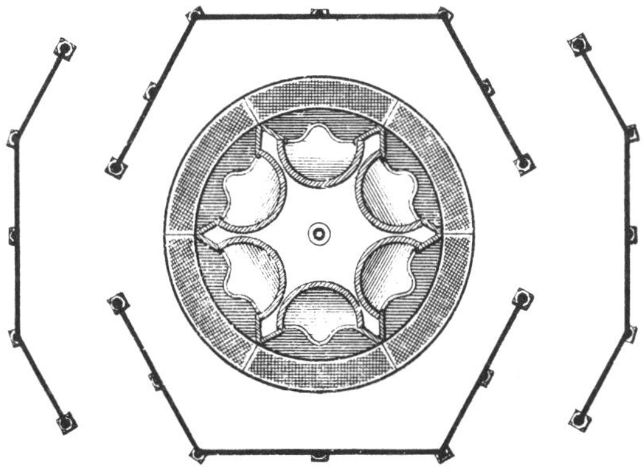

PLAN No. 204,
with No. 198 Urinal.

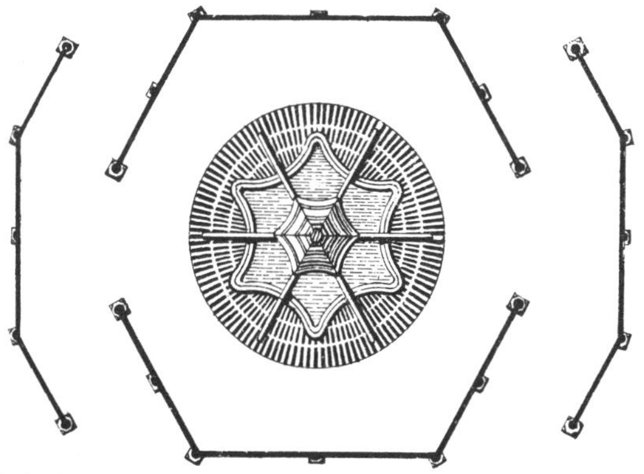

Price complete, including	No. 460 Urinal, Plain Slate and Galvanized-Iron Tank,				-	£155	0	0
Do.,	do.,	No. 137	do.,	do.,	do.,	143	0	0
Do.,	do.,	No. 198 Urinal, with Plain Slate,	-	-	-	117	10	0

DOULTON'S IMPROVED CAST-IRON SHELTERS

FOR TROUGH CLOSETS.

In many large Factories it is desirable to erect Closets and Urinals altogether apart from **Main Buildings**, and this method is both cheap, and economical as regards space. The Shelter forms a complete screen to the closet, and while the passage way is open at the top there is a covering above the closet seats, and also a low cast-iron division between each closet; they are made with 2·6 centres so as to allow plenty of room in each compartment, and can be supplied any length that may be required.

No. 334.

For Prices, see pages 53 and 54.

DOULTON & CO., LAMBETH, LONDON S.E., PAISLEY & PARIS.

DOULTON'S IMPROVED PUBLIC URINALS.

No. 206.

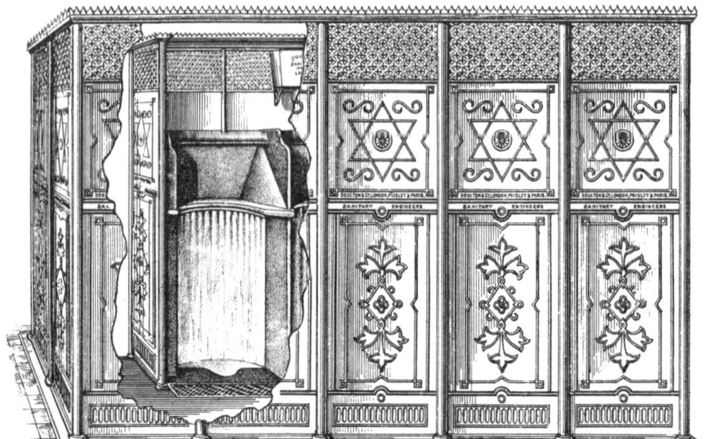

Section

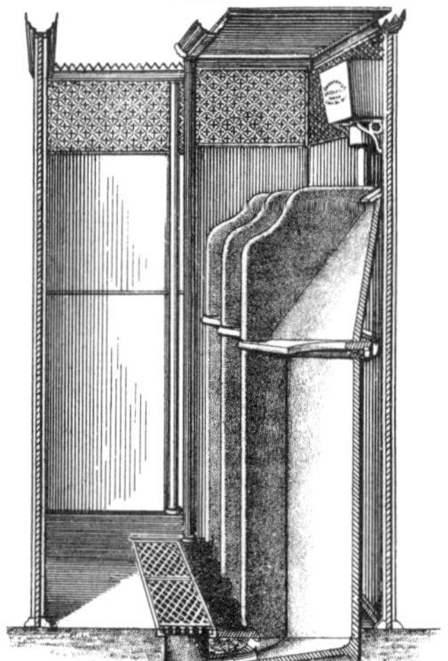

PLAN

The Urinal here shown is somewhat similar to No. 205, but in place of the combined Iron and Slate enclosure the Screen is composed entirely of Cast Iron, and is only partially covered.

In some cases these enclosures are fixed against walls, and this somewhat reduces the cost, as the whole of one side of Screen is then unnecessary.

All parts are fitted together before being despatched, and each is marked so as to avoid any difficulty in fixing; a template showing position of the holes for columns is sent with the work.

For Prices, see page 194.

DOULTON & CO., LAMBETH, LONDON S.E., PAISLEY & PARIS.

DOULTON'S IMPROVED PUBLIC URINALS.

No. 205.

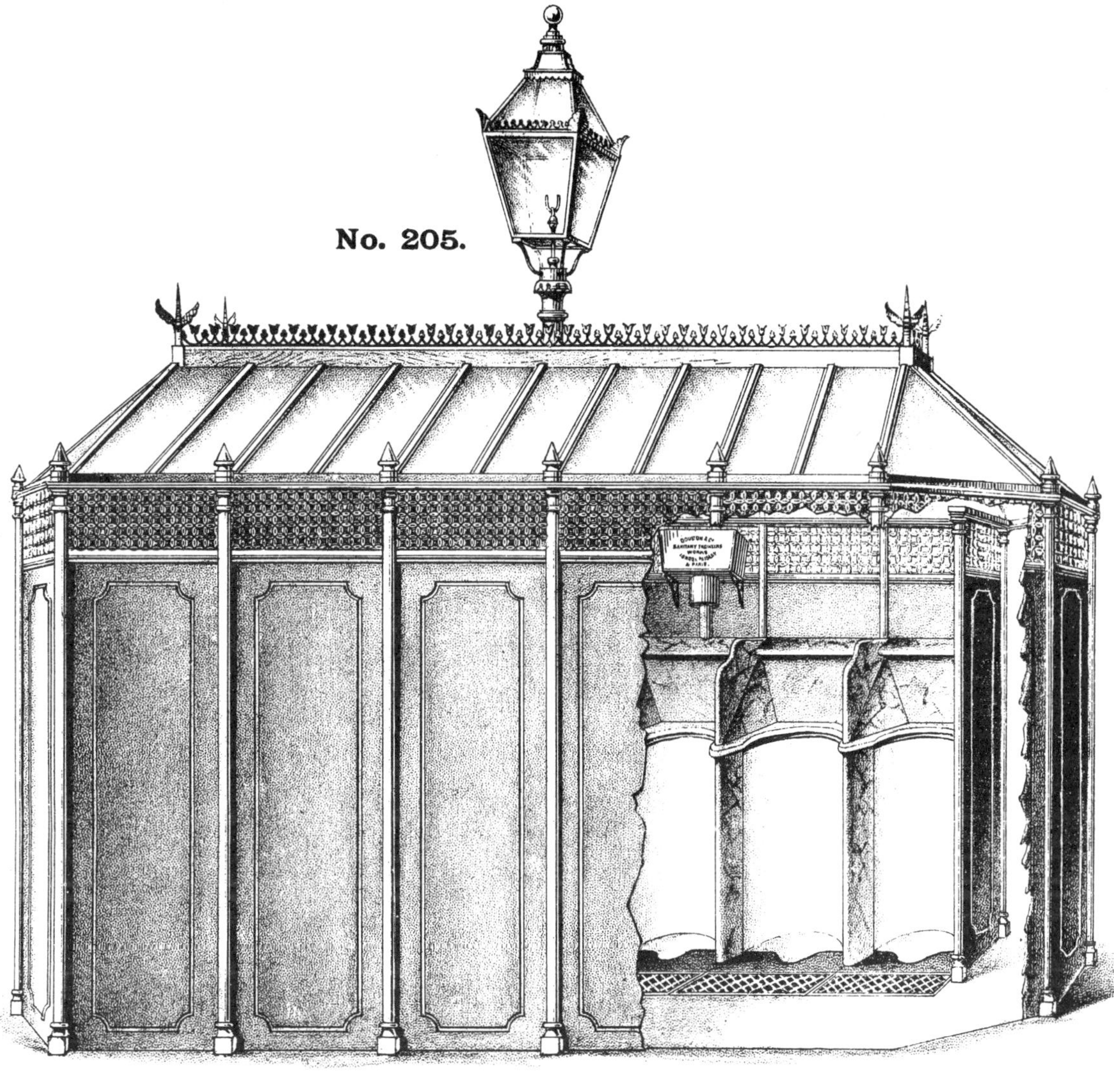

PLAN

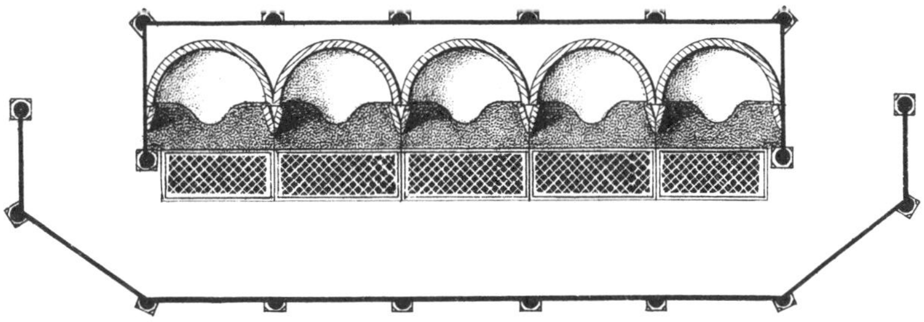

THE above design is specially adapted for narrow streets, the object being to provide the greatest accommodation in the least width.

The Screen is constructed of Slate Panels with Iron Columns, which are arranged so that a Panel can be removed without interfering with the roof or grating. The roof is made of Wrought-Iron Framing, and covered with thick glass, with a grating in the centre for ventilation and gas lamp as shown. It may be varied to suit any position.

These enclosures are fitted up before being despatched, and each part marked so as to avoid any difficulty in fixing; and a template showing position of the holes for columns is sent with the work.

These Urinals may be had for any number of persons.

For Prices, see page 192.

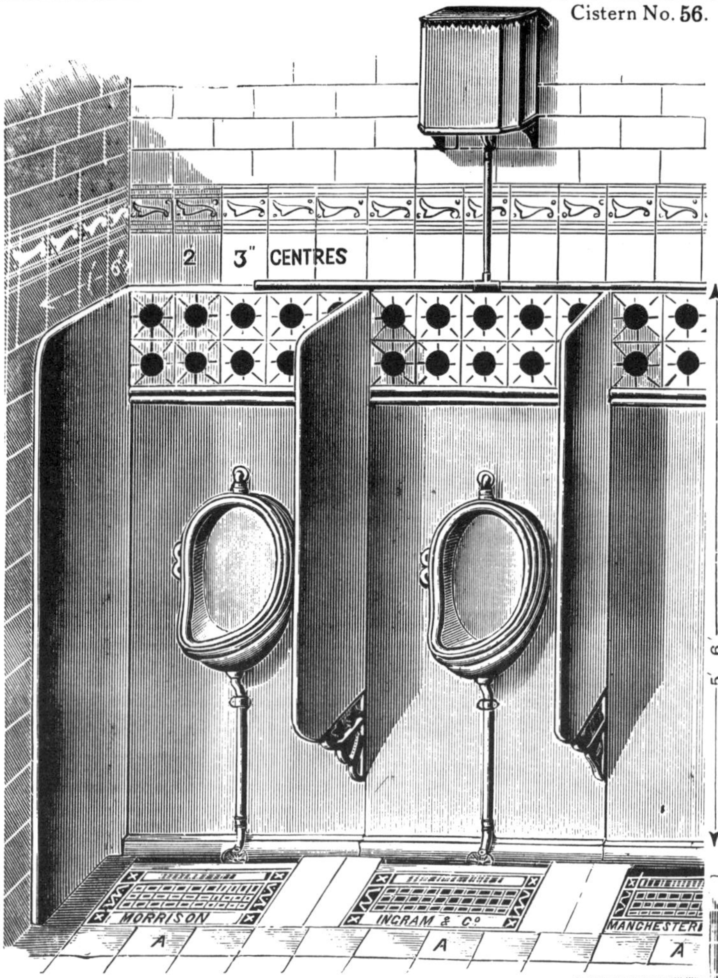

No. 54a.—Marble Urinal.

URINAL RANGES

IN SLATE & MARBLE.

No. **54A** Urinal comprises Polished White Veined Marble Back, Sides and Divisions, with or without Tiles; No. 78 Ivoryware Urinal, large size; Polished Copper Waste Pipes, Combined Soleplate and Channel, White Enamelled Fire-clay, and Cast-brass Hinged Step Grating. The flushing is by means of Polished Copper Automatic Cistern and Flush Pipes. The divisions are supported upon Cast-brass Brackets.

Price per Stall, for 2 or more ... **229/6**

If without Automatic Cistern and Flush Pipes, **193/-**

No. **55** Urinal is made in Polished Slate, Oiled. It is 5′ 6″ high; Stalls, 2′ 0″ Centres, and Divisions 1′ 5″ deep; with Combined Channel and Soleplate, Buff Glazed Fire-clay, and Cast-iron Galvanized Step Grating (A); No. 81 medium size Ivoryware Basin, polished Copper Waste Pipe and Shoe; also Cast-iron Automatic Flushing Cistern and Polished Copper Flush Pipes.

Price per Stall, for 2 or more **118/6**

If without Automatic Cistern and Flush Pipes **90/6**

If without Step Grating as B, deduct **6/8** each.

If Enamel Painted and Polished first-class, per person ... ... extra **25/-**

Other modifications of these Urinals made to order.

PARTICULARS ON APPLICATION.

No. 55.—Slate Urinal.

DOULTON'S PATENT AUTOMATIC TANKS FOR URINALS.

No. 99.

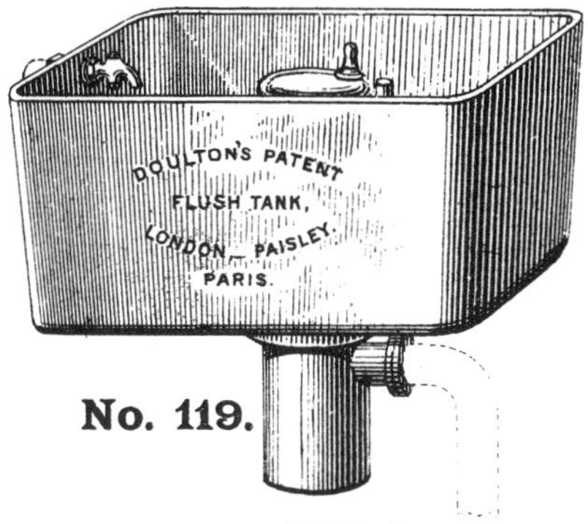

No. 119.

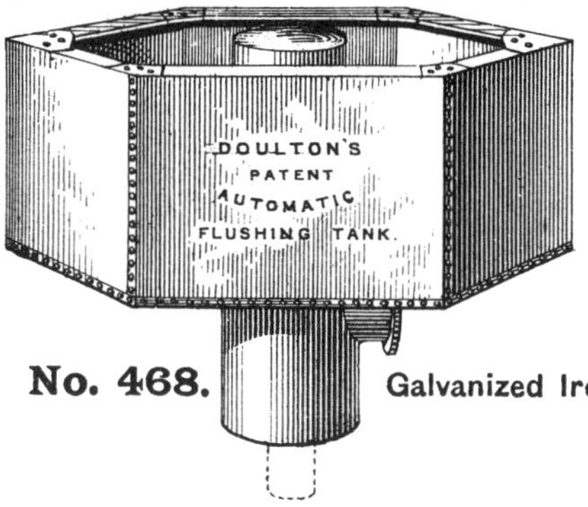

No. 468. Galvanized Iron.

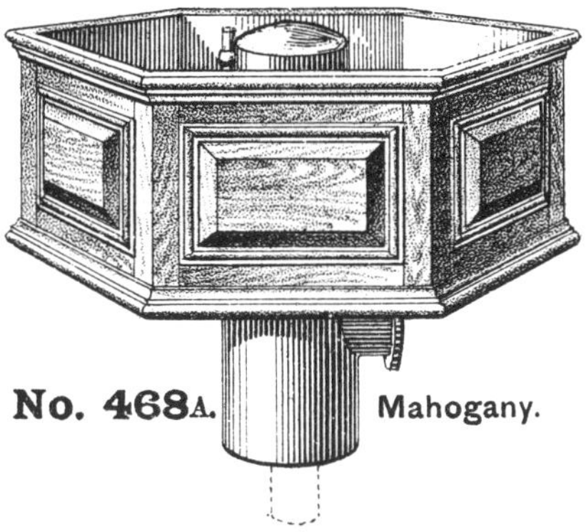

No. 468A. Mahogany.

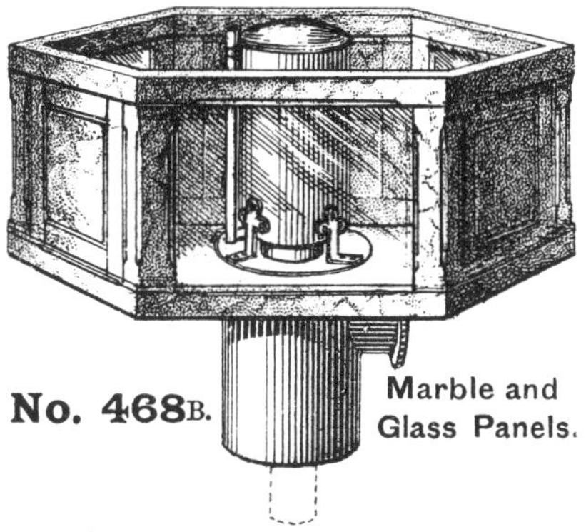

No. 468B. Marble and Glass Panels.

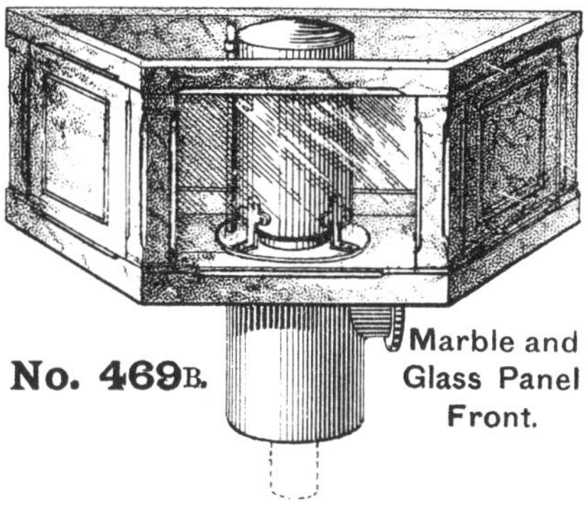

No. 469B. Marble and Glass Panel Front.

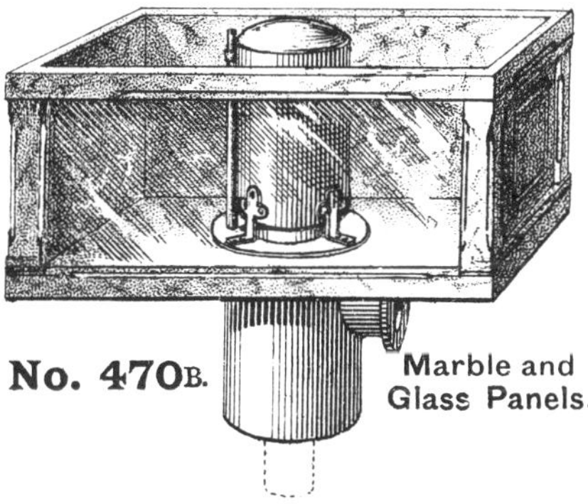

No. 470B. Marble and Glass Panels.

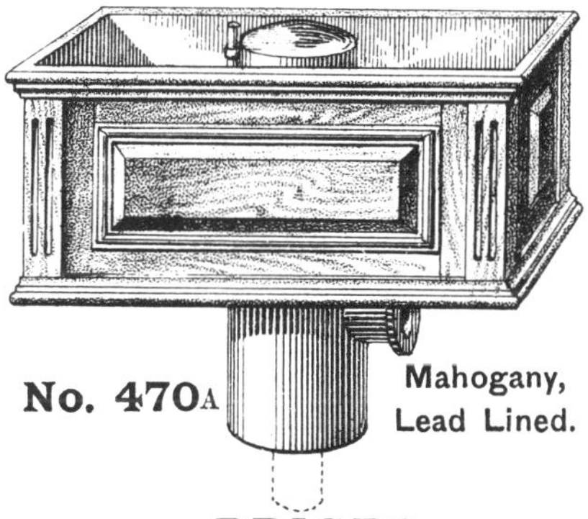

No. 470A Mahogany, Lead Lined.

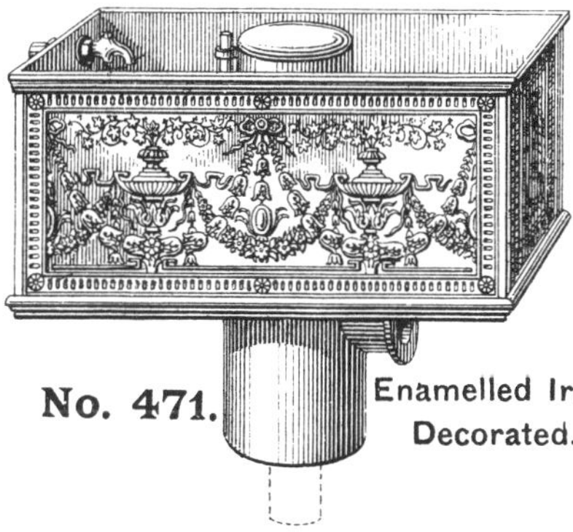

No. 471. Enamelled Iron, Decorated.

PRICES.

No. 119. —3 Gallon Galvanized Cast Iron, including Regulating Valve, - - - - - - - -	each,	£1	15	0
No. 119A.—5 Do., do., do., do., - - - - - - - -	„	2	5	0
No. 119B.—6 Do., do., do., do., - - - - - - - -	„	2	10	0
No. 99. —1 Gallon Automatic, Flat Back, in Copper, including Regulating Valve, - - - - -	„	0	18	0
No. 99A.— Do., do., Angle do., do., do., - - - - - -	„	0	18	0
No. 99B.— Do., do., Flat Back, in Galvanized Wrought Iron, including Regulating Valve, -	„	0	15	0
No. 99C.— Do., do., Angle do., do., do., do., -	„	0	15	0
No. 99D.— Do., do., Flat Back, in Galvanized Cast Iron, including Regulating Valve, - -	„	0	17	6
No. 207. —2 Gallon Automatic, do., in Copper, including Regulating Valve, - - - - -	„	1	10	0
No. 207A.— Do., do., Angle do., do., do., - - - - - -	„	1	10	0
No. 207B.— Do., do., Flat Back, in Galvanized Wrought Iron, including Regulating Valve, -	„	1	5	0
No. 207C.— Do., do., Angle do., do., do., do., -	„	1	5	0
No. 104A.—8 Gallon Galvanized-Iron Automatic Tank, without Regulating Valve, - - - - -	„	2	15	0
No. 104A.—10 Do., do., do., do., do., - - - - - -	„	2	17	6

Special Hexagonal, Half Hexagonal, and 6 Gallon Square-Sided Tanks, without Regulating Valves.

		No. 468. Hexagonal.	No. 469. Half Hexagonal.	No. 470. Square-Sided.
Galvanized Iron, - - - - - - - - - - -	each,	£3 15 0	£3 3 0	
A. Mahogany, Lead Lined, and Polished Brass Trap, - - - -	„	15 15 0	10 15 0	£10 10 0
B. St. Anne's Marble, with Copper Fittings and Polished Brass Trap,	„	19 15 0	13 5 0	13 5 0
C. Rouge Royal Marble, do., do., do.,	„	20 10 0	13 15 0	13 15 0
D. Enamelled Slate, do., do., do.,	„	13 0 0	10 5 0	10 5 0
E. Plain Slate, do., do., do.,	„	9 10 0	7 10 0	7 10 0

No. 471. —Enamelled Cast-Iron Automatic Tanks, Highly Decorated, 3 Gallon, including Regulating Valve, - - - - - - - - - - - - - - - - -	each,	£2 0 0
No. 471A.— Do., do., do., 5 do., do.,	„	2 10 0

AUTOMATIC FLUSHING CLOSETS AND URINALS.

STRONG

DURABLE

CHEAP

Made of Extra Strong Salt-glazed Stoneware, and adapted to the requirements of Child and Adult, in

Schools, Barracks, Dockyards, Factories, Workhouses, Asylums, Blocks of Industrial Dwellings, &c.

Flushing Apparatus, under Control of an Attendant, can be substituted for the Automatic Arrangements, when desired.

A large assortment of various sizes kept in stock.

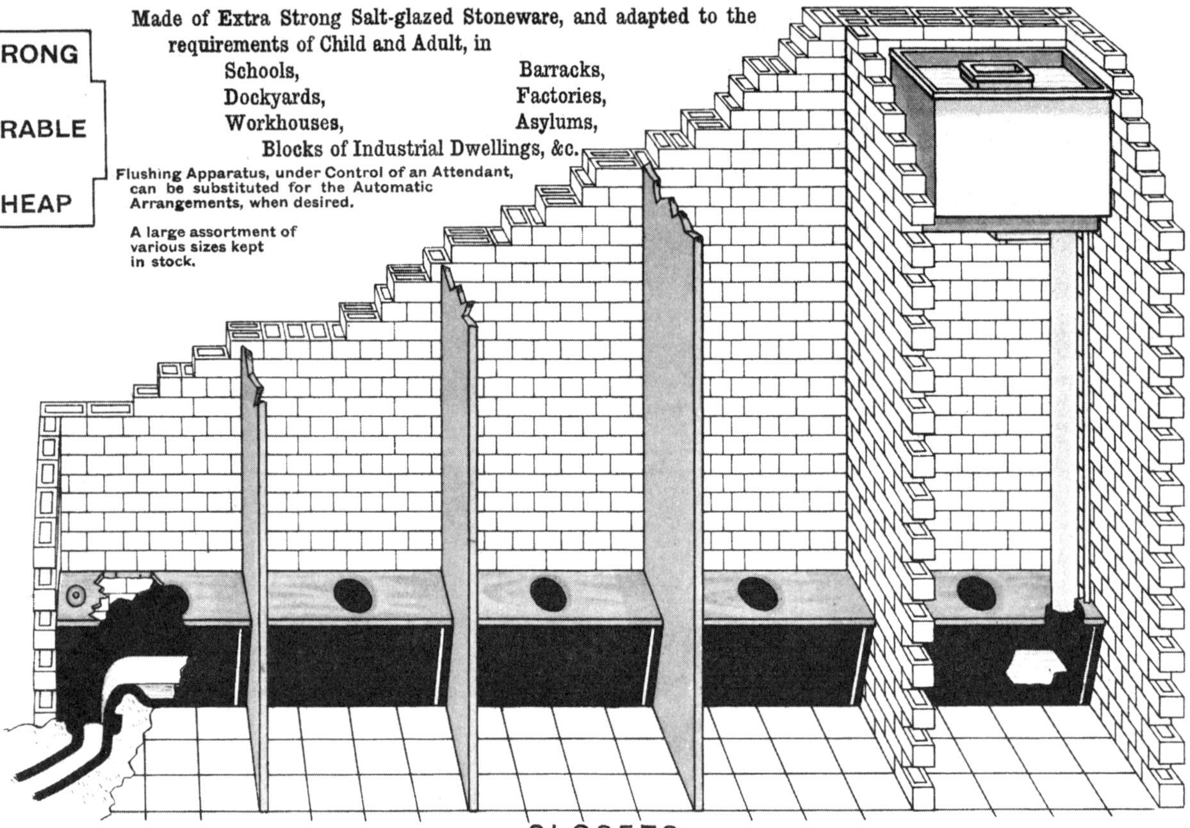

CLOSETS.

The lengths of the various sections are so arranged that the divisions, whether Slate Slabs, or Walls, are built over the Socketed Joints.

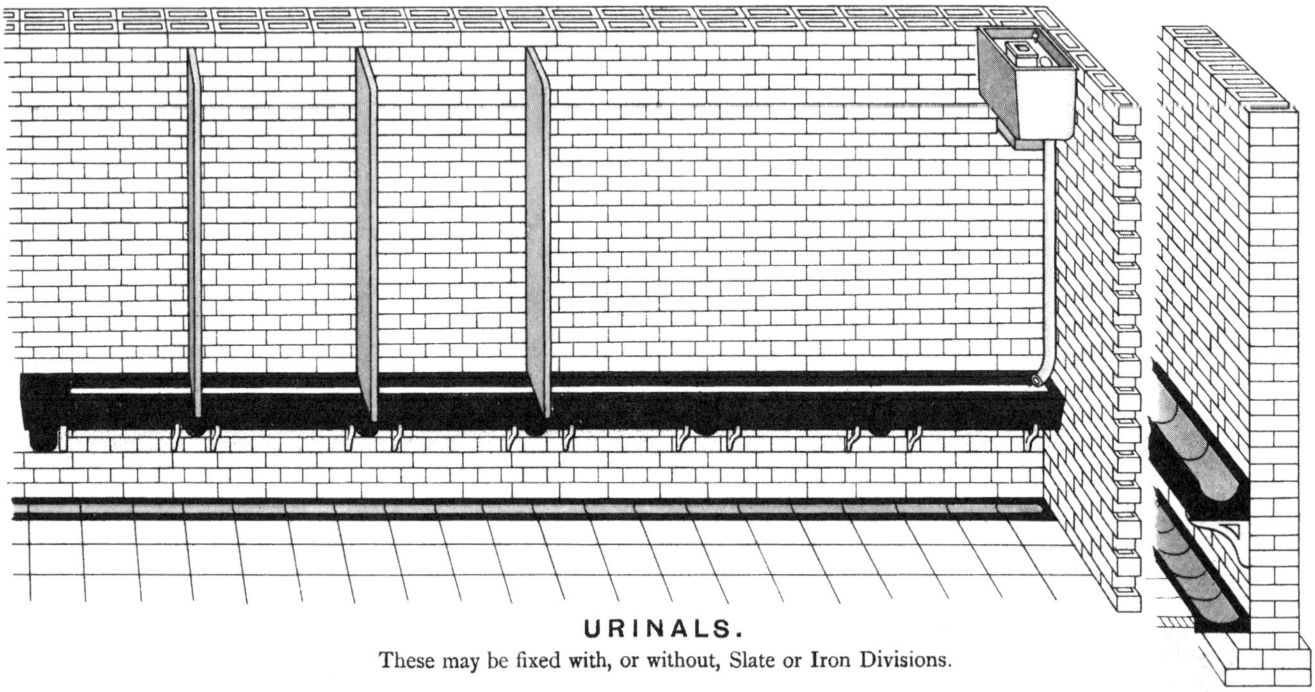

URINALS.

These may be fixed with, or without, Slate or Iron Divisions.

IMPROVED SALT-GLAZED FIRE-CLAY TROUGH CLOSETS,

WITH BUFF-GLAZED FIRE-CLAY DIVISIONS,

Suitable for Schools, Workshops, Barracks, &c.

OUTSIDE SIZES.
2′ 3″ long. 1′ 5″ wide. 1′ 6″ deep.

No. 128.—Salt-glazed Fire-clay Closet, with Supply and Discharge Arrangement, Hinged and Locking Deal Seat, for one person ... ... Price, £2 5 0 complete.

" 129.—Same as No. 128, but without Seat...£1 17 6 "

No. 128.—Closet in Salt-glazed Fire-clay, with Seat, for one person.
" **129.**—Closet in Fire-clay, no Seat, for one person.

HIGHLY RECOMMENDED, COMPLETELY SANITARY.

No. 126.—Trough Closet, with Inlet and Outlet Valves, Divisions and Seats.
" **127.**— Do. do. without Divisions and Seats.

No. 126.—*Salt-glazed Fire-clay Trough Closet, 2′ 3″ centres ; Supply Valve and Discharge Arrangement, Deal Seats, Buff-glazed Fire-clay Divisions (3′ 6″ × 3′ 0″ above Trough), with Cast-iron Pillar, Ramp, and Sill.

For...	2	3	4	5	6	8	10	12	persons.
Price	£6 8 8	10 16 7	15 0 6	19 4 5	23 8 4	32 0 2	40 8 0	48 15 10	complete.

No. 127.—Same as No. 126, but without Seats and Divisions.

For...	2	3	4	5	6	8	10	12	persons.
Price	£2 6 8	3 3 7	4 0 6	4 17 5	5 14 4	7 8 2	9 2 0	10 15 10	complete.

* If with Side Slabs, Cast-iron ¾ Pillar, Ramp and Sill, £3 7s. extra per side.

NOTE.—THESE CLOSET RANGES SHOULD BE FIXED WITH A SLIGHT FALL TOWARDS OUTLET.

ACKNOWLEDGEMENTS & SOURCES

In the following listing, the number of each page of *The Victorian Bathroom Catalogue*, in **bold** type, is listed alongside the page reference of its original source. The original catalogues from which material has been taken appear in alphabetical order.

Doulton: **26** – 90; **27** – 95; **28** – 97; **33** – 4; **43** – 88; **44** – 85; **45** – 86; **61** – 41; **70** – 14; **71** – 12; **72** – 42; **73** – 43; **88** – 144; **89** – 143; **96** – 149; **117** – 109; **122** – 32; **123** – 33; **126** – 35; **130** – 30; **131** – 31; **133** – 121; **146** – 112; **152** – 176; **153** – 190; **154** top – 52; **154** bottom – 193; **155** – 191; **157** – 195.

Morrison: **16** – 65; **17** – 67; **23** – 74; **29** – 91; **30** – 94; **31** – 92; **37** – 145; **40** top – 6; **40** bottom – 7; **41** – 29; **42** – 23; **48** – frontispiece; **50** – 96; **68** – 144; **69** – 148; **78** – 22; **81** – 4; **82** – 1; **83** – 11; **84** – 12; **85** – 14; **93** – 21; **94** – 19; **95** – 26; **97** – 36; **112** – 123; **113** – 124; **115** – 153; **125** – 156; **127** – 158; **132** – 97; **142** – 24; **145** – 51; **147** – 30; **156** – 177; **159** – 151.

Porcher: **46** – plate 108; **51** – plate 55; **77** – plate 77; **104** – plate 35; **110** – plate 53; **118** – plate 19; **119** – plate 45; **128** – plate 173; **135** – plate 134; **136** – plate 174.

Shanks: **6** – title page; **18** – 15; **19** – 8; **20** – 18; **21** – 19; **24** – 25; **25** – 42; **32** – 23; **54** – 41; **59** – 224; **60** – 225; **64** – 214; **65** – 208; **66** – 209; **67** – 204; **76** – 152; **86** – 99; **87** – 100; **90** – 112; **91** – 103; **92** – 115; **98** – 118; **99** – 116; **107** – 166; **108** – 28; **109** – 56; **114** – 229; **116** – 64; **124** – 196; **148** – 254; **149** – 251; **150** – 255; **151** – 256.

Twyford: **34** – 47; **35** – 41; **36** – 45; **38** – 24; **39** – 26; **62** – 62; **63** – 48; **80** top left – 15; **80** – top right 10; **80** bottom left – 2; **80** bottom right – 7; **134** – 17; **158** – 60.

Webb **9** top – facing vi; **9** bottom – facing i; **22** – 207; **49** – 228; **52** – 223; **53** – 225; **55** – 210; **74** – 38; **75** – 39; **100** – 124; **101** – 125; **102** – 112; **103** – 117; **111** – 218; **120** – 304; **129** – 106; **137** – 308; **138** – 176; **139** – 311; **140** – 312; **141** – 313.

These books are recommended further reading; the author acknowledges their use in her research.

The English House by Hermann Muthesius, 1904. English translation by Janet Seligman, 1987.

The English Terraced House by Stefan Muthesius, New Haven and London, 1982.

Life in the English Country House by Mark Girouard, 1979.

The Making of Modern London by G. Weightman and S Humphries, 1983.

Nancy Lancaster: Her Life, her World, her Art by Robert Becker, 1995.

Victorian Things by Asa Briggs, 1988.

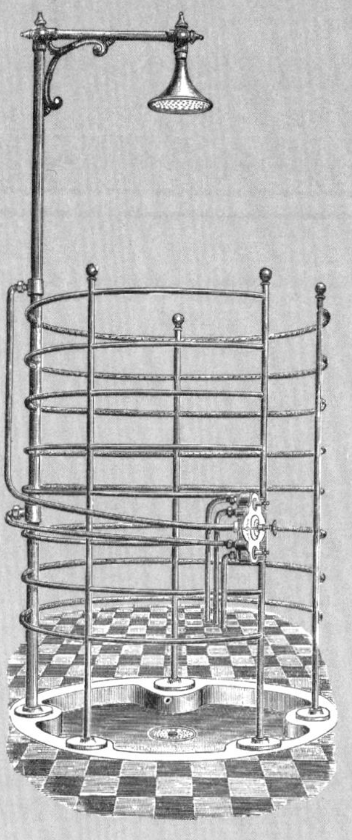
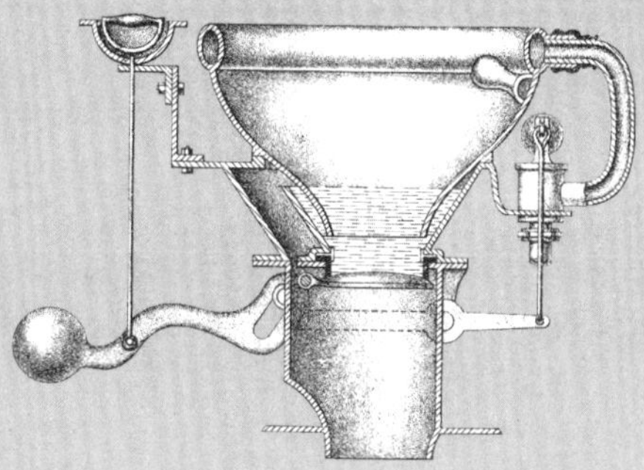

PAT. FEB. 16. 1897.
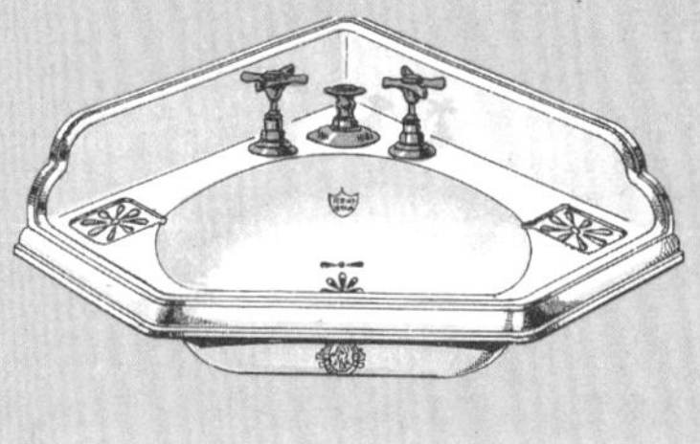
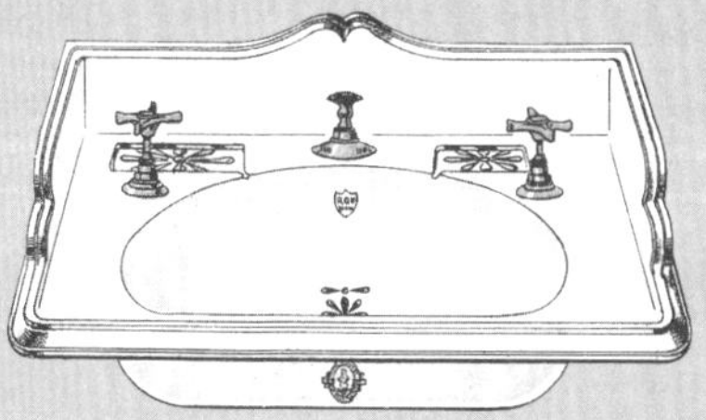
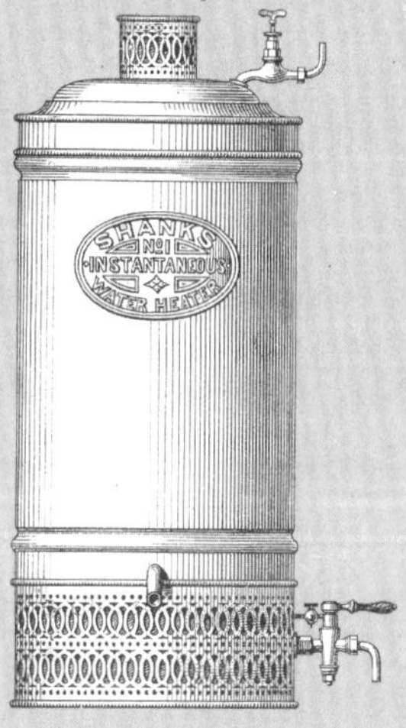
SHANKS
No1
INSTANTANEOUS
WATER HEATER